PAINT LOCKER MAGIC

PAINT LOCKER MAGIC

A HISTORY OF NAVAL AVIATION
SPECIAL MARKINGS AND ARTWORK

WILLIAM TATE AND JIM MEEHAN

FONTHILL

Fonthill Media Language Policy

Fonthill Media publishes in the international English language market. One language edition is published worldwide. As there are minor differences in spelling and presentation, especially with regard to American English and British English, a policy is necessary to define which form of English to use. The Fonthill Policy is to use the form of English native to the author. Jim Meehan and William Tate were born and educated in the USA and now live in the USA; therefore American English has been adopted in this publication.

Fonthill Media Limited
Fonthill Media LLC
www.fonthillmedia.com
office@fonthillmedia.com

First published in the United Kingdom and the United States of America 2015

British Library Cataloguing in Publication Data:
A catalogue record for this book is available from the British Library

Typeset in Mrs Eaves XL Serif Narrow 10pt on 12pt
Printed and bound in England

CONTENTS

APPENDICES

ACKNOWLEDGMENTS

We would like to humbly thank the following veterans and their associations for the sacrifice they made during the Second World War, the Korean Conflict, the Vietnam War, Desert Storm and all after. We also owe them thanks for the extraordinary effort they put forward in helping us to compile this work on Naval Aviation Nose Art. We owe these men and women more than we can ever repay.

Mr Roy L. Balke, Crew 5, VPB-109
Mr William A. Barker, VP/VPB-11 Association
Mr Thomas Edward Barton, NARU Anacostia, MD
Cdr Paul J. Bruneau US Navy Ret., Crew 4, VPB-115
Mr Chris Bryant, Operation Deep Freeze, VXE-6
Mr J. W. Downer, VPB-116
Mr John W. Furey, Crew 4, VPB-115
Mrs Carl E. Godager, VPB-107 Association
Mr Hill Goodspeed, National Museum of Naval Aviation
Mr A. J. Hopkins, Crew 10, VPB-118
Mr Michael Ianuzzi, US Navy Medical Corps
Mr Dion Jacobson, VF-871
Mr Bill Masser, Crew 3 and 10, VP-731
Ms Shayne Meder, www.flygirlpainters.com
Mr Michael and Mrs. Linda Miller, Robert H. Miller 419th NFS
Mr Kenneth Misenheimer, VP-30/VP-93/PATWINGPAC

Mr I. James Morrison, PBY Catalina International Association
Mr Hal Olsen, CASU-44, Tinian, Mariana Islands
Mr Joe A. Palsha, VPB-116
Mr John F. Schneider, 1st Emergency Rescue Squadron USAAF
Mr Dick Shoden, Crew 4, VPB-115/VPB-122
Mr Jonathan Skean, USS *Hancock*/VF-24/VMA-212
Mr Henry J. Thompson, Crew 17, VPB-118
Mr Stan Tokarz, Crew 3, VP-731
Mr Perry Ustrich, VPB-144 and VPB-148
Mr Robert P. Warnock, VPB-131
Mr David D. West, Crew 4, VPB-115
Mr Raymond T. West, VW-11/VP-64/VP-11/VP-8
Mr Richard A. Wilson, VP-83/VPB-107
Mr A. P. (Al) Wiswell, Crew 4, VPB-115
The George Bush Presidential Library
The A-4 Skyhawk Association

Also, to the following list of friends and fellow aviation enthusiasts we would like to add special thanks for their support and research, which assisted us in the collation of this book. If it were not for the work and research that these people do, the history of aviation would be a black hole with little light for understanding.

Mr Stan Adelson
Mr David F. Brown
Mr Tom Kaminski
Mr John R. Kerr
Mr Mahlon K. Miller
Mr Lionel Paul

Capt. Dana 'Smudge' Potts, US Navy
Mr Don Spering, Aircraft In Review (AIR)
Mr Nick Williams, American Aviation Historical Society
Dr and Mrs Stephen Wolf

Special mention should go to John 'Mad Dog' Kerr (MSGT, USAF, retired) a twenty-one-year veteran, who served most of his years in the intelligence field with several special operation (Air Commando) units. John has worked worldwide as a photographer of aircraft and a contributor to numerous magazines and books. Using these skills John was able to ferret out many of the images and details used in the compilation of this publication. Lastly, you will note that many of the beautiful images of aircraft and their artwork are accredited to a close personal friend, Don 'Hawkeye' Spering—an outstanding photographer, and a nose artist in his own right.

In conclusion, I would like to express gratitude to my family for their support and prayers during this twenty-year-long project. I would like to thank my loving wife Pat for her understanding, my son James for his editorial assistance, and my brother John Keith for his technical help and his active role in publishing the manuscript at his office—all these made this book possible.

In addition, I dedicate this book to my co-author Jim 'Mad dog' Meehan and my hero and namesake William Tate III, a single dad who is raising his two sons, Jordan and Logan, while managing a career.

I most humbly thank you all for your patience and assistance.

William Tate

FOREWORD

After I was selected to be an Air Wing Commander I reflected about the common thread that made my success possible throughout my career: the unwavering support of my bride, Pat. Being an aviation history enthusiast, I wanted to celebrate how important her support was to me, as well as a salute to all of the wives of our air wing.

Bob Wills penned a 1938 song entitled *San Antonio Rose*, which has been performed by artists as diverse as Patsy Cline and Clint Eastwood. My wife Pat is a Texan—and a San Antonio native—so a Texas yellow rose was the natural choice. Since I am a Fighter RIO and would conduct most of my flights in the F-14, I asked the commanding officer of VF 103 *Jolly Rogers* in my wing, and my staff, to find an artist within the wing who could render the nose art. I wanted the yellow rose encircled by maroon and white letters (the school colors of our alma mater, Texas A&M). The only other request I had was to use a western-style font, and the only example I could think of was the logo of the San Francisco 49ers. As it turns out, one of my maintenance master chiefs was a superb artist, and he rendered it on the jet.

His work exceeded all my expectations and was a matter of pride for me throughout my tenure as CAG. As far as I know the paint was very durable and never touched up. The *Rose* saw combat over Afghanistan and Iraq, as well as in the Mediterranean and Adriatic. She was a good jet, and she remains a continuing source of pride and fond memory for both my wife and me.

Captain Dana 'Smudge' Potts

An F-14B Tomcat of VF-103, BuNo. 162928; *San Antonio Rose* was attached to CAG-17.

INTRODUCTION:
NAVAL AIRCRAFT NOSE ART

Why another book on aircraft nose art? Most other books on that subject deal primarily with prolific US Army Air Force artwork. For this reason this book will firstly cover the artworks found on US Navy aircraft and secondly the art that is found on US Marine Corps, and US Coast Guard aircraft. The vast amount of nose art carried by the bombers and fighters in the European Theater during the Second World War is well-documented. The art of the USAAF/USAF in the Pacific during the Second World War, the Korean police action, and the conflict in Southeast Asia is also well-documented. However, after reviewing the subject's current resources, we realized that the Navy was not very well-represented. In all the sources we researched, we found only a few examples of naval aircraft nose art. We began a search for naval aircraft nose art. We knew from experience that there was more artwork out there; however, we also knew that US Navy aircraft nose art is not as prolific as Army or Air Force nose art. The period of time covered by this study is from 1941 to the present day. This will afford us the opportunity to examine the wealth of naval aviation artwork which has been created.

We contacted many people while doing our research; some were knowledgeable aviation historians and others were the veterans who flew and maintained the aircraft. In most cases, they agreed that aircraft artwork in the Navy has not been as plentiful as it has been in the Army or Air Force, but it exists in small amounts. Now, over a period of roughly fifty-eight years, it has compiled to a creditable exhibit.

What is the reason for the apparent lack of artwork on the sides of US Navy aircraft? The reasons are numerous, but most sources have suggested that the Navy brass was not as flexible and enforced regulations against the 'defacing of government property' or the personalizing of material. During the Second World War a (Navy) Air Force Pacific Letter No. 12L-43, dated 9 September 1943, was issued. This is one of only a few official documents that might be judged as dealing with naval aircraft nose art. This letter stated that the color red was not to be painted anywhere on the aircraft; not even the officially approved unit insignia. Instructions were also included that the painting of names on aircraft was forbidden. Although a similar letter was issued in the Atlantic about the use of the color red, there was no mention of the prohibition on naming individual airplanes. This restriction was lifted in July 1944 by CINCPAC when it became officially authorized that Unit Commanders could allow pilots to paint miniature Japanese Naval Ensign on his aircraft. These markings were for the purpose of denoting aircraft or ship kills. In September 1944 the Atlantic Fleet followed CINCPAC's lead and also allowed claims made between December 1941 and September 1944 to be displayed. In the case of the Atlantic, the German man-of-war flag was to be used for this purpose. With the end of the war, the restrictions on the use of red paint was cancelled.

It is true, however, that few examples of naval nose art could be found on aircraft that were stationed inside the continental United States, and only a few aircraft were painted with names, kill marks, mission symbols, or artwork. This was done mostly for public relations purposes. It was thought at the time that the public might be offended by the use of off-color slogans and artwork as found on Air Corps aircraft. Also, we must not forget the sensitivity that the mothers, wives, and girlfriends of the sailors might have had toward the genera of pin-up art that adorned many of the Second World War USAAC aircraft.

To understand the reason behind the scarcity of naval aircraft nose art, we must first look at the unique nature of the service. Following a long naval tradition, the Captain, Skipper, or Commanding Officer had total authority over his command and his men. This applied to all aspects of their welfare, both on duty and off. Considering the nature of shipboard duty—which is both isolated and independent—whatever the Skipper said was traditionally obeyed without question. This custom was carried over into the junior elements of the fleet such as Naval Aviation. These formalities applied both to shore-based and ship-based elements of Naval Aviation. Therefore, if there was ever any question as to whether the sailors could paint artwork on the squadron's aircraft it was left up to the squadron's Commanding Officer for approval. The Skipper had to weigh his decision on whether the said artwork would improve morale or offend certain personnel, especially his superiors. Additionally, the Japanese might be offended and take retribution out on captured crewmembers. Jim Morrison, editor for the *PBY Catalina International Association Newsletter*, recalled for me an incident in mid-1942, at Barking Sands, Hawaii:

> When a radioman with artistic persuasions was attempting to adorn the port bow of a PBY-5A he flew most often, it was his Commanding Officer, Cdr. Joseph Paschal (VP-91), who happened to catch him in the act. The nose art came off forthwith and was followed by admonition to all, something to the effect that these aircraft were not to be personalized in any manner.

Also crews were assigned to certain aircraft on a day-by-day basis at that time, so one crew might not appreciate artwork painted on their plane by another crewman.

Other trends were brought to light during our extensive research. First, land-based Navy squadrons were more likely to have elaborate artwork as opposed to carrier-based squadrons. The squadron COs on carriers had a more difficult time getting approval to paint their aircraft due to the long chain of command on board the ships. The Skipper of a carrier squadron was directly subordinate to both the ship's Captain as well as the CAG (Carrier Air Group) Commander. Both of these officers had a lot to say about how the individual squadrons were run. Thus, if a sailor or a pilot wanted artwork on his aircraft he might have to get approval from the squadron CO, the CAG, and the Captain of the ship. This was not usually the case for land-based patrol and fighter squadrons. For instance, a certain reserve patrol squadron—activated for the crisis in the Straits of Formosa—had begun to paint nose art on their P5M Mariners while in the Philippines. An officer on board the Naval Station ordered the sailor to stop work on the painting. After a short conference with the squadron's Commanding Officer, the artist was allowed to complete the work. By the time the squadron left the PI most of its aircraft carried nose art. The shore-based officer was not in the chain of command for the squadron's Skipper, so he had little to say about the aircraft's nose art.

Another problematic trend of Naval Aviation nose art was that even if a pilot, aircrewman, or sailor did succeed in having their aircraft decorated, it might not last long. Accidents and operational losses certainly took their toll, especially on board the carriers. For instance, on October 24, 1944, CVL-23 *Princeton* was sunk during the Battle of Leyte Gulf. On board was an F6F-3 Hellcat squadron, VF-27. The unit's aircraft were painted with a snarling cat's mouth and a glaring, blood-shot cat's eye while in Hawaii, before boarding ship. Some were even christened with names such as Ensign Paul Drury's *Paoli Local*. Many of these aircraft were lost when the ship was sunk. Those that were airborne were of course recovered on other carriers. Apparently, someone on VF-27's new-found home passed down orders that the gaudy nose art must be removed from all the squadron's planes. Few records or pictures remain to document this short-lived effort in Naval Aviation nose art; however, the idea did not end there. In 1961 VF-111 took to painting their F-8 Crusaders with shark mouths, and this custom continued when the squadron transitioned to F-4 Phantoms and, later, to F-14 Tomcats.

VF-27 seems to be the only example where a carrier-based squadron made any effort to decorate their aircraft during the Second World War. Their Skipper during this period was Lt Cdr E. W. Wood, and before the squadron boarded the *Princeton* he became the Carrier Air Group Commander. This may explain why the squadron was able to keep the nose art on their Hellcats. In addition, several other Navy and Marine Corps fighter squadrons made an attempt to paint nose art on their aircraft during the Second World War, but they were all shore-based. The Corsairs of VF-17 and VMF-213 during the Solomon Islands' campaign are two examples—however, their art was not as elaborate as VF-27's.

We will see that they and other island-based Naval Air squadrons were very active in applying nose art to their aircraft. Was it because the land lovers were more gifted artistically? No, the answer to the question lies somewhere between logistics and command approval or disapproval. For instance, the fighter squadrons in the Solomon Islands campaign were at the point of the spear, fighting and dying daily. Squadron *esprit de corps* may have been the edge that the units needed to overcome Imperial Japan in those early, dark days of the Second World War. The squadron's CO would not worry with a small question of nose art, especially if his pilots and ground crew were in favor of it. Also, these outfits were in most cases operating on small, isolated island stations. There were rarely any upper-echelon commanders or general public present to voice disapproval. These island stations also had engineering and construction units that could have building materials, specifically color paints, and experienced sign painters. All material on board ship was critical and rationed, right down to drinking water, so material and personnel might be in short supply while at sea. Thus, land-based air units might have the advantage over their sea-going mates as far as aircraft nose art was concerned.

This advantage is best illustrated when looking at the example set by the shore-based patrol squadrons of the Second World War. Just a glance at the PB4Y section of Appendix A will illustrate how prolific nose art was on this patrol-type aircraft—especially on Tinian—by 1945. The remoteness of these island stations, a more sympathetic command structure, and the availability of materials are just some reasons why the Navy patrol bombing community was more able to apply nose art. There is still another reason for this community's wealth in artwork. Throughout the war in the Pacific, the Navy's long-range patrol squadrons either operated with or in close proximity to the Army's B-24 and B-29 Bomb Wings. In fact, they often shared maintenance facilities. An excellent example of this is in May 1944, when VPB-115 operated a detachment with the Fifth Air Force's 310th Bomb Wing on Wakde Island. So, it is obvious how ridiculous an order not to paint nose art on the PB4Ys would have seemed, especially since the sailors could see Army B-24s just across the ramp exhibiting a cornucopia of color and design. However, when VPB-104 came to the Southwest Pacific in November 1944 to relieve VPB-115, this squadron's CO discouraged the use of nose art. It was justifiably felt that the use of kill marks and provocative artwork might subject captured crewmen to harsher treatment. In this theater of operation particularly, the enemy for the most part took no prisoners. Most of the patrol-bombing squadrons in FAW-10 and FAW-17 all followed this axiom, with the exception of VPB-111 and VPB-117.

The similarity of prolific nose art also existed within the PV-1 Ventura community. However, one unique difference applies to the PV-1; the PV-1s may have come from the factory with artwork already on their sides. Since the Lockheed Vega plant was near Walt Disney's Burbank Studio, it is no surprise that many of the PV-1s awaiting assignment to operational units were found with Mickey Mouse or Donald Duck on their fuselage. In fact, the Disney Studio had a special team assigned just to create art for insignias, as well as other demands for military art. Walt Disney probably realized the morale boost his creations provided for the US Navy, even if the command structure may not have.

We have seen how locale or duty station can be factors working in favor of a unit utilizing art-work on its aircraft, but location can also have a negative effect. Dick Shoden acknowledged that VPB-122, while stationed in Attu, Alaska, found the weather too severe to create an interest in nose art. None of their PB4Y-2s carried nose art, which is unusual for a Privateer squadron. VPB-122 had been formed from the decommissioned VPB-115. Many of the officers and men of the former squadron, which was stationed in the Southwest Pacific, now found themselves in the arctic. The Liberators of VPB-115 had been liberally decorated during their first tour, but the romantic idea of painting the new Privateers lost all appeal in the cold, hostile surroundings of Alaska. This was also the case for VPB-131, a PV-1 Ventura unit, stationed at Attu. VPB-131 had come to Alaska in October 1944 with late model Venturas; although they never painted the aircraft itself, they did paint parts of it. Robert Warnock's crew took the main mount wheel covers off and painted artwork on them. Not all of the Alaskan-based patrol squadrons went without artwork. VPB-136 had been operating from the Casco Bay airfield since August 1943. Their early model PV-1s had come from the Burbank factory with the Disney artwork on the aircraft's sides.

While Ventura and Privateer works of art were abundant, not all of the patrol-bombing community endorsed this concept. Referring to Appendix A, it is apparent that the PBY and PBM nose art is not as plentiful. The only explanation we have come up with is that in most cases these squadrons operated from seaplane tenders in the Southwest and Central Pacific. They had all the logistic and material shortages of a carrier-based unit, and they shared the long chain of command for approval. If approval was granted, the artist would have difficulty painting a shapely beauty on the side of a Catalina while bouncing around in a six-foot rubber raft or small boat.

What could be the reason that a pilot or his crew would want to have their aircraft decorated with some form of art when so many obstacles stood in their way? If, for instance, the enhancing of morale and the building of *esprit de corps* helped to accomplish the unit's goal, then its Commanding Officer would not be against the use of nose art. Late in the Second World War, many of the squadron Commanding Officers were reservist and draftees planning to return to civilian life, and they were less concerned with career gains—either short-term or post-war. Therefore, they had little to fear by promoting nose art, short of a chewing out from higher authority. These lower-echelon officers were concerned with only one thing: getting the job done.

Some of these junior officers also felt that nose art on the squadron's aircraft promoted a sense of unity and team pride. It gave their men, pilots, plane captains, and flight crews a closer identity with the aircraft. This kind of man-and-machine bond improved individual performance and gave the team an edge over the enemy.

By personalizing their aircraft, they were given something tangible in which they could take pride. This boost of morale was sorely needed during those days at the front while sailors were on constant alert, having little sleep or recreation, surviving off field rations, and living in tents. Aircraft nose art improved morale and inspired the sailors, which in turn increased personal performance and peak efficiency. One could look at the pin-up on the nose of an aircraft as a symbolic cheerleader, cheering her team on to victory.

FIGURE HEADS

If there is a historical basis for naval aircraft nose art, it rests in the lost art form of figurehead carvings. Figureheads are defined as folk art sculptures with a nautical twist. Women in most cases decorated the bow of ships, but eagles, other sea birds, dolphins, sea serpents, mermaids, life size human forms of prominent historical figures, and mythical characters were also common. These figures stood looking forward with a serious mien. Gilded or painted wooden carved figureheads adorn the bows of all early US Navy sailing vessels. The figurehead helped establish the ship's identity while in port. The old salts returning to their ship after a night ashore may have had trouble focusing on the stern to read the ship's name, but they would have no trouble recognizing a 40-foot golden eagle or a half-clad damsel protruding from the bow of his ship. The figurehead also helps establish the ship's identity while at sea. William Rush of Philadelphia, Isaac Fowle of Boston, and the Skillins, also of Boston, were all known for their beautiful carved and painted figures. In fact, Boston was the

A gold eagle figurehead from the USS *Lancaster*, one of the ships in Farragut's fleet. (*Author's Collection*)

A partially-clad woman is the subject of this figurehead in the Newport News Mariner's Museum. Compare this pose with the nose art on the E-2C Hawkeye, *Miss B. Havin*, found on subsequent pages. (*Authors' Collection*)

center of a flourishing figurehead business. With the passing of sail and the introduction of steam and iron-clad ships, the figurehead had vanished from the Navy by the beginning of the twentieth century. But, just as the scantily clad figure of 'Liberty' led Admiral Farragut's fleet through the grape shot and torpedoes in Mobile Bay, an Esquire Calendar Girl on a VPB-118 Privateer's nose led a flight through the flak of a Japanese freighter in the Sea of Japan. It is ironic that one of the most prolific nose artists in the Pacific, Hal Olsen, was also native to the Boston area.

DEFINING NOSE ART

We should attempt to define what we mean by the term, 'nose art.' Aircraft nose art usually consists of some kind of colorful painted artwork. The artwork does not have to appear on the plane's nose, but can appear on any part of the fuselage—although 90 per cent of the art will be applied on the forward part of the airplane. The medium used to draw the design on the designated portion of the aircraft's fuselage could be chalk, pencil, pen, ink, or—in more recent times—grease pencil. The paint medium used runs the entire gamut, from water-based, to oils, to lacquer sprays. A name, title, or phrase may also accompany the artwork. This title usually has some meaning for the pilot, crew, or ground pounder connected with a particular aircraft.

The term 'nose art' can be very misleading and confusing. I once had a conversation with a pilot from the 23rd TFW, shortly after Desert Storm. I was admiring his freshly painted A-10 Warthog. I mentioned that it was a shame that they had removed the artwork from the aircraft upon their return from King Fahd Airbase; he seemed perturbed, trying to point out that the artwork was still on the aircraft. He was of course referring to the Flying Tiger motif with which all 23rd FW aircraft are adorned, while I had been referring to the tank kill marks and colorful characters which were applied to some of the Desert Storm A-10s. We were both right, but the term 'nose art' means different things to each individual. Everyone sees art from a different perspective. Naval Aviation 'nose art' is aircraft folk art with a nautical twist.

Nose art could be classified as any of the following types:

(**a.**) a pin-up; i.e. 'Memphis Belle'
(**b.**) a cartoon or caricature; i.e. the 'Road Runner'
(**c.**) shark, tiger, cat, or animal teeth and eyes; i.e. the *Flying Tigers*. (Covered in Appendix D)
(**d.**) a name, a song, a movie title, a phrase or a slogan; i.e. 'Que Sera Sera'
(**e.**) mission symbols, kill marks, or score boards; i.e. Japanese 'meatballs'
(**f.**) memorial or commemorative nose art, i.e. the New York City Firemen's names that adorned the F/A-18 Hornets during Operation Enduring Freedom.

For the purpose of this study, nose art should be defined as either (a.) or (b.) or (f.), and at the least a combination of (d.) and (e.) The artwork shall also be unique to only one of the unit's aircraft. For instance, VAW-33 had a chess knight and a hawk stenciled on the cowlings of all their EA-1s. The squadron's name, *Knight Hawks*, was also painted adjacent to the artwork. At first glance it appeared to be nose art. However, this would not be considered nose art for our purposes because all the unit's planes carried the exact same design; it is merely an elaborate squadron insignia. Shark mouths and the like (c.) would also fall into this category, but because of the visual appeal of this type of artwork it will be covered in Appendix D.

E-2C, *Miss B. Having*, is a good example of pin-up nose art. (*Author's Collection*)

TYPES OF NOSE ART

(a.) The Pin-up

Pin-up nose art was inspired by the art of George Petty and Gil Elvgren before and during the Second World War, and Alberto Vargas later in the war. This particular style of art makes up about 20 per cent of all naval aircraft nose art. In the 1940s, many examples of this type of art could be found on patrol aircraft around the Pacific islands of Guam, Tinian, Saipan, the Philippines, Iwo Jima, and Okinawa. Some of the naval personnel on these islands were already doing this style of artwork for the Army, so the big flat sides of the Liberators, Venturas, and Privateers lent themselves well to this genera of art. Very few examples of this type of nose art have been found in the sea-going commands, like CVEs, CVLs, CVAs, and seaplane tenders. On those rare occasions when this art did appear at sea, it was most certainly small and barely noticeable from the bridge of the carrier. During the Second World War pin-up art was published monthly in the centerfold pages of Esquire Magazine, and in the calendars of Brown & Bigelow and Louis Dow. The pop-culture icons of movie stars like Betty Grable also supplied a stimulus. This type of art was at best voyeuristic in nature, and its images of a pretty girl-next-door, caught in the act of exposing her legs and breast, symbolized the thing that many American sailors felt they were fighting for.

Al Moore, Eddie Chan, and Ernest Chiriaka's calendar art provided the impetus during the Korean police action. Later, Alberto Vargas and *Playboy* Magazine would be an inspiration during the Vietnam Conflict. During Desert Storm, Helmet Newton, Punk fashion, the art of Olivia De Berardinis, and the old 8th Air Force's nose art from the Second World War itself would be the creative source behind the nose art. This trend was best-illustrated by what CVW-8 did on the USS *Theodore Roosevelt*, CVN-71, during Desert Storm. In recent times the partially-clad lady is used rarely, as it is not politically correct and most commands want to avoid any impropriety. It could be said that political correctness was the death of creative expression for the artist; however, a few examples of this type of art did appear briefly during the Gulf War. This would indicate that even though the command structure and public morays may frown on this style, it still flourishes.

A P5M-3 with *Daisy Mae* artwork from the *Lil' Abner* comic strip on the nose. (*US Navy via Kenneth Misenheimer*)

(b.) Cartoon, Comic Strip Art, and Caricatures

This artwork is inspired by the cartoon caricatures of the Walt Disney Studios, Walter Lance, and the Warner Brothers Studios. It is exemplified best by the PV-1 Venturas in the Pacific and Alaska. The movie studios in Hollywood painted many of the aircraft at the Lockheed Vega plant in Burbank, CA. In more recent times, the nose art created by Warner Brothers Studio for VXN-8's aircraft is an excellent example; their Road Runner is the most-used of any of the cartoon characters. The sailors of this particular unit which chose to use this icon probably felt a lot like the bird; always on the go, never stopping to eat or sleep, and dodging all sorts of entrapments. The second most-used cartoon or comic character was 'Snoopy'. The Naval Aircrewman who most likely painted the lovable dog on the side of his airplane could certainly identify with Charles Schultz's small insignificant hero, up against insurmountable odds fighting the mighty Red Menace—I mean the Red Baron. The comic strip *Shoe* by Jeff Macnelly, Milt Caniff's *Terry and The Pirates*, and Al Capp's *Lil Abner* also have provided ideas for naval aircraft nose art. This type of art is easily tolerated by the chain of command because of its public popularity.

A pilot or crewman's personal habits or tastes can inspire other caricatures. Personal and comical caricatures usually have some hidden meaning or a *double entendre*. Numerous shipboard and shore-based examples exist, and were used during both the Second World War and in the post-war years. Many examples found in the Second World War, Korea, Vietnam, and during Desert Storm have only a small piece of art or, in some cases, a name only. This type of art is more accepted because it is short-lived. When the person who is the inspiration for the art is transferred, the art is usually removed. This art is sometimes so small that it is often overlooked. This art form is usually less provocative or controversial, and is also tolerated by the chain of command.

(f.) The Memorial or Commemorative Art

This type of art is meant to be a tribute to a fellow serviceman or a sister squadron/unit. There are many examples found in the Second World War, and the PB4Y-1 Liberator of VPB-115 *Snuffy's Mischief Maker* is a good example. However, the most poignant instance of commemorative nose art can be found in the years 2003–04. Most of the F/A-18E Super Hornets of VFA-115 were named after the fallen New York City firemen and police who were victims of 11 September 2001 terrorist attacks.

Road Runner is the most prolific movie cartoon character used as the subject for US Navy nose art. (*Author's Collection*)

(c.) The Mark of The Beast: This type of artwork will be covered separately in Appendix D. A F6F-3 Hellcat of VF-27, USS *Princeton* (CVL-23), has just landed onboard ship. The eyes and snarling cat's mouth were among the most colorful markings applied to carrier-based aircraft during the Second World War. (*National Archives via Goodspeed*)

(e.) This F2H-2P Banshee illustrates how elaborate score-board-type art could get during the Korean police action, but with no other components (such as a 'name') this will not be classified as nose art in this publication. (*Author*)

An F6F-3 Hellcat at the National Museum of Naval Aviation with kill marks and a name, *Minsi III* illustrates the simplest form of nose art. {Example of a combination of (d.) and (e.)} This is an excellent representation of Second World War carrier-based nose art. (*Author's Collection*)

An F/A-18E Super Hornet assigned to the *Eagles* of VFA-115 is painted with the names and crest of fallen New York City Firefighters of Engine Company 54. Chief Ed Geraghty and Captain Dave Wooley gave their lives to save victims from the World Trade Center on 11 September 2001. VFA-115 was attached to CVW-14 onboard the USS *Abraham Lincoln*. The squadron was deployed for nine months, first to Afghanistan and Operation Enduring Freedom and later to Iraq. The thirteen mission marks were accumulated during Operation Iraqi Freedom. (*US Navy photo by PH3 Michael S. Kelly*)

A PERSONAL CARICATURE

The artwork above is an ideal example of personal caricature nose art. The young pelican or gosling was painted on the side of a Burgess N-9H Jenny, serial number A 2466. When Ensign Harold James Merritt soloed in this plane in 1918; he then cut the fabric off the side of the aircraft. It is now preserved in the National Museum of Naval Aviation at Pensacola, FL. (*NM of NA via Author*)

Aircraft in Training Squadron 2 carried this art, but it is unlikely the caricature was a squadron insignia, as insignias were not authorized until after the First World War. (*NM of NA via Author*)

1

THE SECOND WORLD WAR ERA

Tony Fry, of course, was known by everybody in the area after his brush with Admiral Kester. The old man saw Fry's TBF with twelve beer bottles painted on the side. 'What the hell are those beer bottles for, Fry?' the Admiral asked. 'Well, sir, this is an old job. I use it to ferry beer in,' Tony replied without batting an eyelash. 'Been on twelve missions, sir'. 'Take those goddam beer bottles off,' the Admiral ordered. Tony kept the old TBF, of course, and continued to haul beer in it.

James Michener, *Tales of the South Pacific*, 1946

Michener was out there in the South Pacific during the Second World War, and brought it all vividly home to the American public in his epic novel *Tales of the South Pacific*. In this paragraph he captured the spirit of the Navy men fighting a lonely war in a beautiful but deadly Pacific paradise, far from home. Technically, it did not help the war effort to take the time and materials to paint beer bottles on an airplane—especially an 'old job'—but it must have made the pilot feel proud, and brought a smile to many a scared or bored American kid's face. Cartoons and luscious pin-up girls proved to be even more effective.

The Admiral's order to remove the 'mission marks' was also typical of the attitude of the higher echelon of command with regard to nose art. Art was only permitted on aircraft when the publicity was needed to boost the morale of the home front, the workers who built the airplanes and bought the War Bonds. 'Pappy' Boyington of VMF-214 posed in a F4U-1 Corsair, No. 86, having twenty kill markings and bearing the name *Lucybelle*, for publicity photos. 'Pappy' quickly had the kill markings removed however, as he thought the big scoreboard would 'scare the Japs away.' Also, the name is partially obliterated in most of the published photos, and many sources have recorded No. 86 as *Lulubelle*. Recent research however has confirmed the name was *Lucybelle*. Unfortunately, the art for these publicity photos was often temporary or done on aircraft not actually flown by the aces or squadron commanders, and in 'Pappy's' case, his logbook indicates he rarely, if ever, flew *Lucybelle*.

Many of the published sources on US Navy/USMC markings and camouflage state that nose art and personal names on Navy aircraft are rare. This volume will attempt to show otherwise.

MARINE CORPS AVIATION

The land-based marine units in the Pacific, at the extreme end of the chain of command, were able to get away with a lot more in the way of artwork. Some examples are found in the *Cactus Air Force* operating on Guadalcanal in 1942. Somehow, these marines found time to decorate a few of the F4F Wildcats at Henderson Field. Lt Jim Swett, ace of VMF-221, had the name *Melvin Massacre* stenciled on the rudder of his Wildcat, and for a few days it carried a large cartoon of Hairless Joe on its fin. In 1943 VMF-213 flew early F4U-1 Corsairs from Guadalcanal, many of which also sported artwork. 1st Lt Wilbur Thomas' No. 10 was adorned with a flying gopher cartoon and named *Gus's Gopher*. Another, named *Defabe*, was adorned with a pair of dice. VMF-213's No. 20 had a large eagle design

VT-80 flew a TBM named *Round Trip* with the outline of a ticket in black on the nose. Ensign Higman's aircraft was damaged by flak while flying missions from USS *Ticonderoga* in November 1944. (*US Navy/ National Archives*)

on the starboard cowl, and No. 8 was painted with an eight ball—as was typical of many squadrons. Several other examples of art were noted within the *Cactus Air Force* on Guadalcanal, including a F4F-4, No. 8 of an unknown unit, which boasted an Indian head marking, reminiscent of the First World War Lafayette Escadrille emblem, below the canopy.

In addition to the fighter and attack aircraft, many of the Marine Corps SBD Dauntless aircraft had mission marks in the form of small bombs painted on their fuselages. One such, side number 713 of an unknown VMB unit, was named *Queenie*. The name was painted below the canopy rail, along with 114 bombs to denote its career of combat in the South Pacific. The existing photo shows her engineless in a scrap yard in the Philippines at the end of the war.

The Marines' night fighter units operated in the Pacific up until the end of the war, and managed to paint artwork on many of their aircraft. These radar-equipped aircraft were most often land-based, but on occasion were also carrier-based. Some night fighter squadrons enjoyed great success, and a 5th Air Force report noted that the F6F Hellcats were more effective than the P-61 Black Widows in operations over the Philippines. A photograph of a line-up of Hellcats from VMF(N)-541 shows pin-up nose art on most of the aircraft, with one bearing the name *1 O'clock Jump*. Major Robert Porter of VMF (N)-542 took over a F6F-5N, bureau number (BuNo.) 78669, which had on it a large red heart and the name *Millie Lou*. Porter had the art promptly removed, replacing it with the name *Black Death* and a painting of a bottle of Shenley's whiskey.

THE JOLLY ROGERS OF VF-17

VF-17 was a very successful squadron—downing 152 Japanese planes in seventy-six days of combat and producing thirteen aces—which also had a rich history of nose art. The appropriately named *Jolly Rogers* Corsairs had a pirate flag painted on both sides of the cowling while on the carrier *Bunker Hill*.

Lt 'Chico' Freeman of VF-17 with his F4U-1 BuNo. 17932 aircraft No. 34, in the South West Pacific, 1944. (*US Navy photo*)

This picture of a section of TBM-3E Avengers from VT-34 on the USS *Monterey* was photographed on 29 August 1945, just days before the end of the war in the Pacific. The nearest TBM shows a scoreboard of twenty-one missions and a pin-up varnished to the cowling. (*US Navy*)

When the squadron had their F4U-1s off loaded to Ondonga, they added names to the big vertical fins of the birds. It was here that they became unofficially known as *Blackburn's Irregulars*, after their commander, ace Tom Blackburn. He flew several Corsairs with aircraft No. 1 and the name *Big Hog*. Ace Butch Davenport flew a couple of aircraft with the name *Lonesome Polecat*, while 'Chico' Freeman flew at least two Corsairs with the name *L.A. City Limits*, in honor of his hometown. A little art was added to *L.A. City Limits* when a sign on a post appeared enclosing the name. Although the *Jolly Rogers* of VF-17 already had the nose of each plane decorated, a couple of the Corsairs sported additional artwork. Mel Kurlander's F4U-1, BuNo. 17677, is known to have had a pin-up on the right vertical fin. In the famous shot of a flight of VF-17 Corsairs, with Kepford's No. 29 in the foreground, it appears that No. 28, Bill Popp's F4U-1, also carried some sort of artwork on its tail fin.

VC-10

The escort carriers produced a few examples of nose art during the Second World War. VC-10, serving on the USS *Gambier Bay*, CVE-73, in 1944, personalized many of their aircraft and made use of an unconventional yet effective technique for producing nose art. The CO of VC-10, Lt Cdr Huxtable, flew a TBM-1C with a total of 5 pin-ups cut from various media and varnished on the port cowling. Ens. D. C. Bennett named his FM-2 *Smokey's Lucky Witch* and then decided to have two Vargas girls varnished to the cowling under the name, creating 'instant' nose art. But VC-10 also had some traditionally decorated aircraft like *Mah Baby*, flown and named by future ace Lt Bruce McGraw, which carried three Japanese flags—indicating his kills at that time. Unfortunately, most of these aircraft were lost when the *Gambier Bay* was sunk by Japanese naval gunfire at Leyte Gulf.

Left: Ensign Darrell C. Bennett, onboard CVE-73 in 1944, had two Esquire Magazine centerfolds varnished on the engine cowling of his F4F-4 Wildcat. This was an especially favorite way for the crew to create nose art on their aircraft while onboard ship, where supplies (paint and brushes) were in short supply. (*US Navy photo*)

Right: Two VF-51 Hellcats, from USS *San Jacinto*, flying over the Pacific during 1944. The near aircraft carries the name *Little Joe* and a pair of dice on the lower engine cowling. (*US Navy*)

THE MINSI

Cdr David McCampbell, the Navy's top ace of the Second World War with thirty-four confirmed kills and five probable kills, commanded Air Group 15 aboard the USS *Essex*, CV-9, and flew a series of F6F Hellcats which he named. As CO of VF-15, he flew a F6F-3, BuNo. 41692, named *Monsoon Maiden*, but in June 1944 McCampbell became Air Group Commander and named his new F6F-3 *The Minsi*. Though just a name is not considered nose art by this book, the fact that the F6F-5's *Minsi II* and *Minsi III* were decorated with a single thin white band on the fin, along with the blue letters 'CAG' in place of the modex number, is noteworthy. *Minsi III* was used for most of McCampbell's kills.

THE HANGER LILLY

The Commander of Air Group 19 on the USS *Lexington*, Cdr Hugh Winters, flew a F6F-5, No. 99, named *Hanger Lilly*. It displayed a small painting of a lily and eight Japanese flags representing his confirmed kills. In his autobiography, *Skipper*, Cdr Winters has a photograph of a tow tractor wearing the same flower and No. 99.

VT-51 AND LT GEORGE H. W. BUSH

Future US president Lt George H. W. Bush flew a TBM-1D Avenger from the USS *San Jacinto* while in VT-51. His gunner, Leo Nedeau, lettered the name *Barbara*, in honor of Mrs Bush, just below the right windscreen. (*G. Bush Presidential Library*) Below: In the Atlantic Ocean (26 May 2009), Former US President George H. W. Bush on the aircraft carrier USS *George H. W. Bush* (CVN 77) watches a jet catapult off the flight deck during flight operations. (*US Navy photo by Mass Communications Specialist 3rd Class Dominique J. Moore/Released*)

Former US President George H. W. Bush and Capt. Bob Roth, executive officer of the aircraft carrier USS *George H. W. Bush* (CVN 77), watch as an F/A-18F Super Hornet is launched during flight operations. Bush, the aircraft carrier's namesake, was on hand to watch flight deck operations, fulfilling a wish he made in 2006 at the ship's christening. You can see that the crew went all out for the occasion. They decorated the tow tractor which the former President is sitting on with the same modex and name (*Barbara*) which he had painted on his TBM-3 onboard USS *San Jacinto* in 1944. (*US Navy photo by Mass Communication Specialist 1st Class Michael Tackitt/Released*)

This picture of *Satan's Helper*, VT-83, was taken near Okinawa, 1945. Aircraft '417' carries a drawing of a pin-up sitting in a cocktail glass. (*National Archives*)

AIR GROUP 83

Air Group 83, stationed on the USS *Essex*, CV-9, was in combat from March 1945 until the war ended. CAG-83 accounted for 228 kills shared between the F6F-5 Hellcats of VF-83 and the mix of F4U-1D and FG-1D Corsairs of VBF-83. These aircraft carried the 'fan' 'G' symbol of the *Essex* until the new symbol, a white 'F,' replaced the fan in August of that year. One VF-83 Hellcat, BuNo. 72534, carried the name *Death n' Destruction* and a skull and crossbones in white on the dark, sea-blue finish, along with the *Essex's* fan emblem on the fin. This Hellcat carried nine kill flags, representing the claims of three of VF-83's ensigns.

Several of the VBF-83 Corsairs also carried nose art. *Chow-Hound* had a menu listing 'Tojo on Toast, Meatballs, and Banzai Salad' as its *entrée*. An even more colorful Corsair was *Maggie's Drawers*, which had a drawing of a pair of red bloomers. Sometimes a red flag referred to as 'Maggie's Drawers' was used to stop firing on a rifle range; perhaps the pilot hoped the Japanese might obey the red flag and stop firing.

During this same period on the *Essex*, VT-83 had several personalized TBM-3 Avengers. At least two Avengers carried pin-ups: *Bayou Belle* (BuNo. 23549), with a pin-up on the right side of the cowling, and *Satan's Helper* (BuNo. 23470), with a pin-up in a martini glass on the forward fuselage. A more humorous example was the *Cultured Vulture II*, complete with vulture cartoon.

Left: *Blues in the Night*, a F6F-5N night fighter, was part of VF-83/ Air Group 83 on the USS *Essex*. (*National Archives*)

Right: *Death 'n' Destruction* was a F6F-5 assigned to the USS *Essex*, CV-9. The nine kills were scored by several different pilots from VF-83. (*US Navy*)

The TBM *Cultured Vulture II* of VT-83/Air Group 83 is pictured here over Japan in search of POW camps. The artwork on this Avenger is a cartoon of a vulture in tuxedo. (*National Archives*)

USS HANCOCK CV 19, CARRIER AIR GROUP SIX 1944

Carrier Air Group Six joined the *Hancock* at Ulithi on 14 March 1945. The air group had been in the war since the beginning with the USS *Enterprise*, and would now remain with the *Hancock* until the war ended. It was the opinion of the aircrew and the ship's company that the level of cooperation between the ship and the air wing was a model to be used by all carriers. This excellent level of cooperation led to a cheerful and efficient working relationship.

CAG-6 was able to rack up a score of eleven ships sunk, thirty-nine aircraft shot down, 347 aircraft destroyed on the ground, and thirty-seven locomotives destroyed while operating off of Okinawa and the coast of Japan. The fighters of the *Hancock* on 15 August 1945 had the distinction of destroying the last enemy aircraft of the Second World War, when they shot down a Japanese torpedo plane which was diving on a British task force.

The SB2C-4E, *The Hannah Special*, is pictured in flight over the Pacific Ocean in 1945. The Helldiver operated from the USS *Hancock*'s Dive Bombing Squadron 6 (VB-6). VB-6 operated SB2C-3 and SB2C-4 Helldivers during its combat tour. The letter 'U' on the tail is the *Hancock*'s identification markings for all Carrier Air Group Six's aircraft. The nose art is uncommon on carrier-based aircraft and refers to the ship. (*Robert L. Lawson Photograph Collection, NNAM*)

This collage of photographs of 1945 nose art painted on the aircraft (Helldivers, Avengers, and Hellcats) of Carrier Air Group (CVG) 6 on board the carrier Hancock (CV 19). This collage of images is from the archives of the National Museum of Naval Aviation. (*Courtesy of the Nation Museum Naval Aviation*)

This TBM-3 from CAG-6 has a pair of dice (*Little Jo*) for nose art. (*Robert L. Lawson Photograph Collection, NMNA*)

Here, the unforgettable name *Frumious Bandersnatch*, from Lewis Carroll's *Jabberwocky*, appears on a F6F of VF-15, along with kill markings. Navy ace Ensign John Symmes is pictured here in 1944 after he had scored six kills. (*National Archives*)

USS GILBERT ISLANDS

The *Gilbert Islands* was commissioned on 5 February 1945 and, after a shakedown cruise, departed San Diego for the Hawaiian Islands in April 1945. Onboard was the second all-Marine Close Air Support (CAS) unit, Marine Carrier Group (MCVG-2). This group was made up of two all-Marine squadrons, VMTB-143 and VMF-512—an attack and fighter squadron. By 21 May 1945 the *Gilbert Islands* carrier force was sailing off the coast of Okinawa. For the next ten days they spent their time bombing and strafing enemy positions in support of their fellow Marines on the island. Following this, the Air Group spent its time attacking surrounding Japanese installations and getting ready for the invasion of the home islands. On 1 July the ship gave air support to the Australians, who were invading Borneo. After this the ship and Air Group joined the 3rd Fleet off the coast of Japan, in preparation for the invasion of Japan. After the end of the war the ship spent September and October in a show of force around China and Formosa. She finally arrived back at San Diego in December 1945. CVE-107 *Gilbert Islands* and her units earned three battle stars for Okinawa, Borneo, and the Japanese Home Islands, but it came at high price—the loss of seven aircrewmen.

Another claim to fame for the CVE-107 *Gilbert Islands* was that it was one of the few ships that allowed its crewmen to endow their aircraft with nose art. Also unique to the ship was a famous and very successful commercial artist and illustrator. His name was Alexander G. Raymond, the creator of the very-popular Sunday comic series *Flash Gordon*. In 1930, after completing art school in New York City, Alex Raymond began working as an assistant to comic creators and the King Features Syndicate. During the 1930s Raymond worked his way up in the Syndicate, and he was soon creating his own comic strips like *Jungle Jim* and *Flash Gordon*. By the early 1940s he was quite successful as a comic artist, as well as a popular illustrator for magazines like *Look* and *Cosmopolitan*. In 1944 Raymond joined the US Marine Corps and trained as a ground aviation officer. In his desire to get to the action he managed to get assigned to the USS *Gilbert Islands*. He was already well-known by the youth of the ship, who grew up with the comics, and as 'Flash' he became very popular with the officers and men of the ship, and the men of VMF-512 and VMBT-143. Much like Hal Olsen on Tinian, he brought his artist tools with him onboard the ship. Although it is not known for certain if Raymond painted the nose art on any of the TBM Avengers or the FG-1D Corsair, it is more than likely that he did provide some support and advice for some of the nose art. The answer to this question will remain unanswered, as Mr Alex Raymond died in a car accident shortly after the war. One thing for sure is that the pin-up 'Doris Mae', on VMBT-143's TBM-3E, bears more than a passing resemblance to the beautiful damsel 'Dale Arden' from the comic strip *Flash Gordon*.

The Avengers, from CVE-107 *Gilbert Islands*, sometime after the COMNAVAIRPAC authorized all escort-carrier air groups to adopt the geometric designs to identify various Air Wing. This helped the groups from each carrier to identify each other during formation rendezvous and joining up after attacks. Note that TBM-3 P-78 has nose art of a praying puppy, *Amen*. (*The National Museum of Naval Aviation*)

Aircraft No. P 83 the *Rebel* from CVE-107 *Gilbert Islands*, pictured flying over the Japanese homeland after the war. This nose art also shows the influence of the popular artist Alex Raymond as the *Rebel* favors 'Jungle Jim.' (*The National Museum of Naval Aviation*)

TBM-3 *Fertile Myrtle* P-84 of VMTB-143 inflight from the deck of the USS *Gilbert Islands*, an escort carrier with an all-Marine air wing, in 1945. (*The National Museum of Naval Aviation*)

TINIAN

Tinian, a small, 39-square-mile island in the Marianas group, was invaded and taken from the Japanese in July 1944. This unlikely island became the birthplace for the most creative and prolific period in US Navy nose art history. Just as Paris had been the cradle for the modern art movement during the turn of the century, with its Impressionist and Art Nouveau styles, Tinian was the origin for the development of naval aviation nose art during the Second World War. At the heart of this movement rested Carrier Aircraft Service Unit Forty Four (CASU-44) and an intermediate maintenance unit for Navy Liberators and Privateers in the Central and Western Pacific Theater. This unit had everything needed to repair the Navy's patrol planes, including extensive painting equipment. Navy patrol squadrons like VPB-102, 106, 108, 109, 116, and 118 had many aircraft painted on Tinian. Sometimes the works of art were duplicated two and three times due to attrition. Thus, 115 Liberators and Privateers carried nose art from November 1944 through December 1946. All had operated out of Tinian or passed through Tinian on their way to the war in the vast Western Pacific, and most squadrons would send their planes back to the CASU on this island for overhaul and repair.

HAL OLSEN

Hal Olsen on Tinian, 1945.
(*Hal Olsen*)

Many artists were based on Tinian, both with the Navy and the Army Air Force's B-29 Groups. Hal Olsen served with Instrument Trailer Group Three (ITG-3). He brought oil paints and brushes to Tinian in his sea bag and had planned to improve his painting skills by creating landscapes and still life of local island subjects, much as Gauguin had done in Tahiti. But when a late-night Japanese air raid destroyed the enamel paint locker, putting other nose artists on Tinian temporarily out of business, Hal decided to change from capturing island scenery on canvas to painting nudes on the massive flat sides of Privateers and Liberators.

He did his first airplane for free, and by the time he was finished he had ten others waiting. Whereas most artists on Tinian used enamel spray paint, or used tempera and then sprayed clear enamel over the artwork, Hal was unique in that he used the oil-based paint he had brought from home. Turpentine was used as the extender for the oil-based paint, and flesh-colored paint was mixed by the gallon. Crews would select artwork from pin-up calendars and magazines, and Hal would use the grid method to enlarge the calendar size original into a life-size piece of art. Standing on a 55-gallon oil drum, Hal would paint as a crowd of bystanders watched—often suggesting enlargements of certain portions of the female anatomy. The subject was in most cases a pin-up, and the nudes were frequently adorned with parts of a sailor's uniform or pirate accessories.

Sexy *double entendres* were also much-abused in naming the airplanes. However, when the aircraft returned to the States at the end of the war, Hal graciously painted swimsuits and negligees on the nudes.

It took Hal about four hours to paint the nose art and the crew's names under the cockpit and gun turrets of an airplane. He usually painted from dawn to about 10 a.m., trying to avoid afternoon showers and blowing dust from taxiing planes. On some occasions the aircraft would go on patrol before the paint would dry, and Hal would have to retouch the artwork when the aircraft returned. Hal received about fifty dollars for every aircraft he painted, and out of the 115 patrol planes painted on Tinian, forty-one aircraft, or roughly 35 per cent, were the creations of Hal Olsen.

Before: Hal Olsen's *La Cherie* was painted on Privateer BuNo. 59489 while on Tinian in late 1945. This aircraft was operated by both VPB-108 and VPB-121 during the war. When VPB-108 moved up to Iwo Jima the unit left the plane with CASU-44 on Tinian. VPB-121 took the aircraft on charge when they moved up to Tinian from Eniwetok. (*Don Spering A.I.R.*)

After: this recreation of *La Cherie* was done by Hal Olsen over fifty years later in his Bear Canyon Studio, New Mexico. This oil painting on pressboard gives the viewer a better idea of the coloring and texture that can be obtained with oil paints. These details are not visible in Second World War black-and-white photography. (*Hal Olsen via author*)

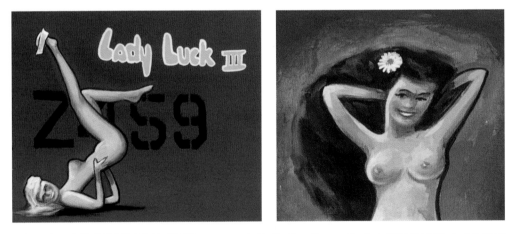

Left: *Lady Luck III* of VPB-108, BuNo. 59459, was recreated in the Bear Canyon Studio in 1996. (*Hal Olsen via author*)

Right: This is a detail look at the girl's face from Hal's recreation of the *Peace Keeper* artwork. Note the detail and brush strokes not normally captured in a war-time black-and-white photograph. (*Hal Olsen via author*)

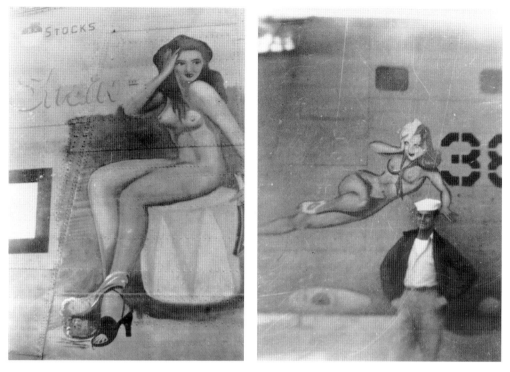

Left: *No Strain* was another of Hal's paintings found at NAS Kaneohe Bay after the war. This Privateers squadron assignment remains a mystery at this time. (*Don Spering A.I.R.*)

Right: The nude in a sailor's hat and neckerchief is a recurring theme in Hal Olsen's nose art. This aircraft was photographed at Litchfield Park in around 1950, but was created by Hal five years earlier. A search of Naval Archives reveals that BuNo. 59382 was in VPB-118, VPB-109 and VPB-123, which other squadrons are known to have used this serial number. (*T. E. Barton via Dr Stephen and Francis Wolf*)

VPB-106

VPB-106 was reorganized on 14 July 1944 at NAS San Diego. Some of the aircraft had nose art applied there, as well as in Kaneohe Bay, Hawaii. By 13 February 1945 the unit finally reached the war zone and Tinian Island. Equipped with fifteen aircraft, the squadron became Tinian's second PB4Y-2 Privateer outfit. In April 1945, the squadron commenced sending detachments to Iwo Jima in order to patrol the Japanese home waters and to support the Okinawa invasion. Hal Olsen painted only a few of the squadron's planes while on Tinian, because in May they were ordered to relieve the Bat-equipped squadron, VPB-109, in Palawan, Philippines. Despite having to move around so much, the squadron did well. On the long patrols out of the Philippines to Singapore they destroyed eleven transports and warships, and splashed five enemy aircraft.

VPB-109

VB-109 started out as a PB4Y-1 Liberator squadron in January 1944, under the command of Cdr Norman M. Miller, flying long-range patrols and bombing missions from the Gilbert Islands against the Caroline, Marshall, and Mariana Islands. At the end of the first tour, Miller's *Reluctant Raiders* had sunk or damaged 134 Japanese ships and downed four enemy aircraft. In October 1944 the

Above: VPB-106 set a precedent of adorning both sides of their planes with pin-ups. This somewhat-erotic piece of nose art was found on the starboard (right) side of its Privateer, BuNo. 59384. The port side of the aircraft was typically reserved for the Patrol Plane Commander, and usually carried the name of the aircraft as well as the crew's mission tallies and kills marks. This plane was withdrawn from use and surveyed for spares by 30 June 1945. (*Michael and Linda Miller in memory of Robert H. Miller 419th NFS*)

Left: Not only did the nose artist use calendar and magazines as a source for their art, but many of the aircrew men would give the artist postcards, like these from Florida and Hawaii, to use as an example for the pin-up art. (*Author's collection*)

The *Superchief* was a Privateer, BuNo. 59563, which moved with the squadron to Palawan, but by 1 June 1945 the aircraft and its entire crew were lost on a raid to Malaya from the Philippines. The small character under the cockpit presents an 'Ol' Salt' Chief Petty Officer, and I would guess his name was 'Lex Loci.' However, the unit's *Superchief* was the nude pin-up to the left of the 'Ol' Salt.' (*Michael and Linda Miller, in memory of Robert H. Miller 419th NFS*)

This PB4Y-1, BuNo. 32238, was a famous VB-106 aircraft belonging to the squadron's first skipper, Cdr John Hayward. The artwork literally caused a traffic jam both on the ground and in the air. The Seabee who created it claimed it was his girlfriend, but the pin-up bore a striking resemblance to a famous California stripper. When VB-106 went back to the States to reform as VPB-106, a Privateer unit, the plane was transferred to VB-115. This picture was taken in Wakde, New Guinea, in late 1944. (*Dick Shoden*)

Left: *Umbriago*, BuNo. 59390, is in storage at postwar NAS Litchfield Park, AZ. (*Mahlon Miller*)

Right: This Privateer had its name changed after the war from *Lucky-Leven* to *Torchy Lena* but it kept the same pin-up artwork. This aircraft was transferred from VPB-106 to a VP-HL unit by 1946. (*Mahlon Miller*)

squadron reformed at Camp Kearney, California, as VPB-109 under the command of Lt Cdr George L. Hicks, and was equipped with PB4Y-2 Privateers.

In February 1945 the Chief of Naval Operations directed that after a short period of training at Kaneohe Bay with VPB-123 and VPB-124, this unit would be equipped with the SWOD Mark 9 BAT standoff weapon. With a small rocket motor and a 1,000-pound warhead, the bomb used radar to lock on to its target and a radio-controlled autopilot to fly it to the target. Since most VPB squadrons launched mast-high skip-bomb attacks against Japanese shipping, this weapon would, in theory, make it easier for the Privateers to launch attacks outside the reach of enemy anti-aircraft fire. The Privateers of VPB-109 were the first aircraft to employ the BAT when, on 23 April 1945, the unit launched its first attack against Balikpapan Harbor, Borneo, from Palawan, Philippines. The results were inconclusive. They attacked Balikpapan again with BATs on 28 April, sinking both an 800-ton tanker and a picket boat as well as destroying a pier and an oil storage tank; however, the object of attack, a large troopship, was not hit by any of the special weapons. While in Palawan the crews painted nose art on most of the aircraft.

VPB-109 moved up to Okinawa on 11 May 1945, where they flew BAT missions in concert with VPB-118. Unfortunately, these missions also saw few successes. Things got worse for the *Reluctant Raiders* on the night of 24 May when, after a late-night bombing raid, some Japanese commandos

The *Miss Lotta Tail* of VPB-109 is seen here after the war at NAF Litchfield Park. The aircraft survived action in and around Okinawa to return home. The squadron lost two Privateers on Okinawa to the 24 May 1945 commando attack by a Japanese Girersu Raiding Unit. (*Roy L. Balke via John R. Kerr*)

attempted to land at Yontan Field, Okinawa. One Sally was able to crash-land, and during the night some of the enemy commandos were able to get in among the squadron's aircraft. By morning the entire enemy unit had been eliminated, but VPB-109 had lost two Privateers. The first success with the BAT was scored on 27 May, when one of the crews sank an enemy destroyer 3 miles from the launch point. The entire bow of the ship was blown off with a direct hit. However, after the recent aircraft losses caused by the 24 May *Giretsu* raiders, VPB-109 was withdrawn from Okinawa and sent to Tinian on 31 May for rest and renovation.

Roy L. Balke was in the *Reluctant Raiders'* Crew Five, and was stationed on Tinian during this period. The *Miss Lotta Tail* nose art and 'that special notation that graced the front end or nose of the aircraft' was born. This also involved the form of a bare lady. In a 30 March 2009 letter to the author, Petty Officer Balke relates the following story of his crew's nose art:

> Our Crew 5 would be no exception to having nose art. With our pilot Lt Joe Jadin's permission, and while on the island of Tinian, we contracted Navy Artist Hal Olsen to do the painting.
>
> Why me, I don't know, but I sketched an outline of the gal we selected and Hal Olsen did the rest. I captured a picture of Hal doing his thing standing on top of a barrel as shown in the photo. Then it came time for a name. Well, the PB4Y-2 Privateer aircraft had a lot of tail, extending nineteen feet skyward from the tarmac. That was it, we all agreed on a name that would fit. *Miss Lotta Tail* it would be.
>
> Upon returning to the States after the war, we landed at Naval Air Station, Crow's Landing, Fairfield, CA, our final destination and point of detachment from the Squadron. As we were unloading our gear from the aircraft, we noticed base personnel pulling tarps over the nose of our aircraft. Suddenly, after all that time in the Pacific, our gal went from being bare to fully-clothed. It didn't seem right. As I recall, when asked for an explanation, the response went something like this. 'Hey man have some respect, we have women, Navy WAVES, on this base!'

The artwork created by Hal Olsen and Roy Balke, *Miss Lotta Tail*, was on a PB4Y-2 Privateer BuNo. 59522. (*Roy L. Balke*)t

Hal Olsen uses a 55-gallon drum as a work stand to create the nose art for Crew Five of VPB-109. (*Roy L. Balke*)

Left: *Blind Bomber*, BuNo. 59514, was assigned to Lt W. A. Warren's Crew Twelve. Warren's crew was responsible for the sinking of one freighter and the downing of two Mitsubishi J2M2 Jacks while operating out of Okinawa. 'Crew 12' was originally painted on the tin cup held by the blind lady, but by 1946 their cup had been painted out and the aircraft was held in a pool of Privateers at NAS Kaneohe Bay, HI. (*T. E. Barton via Dr Stephen and Francis Wolf*)

Right: BuNo. 59502, *Green Cherries*, was Crew Fourteen's aircraft. Hal Olsen did this nose art while the aircraft was on Tinian for periodic maintenance. (*Don Spering A.I.R.*)

Also while the unit was on Tinian, Hal Olsen created the nose art for two other squadron aircraft, *Blind Bomber* and *Green Cherries*. In early July the unit was deployed to Iwo Jima, but by 30 July 1945 the squadron was back on Okinawa. They participated in an attack on a railroad bridge in NW Korea with VPB-118 and VPB-123 on 31 July. They continued to maintain a two-aircraft 'ready alert' on Okinawa, for launching BAT missions against any well-armed ship in open water. The last use of this weapon was 10 August 1945, but the bomb failed to hit its target.

VPB-116

Operating out of Eniwetok Island during March 1944, VP-116 started its war against Japan by flying sorties to Truk. In November 1944 Fleet Air Wing One (FAW-1) was formed, and the unit moved to the Marianas Islands. The land-based, long-range patrol plane element of this wing was composed of Liberators from VPB-102 and Privateers from VPB-118. The Liberators of VPB-116 joined them at Tinian on 10 January 1945. It was not long before VPB-116 had made its presence felt, and one night Tokyo Rose mentioned the squadron on her radio broadcast. She referred to the unit as the *Blue Raiders*, and the men liked the name so much they officially adopted it. In March 1945 FAW-1 began flying Empire Patrols out of Iwo Jima, and the *Raiders* were soon operating from there. They would send six Liberators to Iwo Jima, where they operated from Field No. 2, Motoyama, for temporary duty. Their patrols usually involved a two-aircraft section which covered the East Coast of the Japanese home islands. The squadron would then return to Tinian for a rest and for periodic aircraft maintenance. During July 1945 VPB-116 began to receive PB4Y-2 Privateers as replacements for their battle-weary Liberators. It was on Tinian that some of the squadron's aircraft received nose art. Hal Olsen entertained the crews of VPB-116 by painting full-size portraits of pin-up girls on the sides of their Liberators.

Top left: *Easy Maid*, a PB4Y-1 Liberator, BuNo. 38923, was a creation of Hal Olsen. This is the only original piece of Second World War US Navy nose art that has survived the war and the scrap dealer. The aircraft was turned in to the MCAF Walnut Ridge, Arkansas, in April 1946. While waiting to be cut up for scrap a civilian working at the facility had enough foresight to cut out the artwork and put it aside for posterity. It is now on display at the American Airpower Heritage Museum in Midland, Texas. (*John Kerr*)

Right: Hal Olsen painted *Miss Sea-ducer*, BuNo. 59582, on the island of Tinian while the plane was waiting to be deployed to Iwo Jima. Lt J. W. Anderson's crew did very well for themselves during war patrols, as noted by the two aerial kills and four ship kills. This picture was taken after the war while the aircraft was awaiting a future duty assignment, most likely with the aluminum pot merchant. (*T. E. Barton via Dr Stephen and Francis Wolf*)

Bottom left: Mr J. W. 'Doc' Downer was the plane captain in Lt Leonard Sullivan's Crew Four. The first aircraft Sullivan piloted, named *Willie* after his wife, was surveyed due to battle damage after a crash landing on 19 September 1944. The crew chose a less serious subject for the nose art on their second plane, *Willie's Wildcat II*, BuNo. 38845, and a gunner from the crew, named Pfeiffer, painted it. Later, Doc had Pfeiffer paint the same artwork on the back of his leather A-1 flight jacket. The cat caricature resembles an alley cat from the old comic strip *Smokey Stover*. It was fortunate that Doc Downer saved his jacket. Along with *Easy Maid*, it is one of only a few examples of authentic Second World War US Navy nose art still in existence. Cracked and faded after fifty-four years, this art still reveals some of the spirit of the Navy's patrol-bombing community during the last World War. See Appendix C, Diagram 1, for the artwork's position on the PB4Y-1. (*J. W. Downer*)

At his Bear Canyon Studio in Albuquerque, New Mexico, Hal Olsen created the oil painting (left) in 1996. This work is a reproduction of Lt Cdr Walter C. Michael's Privateer, BuNo. 59755. *Peace Feeler* was the first US Navy aircraft to land in Japan at Atsugi after the Japanese acceptance of the surrender terms, on 27 August 1945. The name was quite relevant considering that the world was finally at peace after six years. (*Hal Olsen via author*)

VPB-117

Tacloban Air Strip (located on Leyte, Philippines) became the home of VPB-117 and FAW-10 on 1 December 1944. The unit became the first Navy land-based squadron to operate from the Philippines. VPB-117 had been operating out of Tinian since September 1944, and some of the Liberators had nose art applied there. VPB-117 not only made use of nose art, but they also had a lot of kill marks and mission marks to add to their aircraft noses. Ultimately, this squadron would have more of the US Navy bomber aces than any other unit.

During most of January 1945 the squadron was not permitted to carry bombs because the unit was considered crucial to keeping tabs on the Japanese fleet. FAW-10 did not want any of their valuable assets to be lost on surface attacks against low-value targets. However, the aircraft still carried plenty of 50 cal. ammo so the crew could defend themselves. During the period of 1 December 1944 through 6 February 1945, the squadron managed to shoot down thirty-one enemy aircraft and claim five probables. On 6 February the unit transferred to McGuire Field, on Mindoro Island. Now under FAW-17's control, the squadron was responsible for shadowing the Japanese task forces and heavy units in Indochina that attempted to interfere with the Allied invasion of the Philippines.

On 17 February 1945 the unit suffered a great loss when Lt Cdr Harold W. McGaughey—the executive officer, a holder of the Navy Cross, and one of the squadron's five aces—was lost with his entire crew over Puerto Princessa, Palawan Island. Finally, on 25 March, all restrictions were lifted on the *Blue Raiders* and they were able to go on patrol fully-armed, returning to wreak havoc on shore installation, railroads, oil tanks, and shipping.

As the war began to wind down in their sector of the Pacific, the unit traded in their old, war-weary Liberators for the newer Privateers. However, they continued to suffer losses until 30 July 1945, when, on a mission over Vietnam, AMM Second Class Frederick F. Thomas became the unit's last casualty of war. On 11 August 1945 the *Blue Raiders* flew their last combat mission. By mid-August they were back at Tinian, and they remained there until September when they were relieved and returned to NAS San Diego, CA. As personnel transferred out of the command, the squadron was disestablished on 15 November 1945.

During the period between September 1944 and August 1945 the squadron claimed fifty-eight aircraft destroyed (fifty-five confirmed by postwar review), 236 enemy ships sunk or damaged, and the destruction of at least 300 ground targets. For these outstanding accomplishments, VPB-117 was awarded the Presidential Unit Citation.

The following is a list of VPB-117's multiengine bomber crew aces:

This aircraft, *Doc's Delight*, was assigned to VPB-111 before being reassigned to VPB-117 on Mindoro, P. I. (*Mahlon Miller*)

Left: BuNo. 38737 was one of VPB-117s Liberators which carried a score of six Japanese aircraft kills and four probables. According to US Navy records, this aircraft was assigned to the *Blue Raiders*. Just to the right of the score plaque, you can see the Disney–designed diving horse squadron emblem. This aircraft was probably not Lt Thomas J. Hyland's aircraft, since the unit's Combat Action Reports list his aircraft as BuNo. 38963, 38757, and 38861. From the artwork under the port window it is easy to see that *Uncle Tom* was the PPC's nickname. One other possibility is that the aircraft might belong to Lt Cdr Thomas P. Mulvihill, who was credited with four confirmed kills and some probables. He was famous for being a very aggressive flyer. (*Don Spering A.I.R.*)

Right: *Naval Maneuvers* was at Tacloban while VPB-117 was there; however, judging from the bare metal finish, this may be an Army Air Force B-24 despite the naval theme. Note the Naval Officer's hat on the pin-up. (*Don Spering A.I.R.*)

1. Lt Cdr Harold W. McGaughey, Crew 4, five kills
2. Lt Daniel Moore, Crew 10, five kills
3. Lt Thomas Hyland, five (six) kills*
4. Lt JG Jan Carter, Crew 16, five (six) kills*
5. Lt JG Sheldon Sutton, Crew 18, seven kills**

* Claimed six kills, but only five kills were verified by postwar review of Japanese records.
** All single engine aircraft

VPB-118

VPB-118 took the first Privateers to the war zone between November 1944 and 6 January 1945. In a hurry to become operational, they received the first Privateers equipped with the old Consolidated tail turrets in the nose, instead of the ERCO ball turrets which were less readily available at the time. Their crews decided on earmarking their individual aircraft in Hawaii with pin-up girls and catchy names. An enlisted man named Rape painted at least two of the unit's planes, *Miss Behavin* and *Flying Fin*, at NAS Kaneohe Bay. As the war went on, squadron loses mounted and replacement aircraft arrived at VPB-118's second duty station, the island of Tinian. But by then some crews had lost interest in nose art, and Hal Olsen only painted a few of the squadron's aircraft. The *Old Crows* racked up an outstanding record while operating from Tinian and, later, Iwo Jima and Okinawa. They earned a Presidential Unit Citation, sank ninety-nine enemy ships and a submarine, and also downed ten Japanese aircraft. However, they lost thirty-one valuable men killed in action and sixteen wounded. *Navy's Torchy Tess*, painted by Hal Olsen, was the only original squadron aircraft to return to the States after the war.

VPB-118's *Miss Natch* belonged to Lt Mark V. Monty Montgomery and Crew Ten. This aircraft was originally named *Marks Farts II* which was the second ship to bear this name and artwork. The first was a VB-104 Liberator which Monty flew during his first tour in the Solomon Islands. However, the Commanding Officer of VPB-118 and most likely some of the crew as well objected to the name. It was then changed to *Miss Natch*. The Skipper apparently recognized *Fart* as obscene but missed or chose to ignore *sNatch*. This photograph was taken in early 1945, probably on Tinian. The *sNatch* caught fire while being serviced on the Tinian ramp and was completely destroyed on 5 June 1945. The Consolidated nose turret identifies this Privateer as one of the fifteen original aircraft assigned to the squadron. (*Photograph courtesy A. J. Hopkins and 'Horse' Thompson*)

The *Modest-O-Miss II*, one of VPB-118's replacement Privateers, was a creation of Hal Olsen. On a bombing mission to Chefoo, China, July 27, 1945, this aircraft suffered damage to the main spar of the right wing. Lt Harry Duba and Crew Fifteen successfully brought BuNo. 59448 back to Ie Shima. The *Miss* was later repaired but was restricted to training flights only. When the squadron left to return to the States from Okinawa in November 1945, 'old 448' was left behind. Somehow, she was later ferried back to Hawaii and subsequently scrapped. This photograph was taken at NAS Litchfield Park after the war. Note the quote 'back alive in '45'. (*Mahlon K. Miller*)

This Privateer, BuNo. 59470, was originally named *Miss Behavin' II* and belonged to Lt A. M. Lodato's Crew Fourteen. Late in August 1945, many of the old timers left VPB-118, and a replacement crew was transferred to Okinawa. Lt John 'J. G.' Lee and his crew took over this plane and renamed it something original: *Sleepy Time Gal*. (*Don Spering A.I.R.*)

On 11 March 1945, Lt Mike Keiser's Crew Twelve smoked a Kawanishi H8K2 on a long Iwo-Connection patrol out of Tinian. The Emily, from the 801st Naval Air Corps, was leading a kamikaze flight of P1Y1 Gingas in an attack on allied shipping off Ulithi. In spite of the loss of their leader, at least one of the bombers succeeded in finding the fleet's anchorage and hitting CV-15 *Randolph*. The pin-up on *Flying Tail*, BuNo 59379, is of interest because this rather-portly beauty bears a certain resemblance to one of the squadron's PPCs. (*Author's Collection*)

VPB-121

Patrol Bombing Squadron 121 was commissioned as a PB4Y-2 Privateer unit on 1 October 1944 at NAAS Camp Kearney, CA. The unit left Camp Kearney for NAS Kaneohe Bay, HI, on 6 January 1945, and after further training they departed for Eniwetok Island at the end of February 1945. There, VPB-121 took on the responsibility of raiding two island groups, Wake Atoll and Ponape, which had been bypassed by US forces in their advance toward the Japanese home islands. The Wake Atoll Island's well-developed air facility could enable the enemy to strike at the supply lines of the US Pacific Fleet, while Ponape's harbor, airfield, and seaplane base were supplying the Japanese held Marshalls. For four months, the squadron bombed and strafed these two island bases, causing great devastation but losing one aircraft and crew in the process. The squadron's success was obvious near the end of June 1945, when the unit found a Japanese hospital ship that was in the process of evacuating over 900 starving and wounded survivors of the allied attacks. When the Japanese were questioned, they said they spent most of their time trying to grow food rather than building a defense.

    The unit was then ordered to Tinian on 3 July 1945. From Tinian the squadron sent nine aircraft and eleven crews to the forward base of Iwo Jima, keeping an average of four crews and three aircraft resting and refitting at the maintenance facility on Tinian. This gave Hal Olsen the opportunity to paint nose art on at least three of the squadron's Privateers. From Iwo Jima, VPB-121 supported the US fleet in its final push to take the Japanese home island of Kyushu. On their patrols the unit

Left: This aircraft carried no name, only a provocative piece of artwork. Hal Olsen repeated the theme of the nude in a sailor's garb on at least three other Privateers, all belonging to different squadrons. (*Don Spering A.I.R.*)

Right: BuNo. 59492, one of VPB-121's PB4Y-2s, displays the popular pirate-themed pin-up. This picture was taken after the war at NAS Kaneohe Bay, HI, in 1946. (*Don Spering A.I.R.*)

BuNo. 59478, another of VPB-121's aircraft, puts a different spin on the pirate theme, which was common to the Privateer patrol-plane community. *Buccaneer Bunny* was at NAS Kaneohe Bay in 1946. (*Don Spering A.I.R.*)

VPB-121's *Tail Chaser* post war after the aircraft has de-mobilized and is ready for storage at a Reconstruction Finance Center field. (*Mahlon Miller*)

sank many transport vessels and performed air-sea rescue work, but the PB4Y-2s also had many opportunities to confront the Japanese Army and Navy Air Forces. In most cases they bested their opponent, claiming two Mitsubishi F1M2s, one Mitsubishi A6M5, and damaging four other fighters. During this time period, until the squadron's last war patrol on 19 September 1945, the squadron lost only one other Privateer to the stiff enemy air defense. The squadron returned to Kwajalein and Eniwetok Islands after VJ day and remained there until May 1946, when they returned to the States with their aircraft. The squadron was decommissioned on 1 June of that year.

VPB-123

Patrol Bombing Squadron 123 was formed on 15 December 1944 at NAS Alameda. Soon after, they moved to NAAS Crows Landing for advanced combat training. When the squadron was earmarked as a BAT squadron, along with VPB-109 and VPB-124, they moved forward to NAS Kaneohe Bay, in Hawaii, to begin training with this complex standoff weapon. VPB-123 did not make it to Tinian until after VPB-109 began to operationally use the BAT, but by 31 May 1945 they had relieved the hard-pressed VPB-109 on Okinawa. They began by flying anti-shipping strikes in the Sea of Japan and the Yellow Sea; however, by this time in the war the other BAT squadrons had given up on this stand-off form of attack, since other patrol units had been much more successful in sinking the small, unescorted Japanese merchant ships by using conventional methods. So VPB-123 reverted to the old way of doing business, and began to achieve successes as well. During the month of June, however, success came with loss. The unit lost two Privateers on the 9th and the 19th, but fortunately these would be their only operational losses during the war. By July, the unit was participating in overland horizontal bombing missions to Korea from Okinawa in an attempt to destroy Japanese shipping and rail facilities. This was part of an overall plan to make life in the home islands very

Left; Privateer BuNo. 59476 flew with Lt Kenny Sanford's Crew Six in VPB-123. This crew was responsible for sinking seven ships and two trains. The artist for the *Pirate Princess* used the pirate motif to decorate this plane, as did many of the other Privateer squadrons. (*Don Spering A.I.R.*)

Right: *Nobody Else Butt*, BuNo. 59520, was a very successful Privateer while in VPB-123, sinking eight ships and downing one aircraft. They also got two trains while on bombing missions to Korea. (*Don Spering A.I.R.*)

The *Vagrant Virago* was photographed at NAS Kaneohe Bay, Hawaii, after the war. This aircraft, BuNo. 59487 also belonged to VPB-123. (*Don Spering A.I.R.*)

uncomfortable for the Japanese people by cutting off the source of food and coal coming from Korea. The squadron also attacked places such as Shanghai and shipping in the Yangtze River. Strikes on Korea and Manchuria continued until the end of the war, with each plane carrying up to 2000 lbs of bombs. VPB-123 sank a total of sixty-seven enemy ships and scored ten aerial kills while in the Pacific.

VD-1

VD-1 was a photoreconnaissance squadron formed at NAS San Diego in late 1942. A self-sufficient six-plane squadron, VD-1 was sent to Carney Field, Guadalcanal, in April 1943, where they flew low-level photo missions. These missions tended to be dangerous, and by the time VD-1 left the South Pacific they had lost at least six Liberators. By June 1944 the war had moved north to the Central Pacific, and the squadron was withdrawn and re-equipped with new or reworked PB4Y-1 Liberators. They joined VD-5 on Guam in May 1945 and would remain there until December 1945. At least three of the squadron's planes made it to Tinian or were transferred there from the CASU during this time, because Hal Olsen painted nose art on the aircraft. Late in the war, the unit began to transition to PB4Y-2 Privateers, and during the post-war period VD-1 flew weather reconnaissance and photographic survey missions in the Central Pacific.

Wild Cherry II was VD-1's aircraft No. 27. This poor-quality but rare photo captures the aircraft just after it has passed through a rainsquall. Note a halo has surrounded the plane. (*Don Spering A.I.R.*)

This PB4Y-1, belonging to VD-1's Crew Three, is unique in that besides its fifteen photo missions it has also flown two bombing missions. This is probably due to the fact that a two plane element from the photo squadron would sometimes require a two or four-plane flight from a patrol-bombing unit to keep the Japanese gunners guessing. The bombing mission was a ruse for the real mission's objective, which was to take photos of some by-passed airfield or invasion beach. This artwork, the nude in sailor's garb motif, was a creation of Hal Olsen. (*Don Spering A.I.R.*)

Wild Cherry's Crew Seven stands in front of their aircraft. This plane has completed seventeen photo recon missions. Note that painted adjacent to each crew position is the name of the crewmember's wife or girlfriend. This aircraft may have been passed on to the unit form one of the Tinian-based Liberator squadrons because the artwork was a Hal Olsen creation. (*Don Spering A.I.R.*)

This is another PB4Y-1P Liberator attached to VD-1 on Guam with fourteen reconnaissance missions to its credit. This nose art was also a creation of the Tinian based artist Hal Olsen. (*Don Spering A.I.R.*)

NAS KANEOHE BAY, HAWAII

NAS Kaneohe Bay, Hawaii, was a significant center for the development of naval aircraft nose art during the Second World War. Some squadrons passed through Hawaii on their way to the war zone, and, while there, would sometimes have their planes painted. For example, VPB-118 had a few of their patrol planes decorated with nose art there before moving on to Tinian. Also, VF-27's Hellcats were painted in Hawaii with their famous cat's mouth before going abroad the USS *Princeton*. The going rate for the decorating of a PB4Y-2 was $75 and a bottle of liquor, a little more than the price in other places, such as Tinian.

In late 1945, as the flight crews in various patrol squadrons earned enough points to warrant separation from active duty, they would fly back one of the squadron's war-weary aircraft. However, the Privateer and Liberator squadrons on Iwo Jima, Okinawa, and in the Philippines might fly to Tinian and leave their aircraft with the maintenance unit for overhaul. They would then fly a war-weary Liberator back to Hawaii, where they would either board a ship back to the States or get selected to fly a patrol aircraft back to San Diego. Thus, after the war a large variety of patrol aircraft from many squadrons were gathered together at Kaneohe Bay, and a unique opportunity could be afforded to see a lot of nose art.

SNUFFY'S MISCHIEF MAKER

VPB-115 was one of the pioneering Liberator patrol-bombing squadrons that came to the South Pacific in 1944. While in training at Camp Kearney, Mesa, CA, and NAS Kaneohe Bay, HI, their aircraft carried no nose art. This changed after the unit arrived at Munda, New Georgia. The crews there usually flew every third day, and when their assigned aircraft was not having maintenance

The above picture was taken in Hawaii at Kaneohe Bay shortly after the war. Note the different variety of patrol aircraft: PBY-5As, PB4Y-1, PB4Y-2s, and PBMs. Right: PBY-5A *Miss Take.* (*Don Spering A.I.R.*)

Right: The following aircraft were at NAS Kaneohe Bay, Hawaii, sometime between September 1945 and December 1946: (*Don Spering A.I.R.*)

Below: PBY-5A, *Homesick Angel* (*Don Spering A.I.R.*)

PBY-5A, *Sleepy Time Gal!* (*Don Spering A.I.R.*)

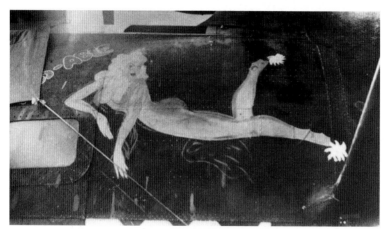

PBY-5A, *Miss-Able* (*Don Spering A.I.R.*)

PB4Y-2, BuNo. 59460, VPB-108 (*Don Spering A.I.R.*)

done another crew might fly it. So, when Lt Bill 'Snuffy' Doerr's Crew Eleven took the *Mischief Maker* (belonging to Lt Paul Bruneau's Crew Four) out on a patrol to Puluwat Atoll on 21 April 1944 and never returned, Crew Four took over Lt Doerr's aircraft. They named it *Snuffy's Mischief Maker* as a tribute to Lt Doerr and Crew Eleven. Crew Four's second aircraft exemplifies the effort to apply artwork within the squadron. A Seabee, 3rd Class Petty Officer A. L. Stephens, painted the artwork and lettering on aircraft BuNo. 32182 while on Green Island. His payment for the task was a bottle of Australian hospital brandy and a ride on one of the crew's patrols (as opposed to the standard fee for painting an aircraft in the South Pacific, which was about $60). Unfortunately, Petty Officer Stephens was gravely wounded during his ride with Crew Four on 19 May.

VPB-115 as a whole managed to destroy forty-four enemy aircraft on the ground and in the air. They also destroyed fifty-five enemy naval and merchant ships, including twelve merchant vessels weighing greater than 4,000 tons. For their outstanding and heroic actions between 26 March and 7 November 1944, the squadron was awarded the Presidential Unit Citation. VPB-115's Crew Four had quite an exciting time while in the South Pacific—they destroyed the following six aircraft on their own:

Date	PPC	Gunners	Claim
10 April 1944	Lt P. J. Bruneau	N/A	One Betty bombed (ground)
23 April 1944	Lt Cdr J. R. Compton Lt P.J. Bruneau 2nd pilot	Furey, Edwards, Wiswell	One Betty destroyed (air)
19 May 1944	Lt P.J. Bruneau	Furey, Shoden	One Zeke destroyed (air)
9 June 1944*	Lt P.J. Bruneau	Furey, Hollis, Shoden, Wiswell	Two Tess destroyed (air)
12 June 1944	Lt P.J. Bruneau	Furey	One Tess destroyed (air)

* The Tess was trying to replenish Palau Island, and later did not fly without a fighter escort.

The 'top guns' of VPB-115, from left to right, are: Al Wiswell, AOMB 1st Class (AB) bow turret; Hank Harmon, AMM 2nd Class (PC) waist gunner; Lee Edwards, AMM 3rd Class belly turret; Lee McKenzie, ARM 2nd Class (FCO) top turret; and not pictured are John Furey, ARM 2nd Class (FCO) top turret, and Dick Shoden, AOM 1st Class tail gunner. Note the six 'meat ball' kills on the side of the aircraft representing the crew's five aerial claims and one enemy airplane destroyed on the ground. Due to battle damage *Snuffy's Mischief Maker* was later withdrawn from service and became a spare-parts locker. Crew Four's final aircraft (Above) was BuNo. 32274, and was named *Mischief Maker III*. This aircraft survived the campaign and brought the crew back to San Diego in November 1944. (*Dick Shoden*)

Dick Shoden is standing by *Snuffy's Mischief Maker* on Green Island after the May 19 action. During this attack on the shipping in the Satawan lagoon their Liberator was damaged by flak, hence the battle damage to the bow turret. Dick was in the bow turret of the Liberator during this mission when a 40-mm fragment shattered the bow turret's azimuth rotation gear. His bottom was literally saved by his folded flak suit on which he was sitting. Crew Eleven probably christened the bow turret on BuNo. 32182 *Princess* since no one on Crew Four seems to have painted it there. In fact many gunners named their guns, i.e. *Murder Incorporated*, but if the plane was shot down and the crew captured, the Japanese might take offense. However, the enemy did not make prisoners of Allied aircrew.

Lt Paul J. Bruneau standing with *Snuffy's Mischief Maker* in the Southwest Pacific in around May 1944. If Mr Bruneau had been flying a multiengine fighter with an air gunner on board, he would be an ace now. Instead, he is just a patrol-bomber pilot who maneuvered his Liberator with the zeal of a fighter pilot. Due to battle damage *Snuffy's Mischief Maker* was later withdrawn from service and became a spare-parts locker.

In 1996, six crewmembers of VPB-115's Crew Four still lived. Five of them, Dick Shoden, Cdr Paul Bruneau, US Navy Ret., John Furey, Albom Wiswell, David West, and Hank Harmon, were kind enough to contribute input to this watercolor. The three areas of question concerning the illustration were the colors in the nose art, the name on the bow turret, and the color of the airplane itself. For the colors in the nose art, most of the surviving members agreed that the lettering and the girl's accessories were white and her hair was auburn. As for the bow turret's name, Dick Shoden came up with the photo (previous page) showing that at the time the turret was named *Princess*. But the color of the PB4Y-1 Liberator proved to be the most difficult thing to reproduce. Everyone gave a different description of the color, varying from light dusty blue to medium or gray blue to dark khaki or olive. However, the majority of the surviving crew said the below rendering, a light sea-blue or gray, was closest to the way they remember *Snuffy*. The confusion on the plane's color is probably due to the fact that the aircraft was originally a USAAF B-24J serial # 42-73104 and, when taken on charge by the Navy, had an Army paint scheme of olive drab. It should have been over-sprayed sea blue, but, in a rush to get these long-range patrol planes into action, it may have been issued directly to the squadron with the Army paint scheme. At some time later, it must have been painted blue because W. W. Rolfes, a plane captain in the squadron, had aircraft No. 82 listed in his logbook as a blue aircraft. But in the end, after the planes were exposed to the harsh conditions in the Solomon Islands the paint may have faded and worn off, revealing an olive drab undercoat. (*Bill Tate*)

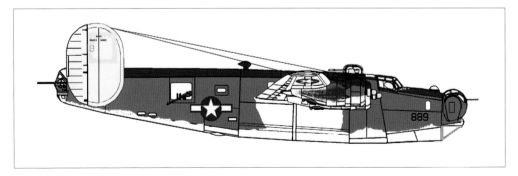

VPB-104, BuNo. 38889. VPB-104's Crew Two and their PPC, Lt Paul F. Stevens, were credited with six Japanese aircraft from 31 December 1944 through 17 March 1945. Their last air-to-air kill was an Imperial Navy Kawanishi H8K1 (*Emily*) which had Admiral Yamagata and his staff on board. The above aircraft was involved in Lt Stevens's first three kills. Because of the barbaric attitude of the Japanese in this unit's op-area, the Skipper ordered 'no nose art' on the aircraft. This could be the miniature Japanese flag kill markings. If the crew had been shot down and captured, they could always claim to be green replacements.

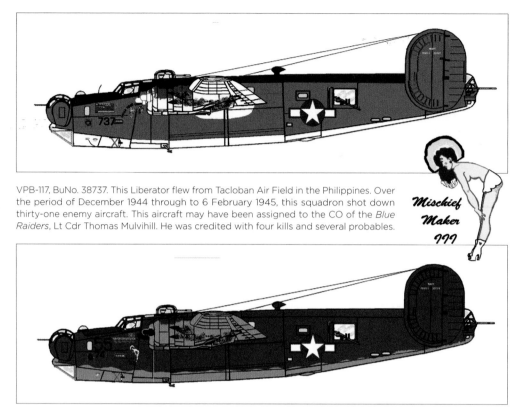

VPB-117, BuNo. 38737. This Liberator flew from Tacloban Air Field in the Philippines. Over the period of December 1944 through to 6 February 1945, this squadron shot down thirty-one enemy aircraft. This aircraft may have been assigned to the CO of the *Blue Raiders*, Lt Cdr Thomas Mulvihill. He was credited with four kills and several probables.

Mischief
Maker
III

VPB-115, BuNo. 32274. *Mischief Maker III* was Lt Paul Bruneau's third aircraft. He and his Crew Four were credited with the destruction of five Japanese aircraft in the air and one on the ground while flying with the unit. This aircraft carries six kill marks as claimed by the crew, July 1944.

MACAHYBA MAIDEN

VPB-107 was reorganized from the PBY-5A-equipped VP-83 during the spring of 1943. The new squadron flew PB4Y-1 Liberators from Natal, Brazil, and Ascension Island during 1943–44. It was here that the squadron found the inspiration for the *Macahyba Maiden*, one of VPB-107's famous Liberators. In late 1944, when the squadron was re-equipped and later transferred to FAW-7 at Dunkeswell Airfield in the United Kingdom, their aircraft had some of the most colorful examples of nose art found on naval aircraft in the Atlantic fleet during the war. It was aircraft like *Heavenly Body* and *Brown Bagger's Retreat* that came closest to meeting the standards set by the nose artist in the Eighth Air Force's B-24 Liberator squadrons.

This unit was more successful against the Axis submarines than any other US Navy patrol squadron. Together with the Enigma intelligence encrypts and carrier-based hunter-killer groups, they made the south Atlantic unsafe for Axis U-boats.

VPB-83/107 was responsible for the destruction of the following Axis U-boats:

1.	*U-164*	6 Jan '43	VP-83
2.	*U-507*	13 Jan '43	VP-83
3.	*Archimede*	15 Apr '43	VP-83
4.	*U-598*	23 Jul '43	VPB-107
5.	*U-604*	11 Aug '43	VPB-107 plus others

6.	*U-848*	5 Nov '43	VPB-107 plus others
7.	*U-849*	25 Nov '43	VPB-107
8.	*U-177*	6 Feb '44	VPB-107
9.	*U-863*	29 Sep '44	VPB-107

In addition, the Liberators of VPB-107 also located the German blockade-runner SS *Wesserlund* and vectored surface ships to the location, where the enemy was sunk. During these actions they lost four Liberators to the enemy. The squadron was one of three patrol squadrons to win a Presidential Unit Citation during the Second World War.

Macahyba, a small village on the Brazilian coast, close in proximity to Natal, was off-limits to US service men during the war. The *Macahyba Maiden*, BuNo. 32056, sank U-598 early in its career on July 23, 1943. After the sinking of U-598 the aircraft's name was changed from *Maiden* to *Madam*. The change to *Madam* not only signified that the aircraft could no longer be considered a virgin but also gives the reader a clue as to why the village of Macahyba may well have been off limits. (*R. A. Wilson*)

Heavenly Body was one of the late-model Liberators equipped with an ERCO nose turret. Lt Sam Taylor, standing third from the left, was the man responsible for sinking U-848 to the west of Ascension Island. (*R. A. Wilson*)

Macahyba Maiden, Natal, Brazil, 1943, with Lt William Ford's crew. Standing left to right are Burgess, Damiano, Butler, PPC Lt Ford, Lt Gentile, and unknown. On the front row, left to right, are Bokon, Rackly, CPO Richter, Meyer, Dupree, and Carpenter. After a twenty-four-hour-long battle between U-598 and six other squadron Liberators, the German boat was so damaged that after surfacing it was unable to re-submerge. Ford's crew then arrived and immediately sank the U-boat. (*R. A. Wilson*)

OTHER LIBERATORS

Dangerous Lady and her crew pose for the camera at some Pacific base during the Second World War. There is no evidence to identify this Liberator other than the name. The Army Air Force serial number is obscured by the pin-up, and there is no modex number visible aside, from the number on the nose turret to identify the US Navy BuNo. Note that the crew members have all posted their girlfriend's names adjacent to their position. (*Mahlon Miller*)

However, this highly decorated Liberator is easy to identify. *Lil Effie*, modex '843,' is the last three digits of the BuNo. 38843, and from aircraft custody cards it was ascertained that the plane belonged to VPB-102 until 23 May 1945. On that date, this aircraft crashed upon take off from Iwo Jima and seven of the crewmen were killed. This aircraft was also named *Boss Burton's Nitemare* and was painted by Hal Olsen on Tinian. (*Don Spering A.I.R.*)

PV-1 VENTURA

The PV-1 Ventura holds a unique place in the story of Naval Aviation nose art. This aircraft was manufactured at the Lockheed Vega facilities in Burbank, California. Wanting to do their part for the war effort, the Walt Disney Studios authorized artists to go over to the Vega plant and paint cartoon characters on the side of Venturas which had just come down the production line. Some of these planes were destined for England and New Zealand, but some were detailed to the US Navy. The Venturas and, later, some Harpoons would be the only Navy aircraft to arrive at operational squadrons with artwork. Once in the squadrons, the artwork might be painted over or it might continue on in use. Some Atlantic Fleet squadrons retained their artwork, while most Pacific Fleet units painted it out—if the plane was downed in Japanese territory the enemy might use it as an excuse to treat prisoners badly. VB-136 was one of these West Coast squadrons which retained its artwork while stationed in the Aleutians.

Pictured is a late-model Ventura from the Lockheed Burbank Factory on a test flight. Note the Disney cartoon adjacent to the national insignia. The artwork depicts one of those moments when Donald is having an angry fit about something. Many enlisted aircrew and sailors identified closely with this type of adolescent art form, since these men were in high school not so long before. (*National Archives via Don Spering*)

This PV-1 is the aircraft that Lt Harry Metke of VPB-148 used to shoot down a Japanese Betty on 1 June 1944. While flying patrols from Emirau, New Georgia, this unit accounted for one more Betty and two Tonys, as well as at least four enemy ships. The name of this aircraft, *Patches*, probably alludes to the many battle-damage repair patches the aircraft carried due to low-level attack missions, which they flew around Bougainville. (*US Navy via Perry Ustick*)

PUNCH AND JUDY

While stationed in Attu, Aleutian Islands LT Bob Warnock established that VPB-131 would not make an effort to paint nose art on their Venturas because of the severe weather conditions. All aircraft maintenance was done in primitive conditions. However, Bob had recently married Julia, and his crew—while preparing for their second tour at Whidbey Island—painted the wheel cover of their PV-1 to commemorate the event. Since Bob had the *Judy*, the crew must have had the *Punch*. In fact, the PV-1 packed quite a punch for being such a small aircraft. From the yoke pickle switches in the cockpit, Lt Warnock could fire the five 50-cal. machine guns in the nose and the eight 5-inch HVAR rockets on the wings. In addition, the aircraft carried twin 50s in the upper turret and twin 30-cal. MGs in the ventral tail position. VPB-131 introduced its new HVAR Venturas into the Aleutian Theater of Operation in October 1944. They operated as a ground-attack squadron, carrying extra fuel instead of bombs in the bomb bay, while flying four plane strikes to Kurile Island.

Punch and Judy was painted on the main mount wheel cover of Lt Bob Warnock's PV-1. See Appendix C, Diagram 4 for the artwork location. (*Robert Warnock*)

THE OTHER GUYS

An enormous number and variety of aircraft supported the Navy and Marine Corps during the Second World War. Transport aircraft were vital to the re-supply of units moving up the island chains in the Pacific. Cruisers and battleships carried float-equipped observation and gunfire-spotting aircraft aboard. Amphibian and float planes performed rescue and support missions. Late in the war, USMC spotter planes observed and directed artillery fire on the islands of Saipan, Okinawa, and Iwo Jima. Examples of personalized aircraft and nose art were found on all of these types of aircraft.

An aircraft famous in the lore of Bataan, Corregidor, and the fall of the Philippines in 1942 was a Grumman J2F Duck named the *Candy Clipper*. The Duck was sunk by strafing Japanese aircraft at Mariveles on Manila Bay, and was later raised by members of the 24th Pursuit Group, USAAC. The floatplane was patched and repaired with parts from other aircraft, and from February to April of 1942, the Duck flew food and medical supplies to beleaguered Army, Navy, and Filipino troops scattered about the islands; thus it acquired the name *Candy Clipper*. Although no known photograph of it exists today, a J2F has been restored using pre-war US Navy markings which have the same name and a candy cane painted on the cowl, as a tribute to the earlier aircraft and the men who kept her flying.

Medical Evacuation or VE Squadrons were formed for the rapid evacuation of wounded troops from combat zones in the Pacific following invasion. The VE squadrons were equipped with R4D and R5D aircraft that were modified to carry casualties. Photos from a former member of VE-2 depict several R4D aircraft in standard olive drab and gray, with names applied. One, the *Back Bay Special*, carried a circular insignia just below the pilot's window. Another photo, which depicts an R4D of VE-2 as having the same insignia and an unreadable one-word name, indicates that other aircraft in the unit may have used the insignia as well.

The Vought OS2U-3 Kingfisher was a scout plane that flew from battleships and cruisers. One, named *Blue Racer* with a snake drawing, operated in the Pacific during 1943. Several of the Marine Corps' Stinson OY-1 spotter aircraft sported artwork. One flew as an artillery-spotter aircraft on Okinawa, and sported a large red-and-white shark mouth. OY-1 *Lady Satan* (with appropriate pin-up) reportedly flew on Iwo Jima in 1945.

This PBY-5A served as a VIP transport in the Headquarters Squadron or HEDRON of FAW-3 in the Canal Zone after the war. Note the flags of all the countries in which the PBY had served: UK, Norway, Denmark, Cuba, the Netherlands, Brazil, the US, and Australia. Is seems unusual that FAW-3's HEDRON would carry this form of artwork while VP-84 and VPB-206, both units that served with the Wing and were in the Canal Zone, discouraged nose art. (*Don Spering A.I.R.*)

The *Back Bay Special* is a Navy R4D-5 of medical evacuation squadron VE-2, pictured here on Guam in 1945. Under the pilot's window is the insignia of VE-2, a winged red cross over a globe with the Latin motto *Auxilium Ab Alto*. (*Ianuzzi via Meehan*)

PB4Y-1 BuNo. 32140 returns from a mission over Puluwat with battle damage. Cdr N. M. Miller taxis the plane to a stop at Eniwetok base. Note that *Climb Aboard* has been censored. (*US Navy via Robert Schaffer and Roy Balke*)

This SC-1 Seahawk was named *Soda H2O* with a small red soda pop bottle just barely discernible below the canopy. This aircraft was stationed at NAF Mustin Field, Philadelphia, PA in 1946 and used for catapult test. (*Don Spering A.I.R.*)

2

THE KOREAN WAR

If the period during the Second World War can be considered the zenith of naval aviation nose art, then the period from 1950–54 can be considered the low point. It would be hard to pinpoint exactly why this happened, but two obvious reasons are that the Korean police action did not enjoy the patriotic support given during the Second World War and that naval aviation was now manned—for the most part—by draftees and reserves recalled to active duty. Korea has been called the 'Forgotten War', mainly because the American public's concern with achieving the 'American Dream' caused them to overlook supporting the war after early 1951. Reflecting this public opinion, the draftees and reservists going into the war were not looking for things to help them take pride in their cause, such as nose art. Not only did the public forget about the war, but also some in the military had forgotten the lessons learned in the previous war, including the fact that the use of nose art facilitated high morale for the pilots and maintenance personnel.

During the Korean conflict, many of the Pacific Fleets' carriers operated off the Korean coast. The years of combat involved the extensive use of US Navy carrier-based aircraft to interdict enemy supply lines and support ground troops. USMC attack aircraft and night fighters also flew from the carriers but were primarily land-based. As Korea marked the introduction of the first carrier-based jet aircraft to war, typical Carrier Air Group attack squadrons mixed the propeller-driven F4U Corsairs and Douglas AD Skyraiders with the jet-powered Grumman F9F Panthers and Cougars and McDonnell F2H Banshees. The larger CAGs were further beefed up by the addition of specialized detachments of photo, night-fighter, night-attack, and anti-submarine aircraft. Unfortunately, the majority of these aircraft were never personalized. Out of the eleven attack carriers that deployed to Korea, only two ships, the USS *Boxer*, CVA-21, and the USS *Princeton*, CVA-37, entertained the use of aircraft nose art. Although quite a few of the squadron aircraft in CAG-101 and CAG-102 were named, adding a scoreboard or artwork was apparently not convenient for most. In some cases, the lettering of these names was done in chalk, making them temporary at best.

The only units that were found to have used artwork on a large scale were Naval Air Reserve Squadrons activated between July 1950 and September 1950. Many of these reservists were veterans of the Second World War and had substantial combat experience. Thirty-five RESFORONs (Reserve Force Squadrons) were called to active duty and were used to augment the regular Navy squadrons. Many of these squadrons had to be supported by a massive amount of personnel and equipment from the regulars before becoming combat-ready; by June 1951 the reservists were flying over 70 per cent of the combat missions in Korea. In order to retain as much of their reserve spirit as possible, these units tried to decorate their aircraft. Their veteran status probably made it easier for them to 'buck the system' and use nose art. The two reserve squadrons that made the most successful effort at using nose art were VF-871 and VP-731.

The Skyraiders flew an enormous number of attack missions during the war, but the small, insignificant scripts on the nose of this aircraft did little to help give these planes a place in nose art history. This simple name, probably done in chalk, is a typical example of aircraft decoration during the Korean police action and is not considered nose art by this study. (*National Archives*)

MARINE CORPS AVIATION

The Marine Corps fighter squadrons—whether land or carrier-based—made great use of color in decorating their aircraft. Several squadrons decorated their Corsairs with cowl bands. VMF-312's F4U-4s were decked out with white checkerboard cowls, while VMA-332's Corsairs were decorated with a white cowl band and red polka dots. The *Death Rattlers* of VMF-323 carried not only a purple cowl band but also a large rattlesnake on the noses of their F4U-4 aircraft. The AU-1 Corsairs of VMF-212 were painted with a long white arrow from nose to tail, and at least two of these carried names: BuNo. 129417 was named *Jody* and BuNo. 129359, LD 10, was named *Miss Penny*.

The F9F Panther and Cougar jets of the Marine squadrons were also decorated in the field when possible. Several Panthers of shore based VMF-311were decorated with either a shark-mouth or a panther face, complete with snarling teeth. VMF (N)-513, the *Flying Nightmares*, flew F7F-3N Tigercat and F3D Skynight night–fighters from Korean bases. Several of the Tigercats had mission markings and simple stenciled names in red on the black finish, like *Linda*.

CVA-21 BOXER

Another ship that our research has shown to have a lot of examples of nose art was the USS *Boxer*, CVA-21. From March 1951 to October 1951 the Naval Air Reserve CVG-101 was aboard this carrier. Many of the squadrons in CVG-101 had nose art, but most were simply names and mission marks. Take, for instance, the VF-791 Corsairs *Dot*, modex A 211, and *Yvonne III*, modex A 207.

Three of the four F4U-4 Corsairs of VF-884, a reserve unit, recalled to active duty from NAS Olathe, Kansas carry some kind of art. All aircraft except A 407 have mission marks. Two aircraft have names, A 406 appears to have *Judy IV* and A 409 may be named *Sweet Sue*. (*National Archives via Jim Sullivan*)

Sweet Sue was one of the legends of VF-884 and the USS *Boxer*; at this time (6 July 1951) the aircraft has accumulated fifty missions and accounted for six vehicles. This aircraft had suffered a hard landing 17 October 1950 but was returned to service by the end of the year. On 3 October 1951, after the aircraft had flown 116 missions, it was placed in storage at NAS Litchfield Park, AZ. (*National Archives via Jim Sullivan*)

Another reserve unit known for its nose art was VF-884, the *Bitter Birds* from Kansas. A photograph shows a formation of their F4U-4s over the ship with many of the aircraft carrying names in white on the fuselage, a squadron insignia, and mission marks. VF-884's *Sweet Sue*, modex A 413, would survive the first year of the war to be retired to NAS Litchfield Park, AZ, in 1951. Then aircraft A 403 would become the second *Sweet Sue* when CVG-101 moved to the CVA 33, *Kearsarge*.

One squadron that used both names and pin-up nose art—a rare thing at the time—was VF-194, the *Yellow Devils*. They flew AD-4 Skyraiders on the *Boxer's* fourth war cruise and had nose art on several of their aircraft. Two confirmed planes with pin-ups on the lower nose were *Miss Mary Jane*, modex B 401, and *Little Miss Rita*, modex B 417. VC-3 also provided night-fighter detachments to the *Boxer*. The F4U-5N Corsair *Sleepless Knight*, NP 6, found there in 1952, had fifteen missions applied to the fuselage.

This AD-4N, VA-194's *Little Miss Rita*, is the night fighter version of the Skyraider. Being used in an attack role, it is carrying a load of bombs from the USS *Boxer* to the Korean coast in June 1953. The diminutive pin-up on the engine cowling is known to have been a nude draped in a confederate battle flag. (*Mr D. Ferrel*)

An F9F-2P of VC-61 is pictured here on the flight deck of the USS *Bon Homme Richard*, near Korea in 1951. The squadron chose to name this aircraft after the popular magazine. (*US Navy*)

CVA-21 PRINCETON

The *Princeton* came to be the center of naval aircraft nose art usage during the Korean War. The Commanding Officer of CV-37 was Capt. William O. Gallery, otherwise known as '30-knot Bill'. He was a highly experienced Second World War aviator, and all the ship's company respected him greatly. This close relationship between the officers and their men may have given birth to the creative atmosphere on board the ship. The high morale of this ship in the dark times of the early 1950s led the *Princeton* and its Air Wing 19 to perform some famous operational successes. The withdrawal of the Marines from Hungnam, the attacks on Koto-Ri, and VA-55's torpedo attack on the Hwachon Dam are but a few examples.

Princeton's VC-3 detachment Dog had several F4U-5N Corsairs with names and mission markings, like the *Yokosuka Queen*, NP 24, with fifteen mission marks. The most famous of these was *Annie Mo*, NP 21, belonging to Guy Bordelon. The *Annie Mo* had pictured a girl in a skirt on the nose in addition to fifteen to thirty-five mission marks, and usually flew from the *Princeton* where Lt Bordelon was the detachment commander. He later became the Navy's only ace from the Korean War while flying this aircraft from Pyongtak Airfield during July and August of 1953.

Another squadron on board the *Princeton* during 1953 was VC-61 detachment Dog. This squadron brought on board three unpainted silver F9F-5P Panthers. The tail section on one of the Panthers was damaged, and VC-61 borrowed a tail section from VF-153, which had an aircraft with a damaged nose section. This became the famous *Blue Tail Fly*, and the name was painted on the aircraft. VC-61 named all of their aircraft, including *Look*, *Life*, and *Look See*, as well as applying miniature camera mission marks on the nose of their aircraft. In addition to the many reserve units called up for combat duty over Korea, the Navy used its famed aerobatic team, the *Blue Angels*, to form the nucleus of a new fighter squadron, VF-191, *Satan's Kittens*. The unit flew F9F-2B Panther jets as part of CAG-19 and operated from the USS *Princeton* during its combat cruise from December 1950 to October 1951. One of the squadrons' Panthers was named *Octane Sniffer*, and had fifteen mission marks.

VF-871

The Naval Air Reserve squadron VF-871 was called to active duty in July 1950 at NAS Oakland, and by June 1951 the men of VF-871 had relieved the personnel of the *Princeton's* CVG-19. Ralph C. Tarleton, a tall, lanky yeoman, had been a commercial artist and sign painter in civilian life, and was activated along with VF-871. After arriving on the *Princeton*, Yeoman Tarleton began painting the names of the plane captains on the squadron's Corsairs, and it wasn't long before he had painted his first

Peg O' My Heart leaves the deck of CV-37 *Princeton* on a strike mission over North Korea, July 1951. (*Dion Jacobson*)

nose art as well. Other squadrons on the *Princeton* would follow VF-871's lead and paint artwork on their aircraft; most were not as detailed as their predecessors, having only a name and maybe some mission marks. Between June 1951 and 29 August 1951, VF-871 carried at least sixteen examples of nose art on their F4U-4 Corsairs. The confirmed nose art is listed as follows. The others are assumed to have had some form of art but are unknown at this time.

Name	Nose Art
After Your Ass	Corsair chasing a donkey
Don's Hopped Up Model	A small car and mission marks
Hot To Go	pin-up
Lorie	pin-up
Louie's Love Nest	small bird's nest and mission marks
Memories	pin-up under a palm tree
Passionate Shirley	pin-up and mission marks
Peg O' My Heart	pin-up and mission marks
Rebel's Delight	pin-up and mission marks
The Princess	pin-up

The following nose art is unknown at present: *Bady's Baby*, *Bakersfield Sheriff*, *Bob's Job*, *Mac's Hack*, *Ray's Roost*, and *Wolf's Witch*. In addition to these, at least one of the unit's Corsairs was reported to have green eyes and big red lips painted on it. Regardless, all the nose art was removed when the *Princeton* returned to the States, in order to avoid offending anyone.

After Your Ass's name was changed when a female correspondent came on board the *Sweet Pea* (CV-37). A red star replaced the word 'Ass.' (*Dion Jacobson*)

Aircraft 312 was titled *Rebels Delight* and was painted in full color. You can just make out the twenty mission marks forward of the cockpit. (*Dion Jacobson*)

Passionate Shirley's name was the idea of the plane captain assigned to A/C 306. Then the squadron's artist, Ralph Tarleton, would get together with the plane captain and design the nose art. You will note that the Corsair in the background, aircraft 210, belongs to VF-821 and does not have artwork. However, some of the other squadrons in the Air Wing and on the Princeton did occasionally use nose art. (*Dion Jacobson*)

Peg O' My Heart was a real trooper; note the thirty-two mission marks on the cowling forward of the cockpit. All the nose art on these aircraft were painted over before the *Princeton* returned the San Diego on 29 August 1951. (*Dion Jacobson*)

VF-871 became part of the regular Navy in February 1953 and was re-designated VF-123 later through a number of re-designations the squadron became *The World Famous Pukin' Dogs*, VF-143. However, over the years the squadron never used nose art again. The closest they came to nose art was the symbol that their F-14s carried during the war on terrorism. The artwork on the nose contains the emblems of the New York Police Department, the Port Authority, and the Fire Department of New York enclosed in a pentagon shape (*Jim Meehan*)

The *Ramp Tramp*, BuNo. 84675, belonged to VP-731's Crew 3. Their original aircraft was a lemon, and spent so much time on the ramp awaiting maintenance that the crew had to fly other aircraft in order to receive the required training before going overseas. Thus, they nicknamed the aircraft *The Ramp Tramp*. After four months of hard work, the first plane was declared operationally ready; however, another crew flew it. After a rough water landing the aircraft was surveyed, and Crew 3 got BuNo. 84675 as a replacement. Once overseas, they decided to keep the nickname and add the artwork. This picture of Crew 3 was taken at NAS Sangley Point in April 1951. Standing left to right are: Joe Esposito, Tom Eierman, Ray Burkett, 1st Pilot, Lt Bill O'Brien, PPC, Lt JG Charlie Dwight, 2P, and Dave Limbacher. Seated left to right are: Lou Clark, Ken Rupp, Norm Howerton, Stan Tokarz, 2nd Mech. and Squadron artist, Art Ring, and Bill Masser, Ordnanceman. (*Bill Masser*)

VP-731

VP-731 was a reserve patrol squadron flying PBYs out of NAS Grosse Ile, Michigan, when they were activated in September 1950 at the beginning of the Korean War. The unit transitioned to PBM-5 aircraft, and in January 1951 it moved to the Philippines, where they remained until September of that year. Flying from either Sangley Point, PI, or the seaplane tenders at Pescadores Island, they operated off the coast of Formosa and Okinawa. During their first deployment of the crisis, the reservists earned a total of seventeen Distinguished Flying Crosses, forty-eight Air Medals, and eighty-one Gold Stars, in addition to the AMs.

Five of the squadron's nine PBM-5s carried beautifully illustrated cartoon characters with names on their aircraft during this first tour. The squadron artist, AD3 Stan Tokarz, a 2nd Mech. with Crew Three, began to paint the aircraft after deploying to Sangley Point. A maintenance officer attached to NAS Sangley Point ordered him to stop, but after a short conference with VP-731's Commanding Officer the work was continued. Each aircraft had the artwork added during a major phase maintenance period because the big boats were brought onto dry land. Doing any kind of work on the Mariners while they were in the water was very difficult. Bill Masser illustrates this well in telling of the time Crew Three was preparing to go home after their first active-duty period. On the homebound preflight of a PBM-5, Stan dropped a piece of the engine cowling into the water. He was then told, 'Dive into the water and retrieve it, or don't resurface,' since the plane needed the part in order to fly the crew home. Obviously, the crew made it home, but it's no wonder Stan decided not to paint nose art on the planes while they were afloat, after seeing the difficulty of performing a daily inspection with the aircraft in the water.

Their second tour, from June to December 1952, was off the west coast of Japan and the east coast of Korea. On 31 July 1952 one aircraft was shot down by two MIG-15s, and two crewmen were killed. VP-731 was re-designated VP-48 on 4 February 1953, and it became a permanent part of the regular Navy. They remained at NAS Sangley Point during the post-war era, transitioning first to the P-5As and later to the SP-5Bs. They continued the tradition of painting nose art on their P-boats up until the 1960s, when they were flying Market Time patrols off the Vietnam coast. After the usefulness of the flying boat ran out, VP-48 returned to the states to become a land-based patrol squadron, using P-3A Orions.

This Crew Ten Jacket Patch was worn during VP-731's second overseas tour to Iwakuni, Japan from June to December 1952. The Japanese scrip can be translated as *Fighting Crew Ten*. The design was also painted on the port side of a PBM-5S2, BuNo. 84713, and *Sam*, PPC Sidney Bailey's nickname, was painted in white just above the artwork. See Appendix C, Diagram 3 for location. (*Bill Masser*)

The above artwork was so kindly reproduced for this publication by Stan Tokarz and Bill Masser. This is the same artwork Stan painted on VP-731's Mariners in 1951. (*All the above via Bill Masser*)
Puddle Jumper, Crew Six, BuNo. unknown. See Appendix C, Diagram 2 for aircraft nose art location.
Zowie! Crew Seven, BuNo. unknown. See Appendix C, Diagram 2 for location.

Left: *Belle Bottom*, Crew Two, BuNo. unknown. See Appendix C, Diagram 2 for location.
Right: *Never Hoppen Twice*, Crew Eight, BuNo. unknown. See Appendix C, Diagram 2 for location.

Lt Guy Bordelon and Detachment Dog of VC-3 flew F4U-5N Corsairs from Princeton from 24 January 1953–21 September 1953. While he was forward deployed to Pyongtak, Korea, Lt Bordelon became the US Navy's only Korean War ace, flying this aircraft—the *Annie-Mo*, BuNo. 124453

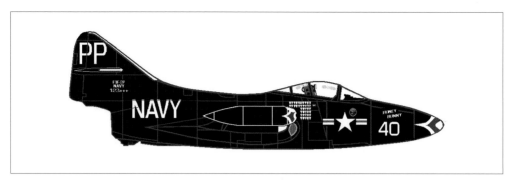

The above F9F-2P Panther belonged to Detachment Easy of VC-61 and operated aboard *Princeton* from March 1952 until November 1952. The *Honey Bunny* flew at least forty photo reconnaissance missions over the Korean Peninsula during this period. BuNo.-unknown.

VF-871 was a Naval Air Reserve fighter squadron called to active duty in July 1950. They came aboard CV-37 on 31 May 1951 and stayed until 29 August 1951. Most of their Corsairs had nose art applied by Ralph Tarleton, a civilian commercial artist, who had been activated with the reserve unit and went with them to Korea. When a lady reporter came aboard ship, the aircraft had its name changed to *After Your*. BuNo.—unknown.

GRAFFITI ARTWORK

Another type of artwork that flourished on the carriers was applied to those aircraft that (through mistake or fuel shortage) had landed on the 'wrong' carrier. Sailors from the host carrier were quick to break out the spray cans of white paint and decorate the visitors before they were able to depart. Many photos of Panthers, Cougars, or Banshees covered in white graffiti exist. One favorite is of a VF-62, F2H-2 Banshee which landed aboard *Wasp*, CVA-18, rather than *Coral Sea*, CVA-43. The white 'NAVY' on its fuselage is sprayed out and replaced by the words 'must be Air Force' in large white letters. Also, the 'F' tail code is modified to read 'Fouled up.' (*US Navy*)

3

THE VIETNAM WAR

The Navy and Marine Corps' long involvement in Vietnam began with air strikes from the Pacific Fleet carriers against North Vietnamese and Viet Cong targets. Air combat evolved to include—in addition to the carrier air wings—the land-based patrol and interdiction aircraft, USMC attack and fighter-bomber aircraft, patrol seaplanes, and Navy and Marine helicopters in attack and rescue roles. A number of the aircraft and helicopters serving over Vietnam with the Navy and Marine Corps were decorated with cartoons, pin-ups, shark mouths, and names, in an attempt to personalize the individual airplane and often to relieve the boredom of drab paint and redundant markings.

A-4 SKYHAWK

The Douglas A-4 Skyhawk flew thousands of missions over Vietnam with Navy and Marine Corps squadrons. One of the most famous of these is the *Lady Jessie* of VA-164. Her story is told in *A Tale of Two Ladies*. The *Blue Blasters* of VA-34 flew one of the oldest A-4Cs, BuNo. 145141, from the USS *Intrepid*, CVS-11, in 1967. The aircraft carried a cartoon, 'Granpaw Pettibone' of Naval Aviation News fame, and the script name *Whiskers* on the fin. Also, the VA-212 *Raiders* had an A-4F, NP 311, painted with R. Crumb's 'Keep on Truckin' cartoon in 1972.

In 1965 Marine pilots of H&MS-15 joined Midway's VA-22 for a two-week operational cruise. One of the aircraft they used, YV 81, was marked as 'VMA-22' and carried mission marks and the script name *Fanny Hill* on the nose. Some of the 'in-country' Marine A-4 Skyhawks carried small, stenciled names similar to those found on the carriers. One of these, A-4E, *Chicken Man*, had mission marks and flew with the 'Avengers' of VMA-211.

F-8 CRUSADERS

Though carrier-based, the F-8 Crusaders of VF-24 and VFP-63 exhibited a vast number of nose art cartoons on their aircraft. In 1972 an artist on the USS *Hancock*, CVA-19, decorated many of the VF-24 *Checkertails* F8-Js with artwork requested by each plane's pilot. The cartoons were placed just aft of the nose modex and were not named at the time. NP 201, the mount of the squadron CO, displayed a bulldog in a pirate costume with a peg leg, while NP 207 was marked with a hound dog in a pirate outfit. NP 203 was decorated with an animated thundercloud and lightning bolts. NP 211 had a cartoon of Yosemite Sam, and NP 213 carried a picture of the alligator from the Pogo comic strip. The most unique one of the bunch, BuNo. 150336, had a John Deere logo on the fin adjacent to the squadron insignia. This Crusader was unfortunately lost in a ramp strike on 12 August 1972.

The RF-8 photo Crusaders of VFP-63 flew as detachments from various carriers off Vietnam, using the host air wing's tail code rather than the squadron's assigned PP letters. Many of the RF-8As and RF-8Gs acquired cartoons located on the fin above the tail codes. They included characters such as

VA-212's A-4F Skyhawks were onboard the *Hancock* during 1972 as the Vietnam War was winding down. This is a facsimile of R. Crumb's artwork, *Keep on Truckin'*. This artwork was more popular with the anti-war movement and underground comics than with the Navy. (*Skean*)

A menacing thundercloud adorns NP 203, an F-8E of VF-24. This was the aircraft of the unit's Operation Officer, whose call sign was *Thunder*. (*Skean*)

Wiley Coyote, Snoopy, and the 'old broad' from Playboy magazine. In 1973–74 the Snoopy cartoon turned an unnatural seasick green on several of the planes. Various cartoon animals with cameras were also displayed on the photo Crusaders' fins, including ducks, alligators, and squirrels.

VFP-63 Crusaders usually carried the squadron name *Eyes of the Fleet* on the forward section of the variable incidence wing—which was visible when raised for launch and recovery—and a pair of blood-shot eyeballs accompanied the logo. VFP-206, a reserve unit that did not see combat, also made clever use of this wing, they put 'happy feet,' two up and two down, on the red section of the variable incidence wing during the 1970's.

A bulldog in pirate regalia decorates the nose of a VF-24 F-8E Crusader on the USS *Hancock*, CVA-19, in 1972. NP-201 was the squadron commander's bird and his call sign was possibly *Bulldog*. (*Skean*)

Yosemite Sam, with sword and pistol, charges across the forward fuselage of F-8E NP 211. (*Skean*)

NP 213, a Crusader of VF-24, wears a cartoon alligator in top hat and tails just above the 20-mm gun ports. (*Skean*)

F-8E NP 207 of VF-24 on the *Hancock* in 1972. The story is that this aircraft was assigned to a pilot who demanded a cartoon on his bird after seeing the pirate artwork on the other Crusaders. The enlisted cartoonist thought the pilot to have a rude manner and executed a cartoon of 'Goofy' the pirate, with his pants falling down. The pilot complained to the Skipper and the CO ordered the art to remain on the aircraft. (*Skean*)

VA-165

The most common method of personalizing carrier aircraft was by using tools that were common to the hangar deck of a carrier, like a stencil cutter and a can of black spray paint. Several squadrons used this medium to inscribe names on their aircraft. The names tended to reflect the rock 'n' roll music, bands, and movies of the era. VA-165, the *Boomers*, named quite a few of their A-1 Skyraiders during a combat cruise on the USS *Intrepid*, CVA-11, circa 1966. Two of these Skyraiders are prime examples of the names typically found on carrier aircraft. *Miss Pussy Galore*, AK 209, makes reference to a character in the James Bond movie *Goldfinger*, and the name *Puff the Magic Dragon* on AK 204 was obviously borrowed from the popular Peter, Paul, and Mary song. Both of these A-1Hs had their names in stencil letters on the cowling, below the modex, and had mission marks.

VAH-21

Several of the AP-2H Neptunes, night-intruder aircraft of VAH-21, were decorated. *Iron Butterfly* was painted on the nose gear door of SL 4, *Napalm Nellie* was painted in oriental-style letters on SL 3, and *Deuces Wild* was painted on SL 2. All of these aircraft carried mission markers and battle ribbons by the end of their service.

VW-1

VW-1 was commissioned in 1952 with the task of flying land-based, airborne early-warning operations for the west coast of the US and Hawaii. Originally using PB-1Ws and one PO-1W, in 1953 this AEW unit became the first to re-equip with the WV-2 Warning Star—more affectionately known as the *Willie Victor*. The squadron moved from Barbers Point to NAS Agana, Guam, in 1957, where they were additionally tasked with weather reconnaissance and became known as the *Typhoon Trackers*. In 1962 the WV-2s were re-designated EC-121K/L/Ps and became unofficially known as Super Constellations or just *Connies*. With the flare up of the conflict in Vietnam, the unit had begun flying daily AEW missions over the Gulf of Tonkin in support of the Seventh Fleet's operations. These missions were flown from either Chu Lai or Da Nang in South Vietnam, or forward bases in the Philippines. VW-1 preformed these operations until 1 July 1971, when its AEW task was taken over by VQ-1. Their *Connies* were either given to VQ-1 or transferred to the bone yard at NAF Litchfield Park, AZ.

Iron Butterfly of VAH-21 as it appeared upon the squadron's return to the states. (*Don Spering A.I.R.*)

The EC-121K *Dragon Lady* of VW-1 at Chu Lai, South Vietnam, on September 1968. (*US Navy*)

Nose art was not used in VW-1 until the end of its existence during the Vietnam Conflict. But their designs would prove to be the most colorful and artistically pleasing nose art of any of the AEW squadrons. Some of the artwork showed an oriental influence, which may indicate that a civilian employee painted these planes in the Philippines.

The EC-121K *Road Runner* of VW-1, BuNo. 145928, in South Vietnam in September 1968. (*US Navy*)

This A-6A Intruder, *Mixed Emotions*, of VMA (AW)-224 was photographed in September of 1972 at Naval Air Rework Facility Norfolk, VA. VMA (AW)-224 flew combat missions over Vietnam from the USS *Coral Sea*, CVA-43, from November 1971 to July 1972. In May of 1972, the A-6s mined the approaches to Haiphong Harbor. (*Jim Meehan*)

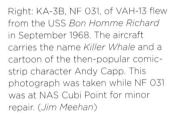

Left: *Mixed Emotions*, NL 512, carried nineteen small, black bomb stencils on her right nose and was severely damaged at the right wing boot by AAA or SAM. Field sheet metal repairs, including loss of the prominent air conditioning intake, allowed the aircraft to be returned to NARF for major repair. (*Jim Meehan*)

Right: KA-3B, NF 031, of VAH-13 flew from the USS *Bon Homme Richard* in September 1968. The aircraft carries the name *Killer Whale* and a cartoon of the then-popular comic-strip character Andy Capp. This photograph was taken while NF 031 was at NAS Cubi Point for minor repair. (*Jim Meehan*)

Left: NP 016 of VAW-111 was marked with a 'smiley face' on the nose. This Grumman E-1B cheerfully sits on the USS *Hancock*, CVA-19, during 1972. (*Skean*)

F-4 PHANTOM

Although the F-4 Phantom was not noted for artwork during the Vietnam era, some good examples do exist among the land and carrier-based squadrons. The VMFA-542 *Tigers'* flew the F-4B Phantom II from Da Nang, RVN, during 1965 and 1966. *Blondie* was a rare bit of pin-up artwork on one of these aircraft, with WH tail codes and unknown modex.

An unusual bit of art, noted at NAS Oceana in 1966, was on a VF-84, *Jolly Rogers*, F-4B that had returned from a combat cruise on the USS *Independence*, CVA-62. AG 202 was marked with seven black bombs, each with a numeral '5' in white indicating five missions flown, and a green tree with airplane wings sticking out of the top. The story was that the Phantom had been called to eliminate a sniper in a tree. Being out of ordnance, they made a low pass, clipped the top of the tree, and, presumably, took out the sniper.

4

A TALE OF TWO LADIES

LADY JESSIE

Two remarkable ladies were honored in a special way for their contributions to Naval Aviation and the morale of its pilots by being commemorated with their own personal nose art.

The name *Lady Jessie* was given to many of the A-4 Skyhawks flown by the *Ghost Riders* of VA-164 and became a long-standing tradition. Photos show several of the squadron's aircraft with *Lady Jessie* painted in large red letters on both sides of the fuselage. The tradition began with Lt Cdr Richard 'Dick' Clark Perry prior to VA-164's Vietnam cruise on the USS *Oriskany* in 1966.

Dick Perry was from Nevada, and during his college years he worked part-time in the Reno casino owned by Mrs Jessie Beck and her husband. After joining VA-164, Perry named his A-4E, BuNo. 151180, *Lady Jessie* in her honor. In return, Mrs Beck hosted parties for VA-163 and VA-164 when the air wing returned to NAS Lemoore. Photos indicate that Dick Perry named at least one more A-4, BuNo. 152048, for Mrs Beck. Sadly, Lt Perry was lost in combat on the *Ghost Riders'* 1967 cruise to South East Asia. He was shot down in BuNo. 151991, AH 402, by a SAM missile over Haiphong, NVN. His remains were returned in 1987, the same year Mrs Jessie Beck passed away.

After the loss of Lieutenant Perry, the name *Lady Jessie* was carried on each squadron CO's aircraft until the squadron was disestablished in December of 1975. Pictures of BuNo. 155018, NP 401, and BuNo. 155022, also NP 401, indicate this to be true.

A-4E Skyhawk of VA-164 returning from a mission over the North. This was the third squadron aircraft to be named *Lady Jessie*. (*Don Spering A.I.R.*)

Lt Dick Perry is flying the original *Lady Jessie* over California in 1966. The aircraft is A-4E, BuNo. 151180 of VA-164 Ghostriders. (*US Navy via Skyhawk Association*)

VA-164's squadron commander's A-4F *Lady Jessie*, BuNo. 155022 from the USS *Hancock*. The tradition of naming the CO's plane continued until the unit was disestablished in 1975. (*Don Spering, A.I.R.*)

Lady Jessie number three is all dressed up to go downtown with six Mk-82 bombs and a 300-gallon external tank. (*Don Spering A.I.R.*)

USS *Carl Vinson*'s C-1A, COD was the first of that ships aircraft to be named *Miss Molly*. You can just make out the name painted on the number one engine's aft nacelle. (*Raymond West*)

MISS MOLLY

The second remarkable lady was Mrs Amalia 'Molly' Steman Snead, who, after completing nurse's training, joined the Navy. She was commissioned a Navy Nurse and was eventually stationed at the Navy Medical Center in Bethesda, MD. She became the nurse for Mary Vinson, Congressman Carl Vinson's wife. The two ladies became lifelong friends and she later cared for Congressman Vinson until his death. She became the sponsor for CVN-70 at the suggestion of Congressman Vinson. The *Vinson* would be the first ship to bear the name of a living person. Originally, a C-1A COD aircraft for the *Vinson* carried the name *Miss Molly*, but the name was passed on when the Trader was retired. The name *Miss Molly* was picked up by the *Sundowners* of VF-111 while serving on the USS *Carl Vinson*, CVN-70, in December of 1989.

Lt Mark Conn painted on both sides of F-14A, BuNo. 161621, NL 200, a pin-up of a red-headed nurse and the name *Miss Molly*. The aircraft also carried the red-and-yellow sunbursts and the aggressive shark mouths of VF-111. The Sundowners continued to operate from the *Vinson* through 1990 and were disestablished in March 1995. Thus, Naval Aviation lost one of its most colorful Tomcats when it retired *Miss Molly*.

F-14A, BuNo. 161621, of VF-111, *Miss Molly* at NAF Washington DC in December, 1989. Artwork is on both sides of the aircraft and was painted by Lt Mark Conn. (*Handelman via David F. Brown*)

5

THE COLD WAR ERA (1954–1990)

During the long Cold War period of American defiance of the 'Communist Menace', a few examples of nose art appeared in the Naval Aviation community. This section notes the artwork not covered in the Korean War and Vietnam War chapters. Some of the art on the PB4Y Liberators and Privateers survived for a few years after The Second World War. These usually vanished with the introduction of the overall gloss sea-blue finish on the aircraft.

TEST AND EVALUATION AIRCRAFT

One area of Naval Aviation that made use of nose art during the Cold War was the test and evaluation units. These units were based at both NAS Patuxent River, MD, and NAWS China Lake, CA. This nose art occurred mostly on one-of-a-kind test aircraft, and usually had a cartoon and/or name related to its mission. The Snoopy character was a favorite of many of these aircraft. The Naval Weapons Center had an NTA-4F with a Snoopy wearing goggles and a scarf on the nose; the Weapons Test unit at Pax River had an EA-1E with Snoopy's silhouette in 1969, and the Naval Air Development Center had an NOP-2E Neptune with Snoopy on it in 1971. In addition to these, many of the F9F and F-4 drone aircraft had painted on shark mouths.

P-2 NEPTUNE

Neptune managed to gain some artwork, usually when deployed overseas. The famous P2V-1 *Truculent Turtle*, now preserved at the Naval Aviation Museum in Pensacola, was decorated specifically with a pipe-smoking turtle cartoon for its record-breaking mission.

F-4J PHANTOM II

The VF-31 *Tomcatters* painted cartoons and names on the outer-nose-gear doors of their F-4J Phantom II jets in 1975 for a Red Flag exercise at Nellis AFB. Two interesting examples were *Bud Man* and *Mig Eater*, both with appropriate art. Detachment '66', for CVA-66, of the VF-101 *Grim Reapers*, served aboard the USS *America* during a Mediterranean deployment in the fall of 1971. The F-4J Phantom IIs carried a not-too-flattering Mickey Mouse head on the intakes, with the legend *Mickey Knause Club* referring to the Detachment Commander.

This EA-1F of VAQ-33 was photographed at NAS Norfolk, VA in August 1970. The 'postmarked' side could indicate that the old electronic Skyraider was to be retired at the Smithsonian's Air and Space Museum. It's interesting that the USS *Kennedy* decided to mail the Spad to the Smithsonian because, when not doing the ECM mission, this aircraft would fill its large carrying capacity with mail and deliver it to the *Kennedy*'s personnel. (*Don Spering A.I.R.*)

An SP-2E Neptune of VP-661 is shown here with a larger Snoopy drawing on the nose. (*Jim Meehan*)

AD-5W SKYRAIDER

In 1958 an AD-5W Skyraider of VAW-12 on the USS *Forrestal*, CVA-59, carried a cartoon on its cowling below the modex 723.

CRUSADER

The Vought F-8 Crusader, *Last of the Gunfighters*, received a few examples of art in its long career. Many of the RF-8 Photo Crusaders carried cartoon art. One RF-8G of VFP-63, modex AB 601 from the USS *Kennedy*, was decorated with the 'Wiz' cartoon from the *Wizard of Id* comic strip while on a visit to England in 1976.

These two Crusaders are from CVW-19 onboard USS *Oriskany*. The F-8Js pilot, LT 'Shoe' Garnett had a flying 'boondocker' painted on his aircraft's nose. Another 'photo' Crusader from VFP-63 Det. 4 attached onboard USS *Oriskany* between October 1973 and June 1974. This time the artwork is on the nose of the aircraft rather than the tail. The 'playful bunny' character from *Playboy* magazine was popular during this time period. The 'Playful Bunny' from *Playboy* magazine adorns both sides of this VFP-63 photo Crusader. This is a far cry from the pin-up art found with the Second World War photo outfit VD-1 in the Pacific. (*Don Spering A.I.R.*)

F-4D SKYRAY

The exotic Douglas F-4D Skyray had a short career with the Navy, but it managed to pick up a few bits of nose art along the way. Most examples could actually be called 'intake art,' since a black radome, large national insignia, and modex took up most of the small nose of the Skyray. A F4D-1 of VMF (AW) 114, modex AB 208, carried a portrait of Alfred E. Neuman aft of the canopy.

HSL SQUADRONS

Just as they did in the Second World War, the 'Airedales' went back to sea on cruisers, frigates, and destroyers when these smaller surface ships began transitioning from the DASH ASW system to the LAMPS system in 1971. The Air Department on these ships consisted of two aircraft, with twelve aircrew and aircraft maintenance personnel each. All in all, this was a very small per cent of the ship's company on a destroyer, and was not even a permanent establishment of the ship. Their parent command and

Above and right: Photographed in October of 1959, *What? Me Worry* is a great motto for a Marine F4D-1 pilot. Mad magazine's Alfred E. Neuman adorns the fuselage of this Skyray, at MCAS Cherry Point, NC. This aircraft was deployed on the USS *Franklin D. Roosevelt* from February to September of 1959. The yellow sash on the tail fin of this Skyray contains the Latin phrase '*Primus Principus*,' the motto of CVG-1. (*Williams*)

The two vultures were painted on the nose of a NAF Washington D.C. T-1A BuNo. 144214. The quote 'Patience my foot—I'm going to kill something' was probably the sentiment of some Pentagon bureaucrat who was doing a tour in DC and used NARTU's Seastar to fulfill annual flight-time requirements.

support remained shore-based, either in Norfolk, Mayport, or North Island. Therefore this tight-knit organization was considered just another weapons system (like the towed sonar array system) by a ship's Commanding Officer. To establish a since of identity, the small LAMPS detachment would spend many hours of a long sea cruise developing artwork to adorn their SH-2 Seasprite, LAMPS I, or SH-60B Seahawk, LAMPS II, aircraft. In most cases this artwork was painted on the sonobuoy storage-access door of the SH-2s and SH-60s, but they sometimes chose to paint the design on the helicopter itself. Most of the time the detachment would select a suitable pseudonym—for example, *Ocean Scanners*—and then develop the artwork around that theme. Over time, this became a custom throughout the HSL (Helicopter Light Anti-Submarine Warfare) community. From the mid-1990s, with the advent of both HS and HSL squadrons fulfilling the same role and with the introductions of the SH-60 Seahawk into both types of squadrons, the attitude toward nose art changed. The HS units had little use for aircraft artwork, as they had operated from carriers and deployed as a squadron size unit with Sea Kings. However, both units began to adopt the practice of painting the Commanding Officer's aircraft.

An SH-60B modified LAMPS III aircraft, belonging to HSL-42, is pictured above at their homeport in Mayport, FL. In late 1992 the detachment was assigned to the USS *Normandy*, CG-60, which was named to commemorate the great Second World War battle. Therefore, Detachment Five's SH-60 took the name *Overlords* from the D-Day Operation, which took place on Omaha Beach on 6 June 1944. (*Tate*)

The three US Army units that participated in the initial Omaha Beach landing in Normandy, France were the First Infantry Division, the 29th Infantry Division and the Fifth Ranger Battalion. (*Tate*)

Above: The only things missing on this Seahawk are invasion strips, which would have been appropriate to commemorate the fiftieth anniversary of D-Day. (*Tate*)

Below: This SH-60B, BuNo. 163905, of HSL-48's Detachment 1 is at NAS Oceana, VA, in May 1996. To the right is a close-up view of HR 510's door art. (*Meehan*)

The *Ragin Bulls* helicopter of HSL-32, Detachment Four, is pictured here in June 1992. (*Don Spering A.I.R.*)

Zulu Invader was a Seasprite belonging to the Zulu Detachment of HSL-32 in September 1990. (*Meehan*)

Fifi of HSL-32 was a Seasprite, BuNo. 161642, photographed in April 1986. This aircraft was very successful in the prosecution of ASW targets, obtaining eleven kills during the squadron's annual SLAM Ex. The red and white 'subs' have to do with different types of simulated ASW exercises prosecuted against live 'Red' Forces. (*Meehan*)

Woody Woodpecker and the rebel flag compose the sono-door art on this SH-2F of HSL-32 during 1982. Art like this would not have been done a few years later because in the nineties politics began affecting artistic expression, and the rebel flag would become politically incorrect—just like pin-up art. (*Meehan*)

The *Ocean Scanners* SH-2F LAMPS I helicopter of HSL-34, Detachment One, from NAS Norfolk, VA was attached to a Knox Class Frigate, the USS *Elmer Montgomery*, FF-1082. (*Meehan*)

Pictured is the *Sub Hunter* beaver sono-door art for the SH-2F, BuNo. 149748, of HSL-34's Det. 3 from August 1980. (*Meehan*)

HSL-34's Seasprite sono-buoy access door was painted sometime before April 1990 while Detachment Four was attached to FF-1085, the USS *Donald Beary*. (*Meehan*)

The Titans of HSL-94 were a Naval Reserve LAMPS squadron established in 1985 and based at NAS Willow Grove, PA. This over size character of the titan is painted on the squadron commander's aircraft. Note that HSL-94 is the recipient of COMHELWINGRES's 1999 Safety 'S.' (*Meehan*)

Even though the titan is the unit's emblem, this rendition (left) is not in the approved format for a squadron insignia. (*Meehan*)

A MH-60S from HSC-6 after refueling takes off from the USS *Nimitz* CVN-68 on 4 April 2013. Observe the Indian brave tail art which symbolizes the unit's name, *The Indians*. The squadron's duties include search and rescue, drug interdiction, anti-ship/submarine warfare, and VOD missions. Take note of the name in red, *Crazy Horse*, barely visible on the forward nose cone below the windshield. This aircraft art is the work of one of the most prolific aircraft artists at this time, Shayne Meder. (*US Navy photo by Mass Communication Specialist 3rd Class Raul Moreno*)

The *Grim Reaper* is on world tour with HSL-44. One of the more colorful works of art found on a SH-60 sono-door. (*Don Spering A.I.R.*)

The tail art on this SH-60B *Warlord 02* is a concept combining HSL-51's squadron patch of 'Musashi', a seventeenth-century Samurai warrior, and Mt Fuji, which is located near NAS Atsugi, Japan—the squadron's home base. This idea of the lone warrior signifies the squadron's Commanding Officer and his unifying force. Note that the warrior is not using his traditional Samurai sword but a trident from Greek mythology, which is more in keeping with HSL-51's anti-submarine and surface warfare role. This aircraft's tail art was created and is maintained by the squadron's Detachment Oscar, based at NAS Atsugi. (*US Navy, courtesy of HSL-51's commanding Officer via LTJG Jeremy Casella USNR*)

The tail art on the Skipper's bird certainly reflects the influence of Mt Fuji, Japan, in the background during 2001, before the unit deployed to the IO. (*US Navy; via LTJG Casella*)

VF-43

The present VF-43 started life as VF-74A, which was established on 1 May 1945 and was re-designated VF-74 in August of 1945. This is not to be confused with the first VF-74, which had served in the Mediterranean Theater in support of the invasion of southern France and was decommissioned upon its return to Norfolk in October 1944. The 1945 VF-74 was transformed first into VF-1B in November 1946, and then into VF-21 in September 1948. Fighter Squadron 21 remained unchanged for the next eleven years, and during this period the *Mach Knockers* converted from the F4U-4 Corsairs to a series of jet aircraft. In July 1959 the unit's designation was altered once again, this time to VA-43, and in June 1973 the unit was finally re-designated to VF-43.

In June 1957 VF-21 became the first AirLant squadron to operate the F11F-1 Tiger, and with the introduction of this new aircraft came the squadron's first use of nose art. All of the squadron's Tigers were painted with tiger mouths and eyes in honor of the revolutionary new aircraft. Soon after July 1959, the squadron, now VA-43, became a replacement pilot training squadron for both the F11F-1 and the A4D-1 Skyhawk. They continued to use the tiger-mouth art on both the Tiger and the Skyhawk until 1964. With the change once again to VF-43 the unit became an adversary squadron, flying A-4s, TA-4s, F-5s, F-21s and F-16s. During the mid-1990s the squadron began its second flirtation with nose art. This time all of the A-4s and TA-4s were given names or call signs, and these were painted in script on the nose of each Skyhawk.

This is an example of VF-21's F11F-1 Tigers with the tiger nose art during late 1957. The aircraft line up makes an impressive sight. (*US Navy via National Museum of Naval Aviation*)

Bullet an A-4F, BuNo. 154172, was VF-43's aircraft No. 25 during September 1993. (*Meehan*)

Soon after this photo was taken at NAS Oceana in September 1993, VF-43's Skyhawks ended their long years of service at Oceana. The aggressor lineup includes the A4-Fs *Magnum* No. 24, *Bandit* No. 22, *Trigger* No. 23, *Rufus* No. 29, *Cujo* No. 20, *Bullet* No. 25, a TA-4J *Patsy* No. 43, and an unnamed No. 42. (*Meehan*)

An A-4F Magnum, aircraft No. 24, at NAS Oceana.

Skyhawk AD 320 at NAS Quonset Point, RI in the early 1960s, soon after the squadron became a replacement pilot training unit. Note the similarities between the tiger-mouth art on this A4D-1 and the art on the F-11F-1 Tiger. Notice that the squadron is now designated VA-43. (*Don Spering A.I.R.*)

This TA-4J of VF-43, a Navy adversary squadron, was conducting air-combat-maneuvering (ACM) training flights for the Atlantic Fleet in the 1980s and '90s. Note the five F-8 kill marks next to the *Mach Knocker* unit emblem. The emblem had formerly belonged to VF-21, the *Mach Busters*, and dates back to 1952 when that squadron transitioned to F9F Panthers. (*Don Spering A.I.R.*)

VF-74

Established as VBF-20 on April 16, 1945, this fighter unit was re-designated VF-10A on 15 November 1946, and then became VF-92 on 12 August 1948. Before the Korean police action the squadron left Air Wing Nine and joined Air Wing Seven, becoming VF-74 in January 1950. By July 1961 the *Be-Devilers* became the first Navy fighter squadron to fly the F-4J Phantom II with its improved AWG-10A weapons system. The squadron's task was fleet air superiority and defense. The squadron, as part of CVW-17, was aboard USS *Forrestal*, CV-59, during 1981, however it was reassigned to USS *Saratoga*, CVA-60, by 1985. NAS Oceana, VA was the unit's homeport when not at sea with CVW-17.

1961–81 First in Phantoms, commemorating twenty years of Phantom II service in Fighter Squadron 74. (*Don Spering A.I.R.*)

F4D-1, BuNo. 139113, of VF-74 carries a faded pin-up and the name *Sexy Six* on its intake. VF-74 flew the Skyray from May 1956 to mid-1961, when it transitioned to the even-sexier F-4H Phantom II. (*Luckenbaugh via Williams*)

Sexy Six was photographed in April of 1961 in downtown Norfolk, VA. Perhaps it was there as part of a military parade, since this was the end of the Skyray's career with the *Be-Devilers*. This was quite unusual for the Navy at the time because female pedestrians could have been offended by the artwork. (*Luckenbaugh via Williams*)

From 20 May 1952 through to January 1953, VF-74 flew F4U-4 Corsairs over Korea from the deck of the *Bon Homme Richard*. The unit had a dual role in that it flew to cover for VA-75's Skyraiders while also carrying an ordinance load for the suppression of ground and anti-aircraft fire. Many of the squadron's birds were decorated with bomb and mission marks and given names. Aircraft L408 has the name *Babe* on the engine cowling. (*US Navy via the National Museum of Naval Aviation*)

On 20 September 1974 VF-74 returned to Oceana from CV-59 *Forrestal* with artwork on their splitter plate. (Above and Below) The *Sound of Philly Bro db* is an F-4J from VF-74 returning with CVW-17 to NAS Oceana. Someone must have been a music fan from Philadelphia. (*Don Spering A.I.R.*)

Another F-4J Phantom II belonging to VF-74 (The *Be-Devilers*), after returning from a Med-Cruise to NAS Oceana, VA. The significance of the two fish is not known, and the banner remained unfinished by the time the unit came ashore in September 1974. (*Don Spering A.I.R.*)

The WP-3A *Edith*, BuNo. 149674, illustrates that even after the squadron transitioned to the Orion, the naming of planes after major hurricanes continued. Even though the Orions were later prevented from penetrating these storms due to structural problems, the tradition of applying nose art continued. Note the hurricane warning flags used as the unit's tail marking. (*Bill Tate*)

VW-4

The *Hurricane Hunters* of VW-4 were based at NAS Jacksonville, FL, and had a tradition of using a hurricane symbol on the side of their aircraft. In the early days, 1956–58, the unit merely stenciled small, red hurricane symbols, representing each storm the aircraft had penetrated, on their P2V-5F Neptunes. However, new art, which consisted of a larger stencil of the hurricane symbol and a name, was later developed. The large hurricane icon was painted red or white on the nose of the aircraft, and the aircraft was then named after a major tropical storm that the squadron had tracked or flown through. Since this was before the ERA's time, the entire unit's aircraft had female names.

VW-11

Shortly after the end of the Second World War, the United States became increasingly aware of its vulnerability to surprise air attacks from the Soviet Union by long-range, high-speed bombers. Expanding America's radar horizons beyond her territorial borders was necessary in order to provide adequate warning of attack. The US Navy was responsible for extending radar coverage at sea. The Navy Department realized that it would be some time before they had enough radar picket ships to cover America's seaward approaches. So, in July 1955, they accepted the responsibility of manning the North Atlantic Barrier, and three new squadrons were commissioned. Airborne Early Warning Squadrons VW-11, VW-13, and VW-15 joined the existing VW-2 and began training. By March 1956 these units began operating a 2,100-mile early-warning barrier between Argentia, Newfoundland and the Azores Islands. They covered the over-water gaps in NORAD's Distant Early Warning, or DEW, Line.

Of all the East Coast squadrons, VW-11 was the only one to carry nose art on their EC-121 Super Constellations. However, this art was not nearly as complicated as the nose art carried by some Second World War patrol planes; it consisted of a stencil in white of a three-mast sailing ship. Lockheed's

The NC-121K *Super Connie*, BuNo. 143198, was named after hurricane *Dora* in August 1967. (*US Navy*)

Trade Wind, BuNo. 141308, is a WV-2 at NAS Argentia, Nfld., in 1960. The snowy, windswept ramp was normal for this isolated, fog-shrouded part of Newfoundland. (*Author's Collection*)

Constellation had the same romantic appeal as the old clipper ships that plied the Atlantic during the golden age of sail, so each aircraft in the squadron was christened with the name of a clipper ships. Capt. R. C. Lefever said that the squadron 'was upholding the clipper ship tradition of efficiency and reliability'. The artwork was usually done by Lockheed Air Services in New York, and when the planes were repainted the artwork was stripped off and not always reapplied. During 1965, however, one example of the clipper ship artwork was repainted in full color. After ten years of continuous AEW barrier operations, the Department of Defense decided that the AEW barrier was outdated and too costly to operate. By July 1965 the Navy's entire AEW fleet was decommissioned, except VW-11. This squadron would be the only one to operate the North Atlantic Barrier from beginning to end in October 1965. As proof of the outstanding reliability and efficiency of both the men and aircraft of this squadron, they maintained a plane in the air, patrolling the barrier, every hour of the day for 145 days straight.

VW-11's EC-121K *Golden Light*, BuNo. 141320, is pictured at NAS Keflavik, Iceland, *c.* 1964. (*Ray West*)

EC-121K, the *Cutty Sark*, is at Harmon AFB, Nfld. for a 1965 Armistice Day air show. The only VW-11 Connie with color nose art, its sails and letters are white; the ship's hull is brown, and the cloud field is insignia blue. (*Ray West*)

Que Sera Sera was the first aircraft ever to land at the South Pole. The song by the same name, made popular at the time by Doris Day, is translated as 'whatever will be, will be'. This title was probably chosen to reflect a cavalier attitude toward arctic exploration. On 31 October 1956, Lt Cdr Conrad S. Shinn landed this LC-47 on the 56-degrees-below-zero plateau of the South Pole. The aircraft almost became frozen to the ice, making the takeoff and return flight a very dicey operation. BuNo. 12418 is now on display at the Naval Air Museum in Pensacola, FL, and appears today much as it did in 1956, except that the VX-6 tail code 'XD' is missing. (*Tate*)

VXE-6

In anticipation of the International Geophysical Year 1957–58, twelve nations agreed on the peaceful exploration and scientific research of Antarctica. The Office of Naval Research had organized operation Skijump II in 1952, which supported Antarctic research using personnel and aircraft from the Arctic Research Laboratory based in Point Barrow, Alaska. A unit was formed which brought together ski equipped R4Ds, P2V-2s, UF-1s, UC-1 Otters, and three HO4S-3 helicopters to support Skijump II. This unit was later commissioned VX-6 at NAS Patuxent River, MD, in January 1955, and in May 1956 it was relocated to Quonset Point, RI. The mission of the unit was to support Rear Admiral Byrd's Task Force 43, which was transporting supplies to the continent of Antarctica for IGY's use. Specific missions included aerial photography and mapping, ice reconnaissance, air rescue, logistic support, and magnetic earth field readings.

Some of the aircraft taken over from the civilian-run Arctic Research Laboratory already had names and nose art, but VX-6 soon assumed a character of its own. The emperor penguin, an inhabitant of the harsh and challenging climate of the South Pole, became the mascot and symbol for the squadron. The penguin art first appeared during Operation Deep Freeze I in 1956, and this penguin in one form or another adorned almost every aircraft type operated by the unit. Many names for the unit's aircraft were inspired by the unique bird, i.e. *King Pin*, *Penguin Express*, *Lou Bird*, and *The Emperor*. The unofficial *Puckered Pete* insignia also became a part of VX-6's legacy. 'Pete' typifies the Antarctic veteran aviator, having too much booze, brawling, and bimbos in Chee Chee, or Christchurch, NZ, the squadron's forward staging area. Also, Pete's bloodshot eyes and chain smoking were symptoms of long hours of flying in whiteout conditions. Because of its questionable nature, the *Puckered Pete* insignia would not receive official design approval. Squadron emblems were becoming a serious business, and the Navy would not support the use of anything, especially a cartoon character, that could imply some impropriety. In spite of the official attitude 'Pete' became a squadron icon. Much like his namesake, the emperor penguin, he has been able to survive in a hostile climate.

On 1 January 1969, VX-6 became VXE-6, changing from an air-development squadron to an arctic-development squadron. They were part of the civilian-organized and funded United States Antarctic Research Program (USARP), which is under the auspices of the National Science Foundation. Thus the squadron personnel spent long, isolated winters in close proximity with a civilian scientific community. The fact that the unit was somewhat out of the normal military chain of command, and that its duty stations were without a doubt isolated may explain why the official negative attitude of the US Navy brass had little influence on the squadron's use of nose art. In the winter of 1999–2000 the responsibility for supporting the scientific community's research in Antarctica was assumed by the New York Air National Guard's LC-130Hs. VXE-6 had a history of nose art utilization, going back to 1956, and with the decommissioning of Antarctic Development Squadron 6 a forty-four year tradition of Naval Aviation nose art came to an end.

This Neptune displays one of the earliest forms of penguin art. The P2V-2N was named *Amen* and served with Operation Deep Freeze during December 1955. (*US Navy*)

The emperor penguin is a recurring theme in VXE-6 aircraft nose art. This aircraft was also on display in Pensacola. (*Tate*)

King Pin II, an LH-34D, was used for transportation, rescue, and logistical support for the many outlying base camps around McMurdo Sound. LH-34s lacked range and high-altitude performance, and were replaced in 1971 with UH-1Ns. (*Tate*)

Above: C-121J, BuNo. 131624, is flying over Christchurch, NZ. This Connie was first used as a transport to support Deep Freeze 64. This aircraft was also used on bug runs around Ross Island. Nets were towed behind the aircraft in flight to trap rare insects that existed on the frozen continent. The phoenix is a noticeably different type of bird art when compared to the penguin art used by most in the squadron. (*US Navy*)

Left: Even the USAF joined in the act of painting penguins on their aircraft. This C-124 made ten logistic flights to Antarctica during Operation Deep Freeze III. The wopple-jogged penguin represents a landing accident at NAF McMurdo on Ross Island. (*USAF*)

Below: LC-117D, BuNo. 17156, of the Naval Arctic Research Laboratory at Point Barrow, AK was a forerunner to VX-6. The nose art is taken from the *Shoe* comic strip antd might well illustrate how it felt to fly a Gooney Bird on and off the ice: (*Tate*)

Above: *City of Christchurch*, LC-130R, BuNo. 148318, was used on WINFLIES (winter-supply flights of men and material) in preparation for Deep Freeze 70. (*Williams*)

Right: The artwork on LC-130R, BuNo. 155917, illustrates another recurring theme of VXE-6 nose art. Many of VXE-6's aircraft names and art reflect a close relationship with the people and places of New Zealand. Note the kangaroo zap from the RAAF and the kiwi bird zap from the RNZAF No. 5 Squadron. (*Williams*)

Above: When deployed to Antarctica these aircraft would perform what the crews called *Rickety Rack to the Pole and Back* supply flights. *AO TE'A ROA* of VXE-6 was photographed in July 1969. (*Williams*)

Left: This LC-130, BuNo. 159129, at Mc Guire AFB, NJ, during September 1983, has diminutive penguin nose art. (*Don Spering A.I.R.*)

An LC-130R (BuNo. 160741) of VXE-6 with a small penguin symbol over the forward crew-entrance hatch, was transferred to the New York ANG in 1999 after VXE-6 was decommissioned. Most of the squadron's Hercules carried penguin art at one time or another between 1961 and February 1997. (*Meehan*)

Above: *The last plane out*, LC-130R (BuNo. 159130) departed Williams Field, Antarctica early on 17 February 1999. This Hercules was appropriately named *Spirit of Willy Field* and marked the end of the US Navy's mission with Operation Deep Freeze. (*US Navy, photo by PO 1st Class E. G. Martens*)

Right: This is a close up of the *Chilly* nose art. (*Chris Bryant via Joe Hawkins, www.vaq34.com*)

VXN-8

During 1965 several projects under the supervision of the US Naval Oceanographic Office were reorganized into one assignment for a single unit. These projects were: Magnet, Birdseye, Seascan, and Jenny. Project Magnet, formed in 1951, collected geomagnetic data used to annotate oceanic navigation charts and to calibrate ASW equipment. Project Birdseye began in 1958 and collected ice flow information in support of US Navy surface and subsurface operations. During 1962 two more projects were started. Project Seascan observed geothermal, acoustic, and ambient noise, applying this information to submarine detection. And Project Jenny, a contemporary of the Cuban Missile Crisis, provided an airborne platform for the broadcasting of radio and television programs under combat conditions. On 29 July 1965 the Oceanographic Air Survey Unit, OASU, was commissioned to perform all these tasks. This unit reported to COMPATWINGLANT for administrative purposes and also to COMNAVAIRLANT for operational tasking and providing technical support to the COMNAVOCEAN Office. Oceanographic Development Squadron 8, VX-8, was formed from the OASU.

Since the late 1960s VX-8 (later VXN-8) operated a mixed bag of C-121 Super Constellations and P-3 Orions. Most all of the aircraft were painted international orange, identifying them as non-hostile, and also had nose art sanctioned by the Warner Brothers Studio, depicting the popular *Loony Toons* characters. Since 1958 the 'Road Runner', 'Wiley Coyote', and 'Taz' have adorned the Connies and Orions used by the squadron and its predecessors. The studio even developed the 'Arctic Fox' character for use on the Project Birdseye aircraft. This agreement was reminiscent of the early days of the Second World War, when Walt Disney Studios co-operated with Lockheed-Vega and the US Navy to provide art work for the PV-1 Ventura and US Navy squadrons. The VXN-8's PAO Officer felt that the use of these cartoon characters was excellent for the organization's *esprit de corps*, just as these cartoon characters had done in the Second World War. Only one VXN-8 aircraft carried artwork that was not based on a Warner Brothers character, and that was the squadron's utility and logistics aircraft, *World Traveler*. At different times in its life this aircraft was adorned with either Charles Schulz's 'Snoopy' or Jeff MacNelly's 'Loon' from the *Shoe* comic strip. VXN-8 like VXE-6 had a long-standing tradition in the use of nose art, going back thirty years, but in October 1993 the squadron was ordered to stand down due to economic considerations.

By June 1986 *Loon* was chosen as the World Traveler's mascot artwork. This character is from Jeff MacNelly's comic strip *Shoe*. This lovable old flyer's motto is: 'Any landing you can walk away from is a good landing'. This plane was probably the unit's pilot training bird and trash-hauler.

An RP-3D, BuNo. 158227, is at NAS Rota, Spain, in July 1974. While taking magnetic readings in the Southern Hemisphere in March 1973, this aircraft would become the first P-3 to fly around and across the South Pole. (*Author's collection*)

Blue Eagle Three, an NC-121J, BuNo. 131655, is in a revetment at Da Nang, South Vietnam in October 1967. In April of 1966 this aircraft was damaged in a mortar attack at Tan Son Nhut. The aircraft was repaired and became instrumental in maintaining radio and television communication with the people of South Vietnam during the Tet Offensive. It appears that someone in the unit was an Auburn University alumnus. The Blue 'War' Eagle was applied to all three of Project Jenny's aircraft. (*US Navy*)

An EC-121K, BuNo. 141325, of Project Birdseye, was adorned with the *Arctic Fox* on a block of ice. This character nicely represents the aircraft's mission—monitoring polar ice flows. (*US Navy via Ray West*)

Project Birdseye's aircraft is at its homeport, NAS Patuxent River, MD, in October 1986. The artists at Warner Brothers Studios created the artwork on BuNo. 151384 for the unit. This aircraft was an auxiliary back up for the regular RP-3D project aircraft. (*Dr Stephen Wolf*)

This is the first *El Coyote*, an NC-121K of Project Seascan, BuNo. 145924, as it appeared in April 1971. (*Don Spering A.I.R.*)

The second *El Coyote* was an RP-3A of Project Seascan, BuNo. 149667, and is pictured on a RON at NAS Brunswick, Maine, in January 1978. (*Ray West*)

El Coyote number three was a former YP-3C prototype, modified to RP-3D standards. However, this Orion was dual-mission capable, able to perform for Project Seascan and the Project Birdseye mission. (*Author's collection*)

Here is a close-up view of the nose art on the second *El Coyote*, BuNo. 149667. (*Ray West*)

Here, the *Road Runner* nose art is compared over a twelve-year period. Above: BuNo. 158227, the Project Magnet aircraft is pictured here as it appeared in July 1974. This aircraft was responsible for locating the Union ironclad USS *Monitor* off the East Coast of the United States in late 1973–74. (Bill Tate) Below: The same aircraft in October 1986 is now named *Paisano Tres*. The first two *Paisanos* were Super Constellations. (*Dr Stephen Wolf*)

Snoopy was VXN-8 World Traveler's mascot in October of 1982. BuNo. 150520 is the squadron's bounce bird, used for logistic support and flight crew training. (*Dr Stephen Wolf*)

BuNo. 150500, an RP-3A, was the second *Arctic Fox* to fly the Birdseye mission. It was fitted with a cryogenic radiometer, a research and development sensor, in 1976. The aircraft not only sported nose art but also three-dimensional nose sculpture. (*Bill Tate*)

PHANTOM ARTWORK

VMFAT-101 was an operational conversion unit, which occasionally did AMC training at NAS Miramar, CA, with Topgun. The squadron's tail code, 'SH', was understood to mean *Sh-t Hot*. But the Topgun Instructors and the F-14 drivers interpreted it to mean *Sh-t House*, hence the tail art. By this date the obsolescent F-4N was somewhat sluggish compared to the faster Tomcats and agile Skyhawks. Needless to say the artwork was removed when the aircraft returned to MCAS Yuma, AZ. (*Dr Stephen Wolf*)

BuNo. 152230 was an F-4N Phantom of VMFAT-101, photographed in 1979. (*Dr Stephen Wolf*)

Bloodhound 40 of the Naval Weapons Test Squadron was stationed at NAWS, Point Mugu, CA. This QF-4N was modified for the advanced testing of an airborne missile countermeasure system. This system (Generic Electronic Warfare Platforms, or GEWP) was installed in this aircraft in 1994. (*David Brown*)

In reference to the experimental countermeasure system, the roadrunner is saying *GEWP GEWP* instead of 'beep beep' and dropping flares out of his back end. This aircraft has evaded several Stinger missile firings. (*David Brown*)

QF-4 Phantom attached to the Naval Weapons Test Squadron, Point Mugu, California, begins another weapon simulation test with Navy surface units in the Puerto Rican Operation Area on 2 July 1999. As you can see, this nose art is identical to the nose art on *Bloodhound 40*. The first road runner's BuNo. is 150465, while this road runner aircraft's BuNo. is 152970. (*US Navy JO1 David Rush*)

The road runner on the second *GEWP GEWP* is the same as on the first aircraft, which leads one to believe that rather than painting artwork on each aircraft the maintenance personnel just transfer the radome to another aircraft as required. (*Frank Hamby*)

VMFA-321

VMF-321 was formed on 1 February 1943 at MCAS Cherry Point, NC, and after work-ups and intensive training the squadron was transferred to the Southwest Pacific. They arrived on Vella La Vella and began operations against Bougainville on 23 December 1943. They then moved to Green Island and continued flying sorties in the Solomon Islands' OP area between March and April 1944. While in the Solomon's the *Hell's Angels* scored thirty-nine kills against the Japanese for a loss of only eight Corsairs. Major Edmund F. Overend, the squadron's Commanding Officer, was the unit's leading ace, with eight kills to his credit.

By August 1944 they were flying out of Guam, and on occasion from carriers (like *CVE-98 Kwajalein*) that passed through their theater of operation. While on Guam, the unit flew missions against the bypassed Japanese islands of Rota and Pagan until mid-December 1944, when they returned to the States. It was while on Guam that the squadron began to use nose art. Major Overend, an ex-Flying Tiger from China, was probably the influence behind the unit's emblem of the *Hell's Angles*. The emblem, a nude silhouette of a woman with wings, closely resembled the emblem of the 3rd Pursuit Squadron, AVG, of which Maj. Overend was a former member. From this rather *risqué* symbolic start, it did not take long for the squadron members to add pin-ups and names to their aircraft.

Following the war the VMF-321 was disestablished. In 1946 a group of ex-Marine aviators and some wartime veterans of VMF-321 decided to reform a Marine Air Reserve squadron in the Washington DC area. They adopted the linage and squadron emblem of the Hell's Angels, and the unit stood up in July 1946 at NAS Anacostia, Maryland. Again they would be equipped with the FG-1D, and later models of the Corsair. The unit was re-equipped with more modern aircraft as time passed, from F8F Bearcats, to AF-1E Furys, to F-8 Crusaders, to F-4 Phantom IIs. By 19 October 1961 VMA-321 had to move to NAF Andrews AFB in order to operate the more sophisticated jet aircraft. It was December 1973 when the squadron, now VMFA-321, re-equipped with the Phantom. These aircraft would stay with the unit for eighteen years, until the squadron transitioned to F/A-18 Hornets. This Marine Reserve squadron at times over those years would use aircraft artwork on more than one occasion, first in 1975–76 during the Bicentennial, then in April 1990 on an Advance Combat Maneuvers ACM Det. to Key West, FL. The last occasion was when the unit was about to give up its beloved F-4S Phantom II in July 1991.

This artwork was specially created for VMFA-321's F-4S Phantom II, which commemorates the Phantom's eighteenth year of operations with the unit. One of the creators of this art was the talented Don Spering. VMFA-321 is stationed at NAF Washington DC, but maintains a detachment at NAS Key West when warranted. Don Spering took this beautiful airborne picture of MG 000 in July 1991 over the Atlantic. (*Don Spering A.I.R.*)

Aircraft BuNo. 153904 is the Marine Air Group Forty-One Commander's mount, as signified by the 'triple nuts' on the nose. Notice the incorporation of the Phantom 'Spook' character into this design. This imaginative little character was born at MCAIR in 1962, during the research and development phase of the Phantom II. His creator, Tony Wong (a technical artist for MCAIR), endowed this faceless little guy with the mystifying and stealthy qualities which symbolize the McDonnell F-4 Phantom II. (*Don Spering A.I.R.*)

Don 'Hawkeye' Spering began building aircraft models with his father and brothers at an early age, and in the 1970s he became an aircraft painter at McGuire AFB. Don and his brothers collected over 1,300 scale models by the time he was eighteen. From these experiences he moved on to creating nose art for certain Air Force commands, chiefly the Air National Guard. In 1991, after painting numerous ANG F-106s and F-4s, he was asked to work with the Marine painters at Andrews AFB in creating the squadron's anniversary aircraft. Don makes abundant use of the McDonnell Douglas 'spook' character, which is a hallmark for all Phantom Phans. Don's lifelong dream was to fly in jet aircraft, and in 1972 the USAF gave him his first ride in an F-106B. From then on he had the bug to fly and to photograph aircraft in flight. Over the years he has amassed over 2,000 flight hours in T-33s, F-106Bs, F-105s, F-100s, A-3s, F-15s, and F-18s. However, his favorite aircraft is the F-4 Phantom, in which he has over 130 flight hours. Don had his camera on hand during every flight to document it, and on many occasions he would photograph the very planes he had painted. Most of the aircraft Don painted with commemorative nose art belonged to the USAF and the Air National Guard; however, because of his experience in painting Phantoms, he was asked to paint some USMC aircraft. Don has been rewarded for his achievements on more than one occasion. Many of Don's pictures appear in aviation books and publications, and he continues to work in the field of aircraft nose art whenever an interested party commissions him to work his magic. (*Don Spering A.I.R.*)

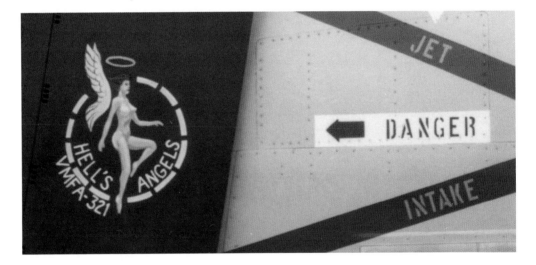

These are two pictures of the splitter plate on MG 000, before and after the Clinton Administration's campaign to make everything politically correct in fall 1991 (above). You might note that after the angel has been robed she has grown gray hair. Is this a sign of stress? Actually, this squadron insignia has had a long-running disagreement with the official guidelines for Navy/Marine Corp insignias. During the Second World War everything was pretty much fine, but by December 1952 things had changed. A new directive came out with more stringent rules. For example, the Disney-created cartoons of the past were no longer acceptable; everything had to be standardized and dignified. Later in the 1970s, the dignity of the service was clarified in that no references to games of chance, alcoholic drink, nor most certainly naked women would be allowed. However, since VMFA-321 had adopted the insignia of the former VMF-321 in 1946–47, they could officially carry on the tradition. The 'official' patch for the squadron now is the pitchfork through the halo over flames. So, it would seem that the devices of Satan are more acceptable to a bureaucracy than female nudity. Below is the *Hell's Angels* before the Clinton-era changes. (*Meehan*)

This is a VMFA-321 F-4S at Boca Chica Field on an ACM detachment. The artwork on the splitter plate illustrates the unit's insignia, the *Hell's Angel*, under a Florida palm tree. Below is a close up of the artwork on Phantom MG 06, BuNo. 156980. (*Don Spering A.I.R.*)

This VMF-321 F4U-1 Corsair was stationed on Guam Island in 1944. Notice the name *Luscious Lil-Nan*, and the small pin-up just in front of the cockpit and below the windshield. This artwork was probably cut out of a magazine or calendar and doped on to the aircraft fuselage. Many of the Corsair's control surfaces and part of the wings still used dope and fabric to cover areas, and the maintenance department was more than able to accomplish this job as long as the pilots could keep them supplied with pin-ups. Below the pin-up is the squadron's 'Hell's Angels' insignia, highlights added. (*National Archives via NMNA*)

The Marines had come to NAS Boca Chica Field in Key West for some ACM training in the less-crowded sky over the Caribbean. This is 'Hell's Angels' MG 04 on the ramp at Boca Chica, April 1990. (*Don Spering A.I.R.*)
 This is another rendition of the ACM Det. nose art on aircraft MG 04, BuNo. 157261. (*Don Spering A.I.R.*)

THE F-14 TOMCAT

The powerful F-14 Tomcat first flew in December 1970, and entered operational squadron service with the VF-1 Wolfpack in June 1973. The Tomcats' first combat cruise, in which they provided cover for the evacuation of Saigon and the Mayaguez Incident, was aboard the USS *Enterprise*, CVN-65, in 1975. But the Tomcats did not fire their weapons in anger until 1981, when the Black Aces of VF-41 splashed two Libyan Su-22s. During almost thirty years of service the Tomcat has evolved through F-14A, F-14A+, F-14B, F-14B (upgrade), and the F-14D. It has gone from a pure fleet-defense fighter to an attack-bomber, carrying laser-guided bombs and a reconnaissance platform with the digital TARPS pod. The Tomcat has also received a fair amount of 'nose art' during its long career.

AD 102 of VF-101 was photographed at NAS Oceana in April 1982, and bears the personal making of 'Rattler' Rucker under the rear seat. (*Jim Meehan*)

VF-101

One early form of F-14 art was the black stenciled rattlesnake on several aircraft flown by Lt Alexander 'Rattler' Rucker. The snake was first recorded on an F-8 Crusader flown by Rucker with VF-111 off Vietnam. The first F-14A to carry it was modex AE 204 of the VF-142 *Ghostriders*, photographed in 1978 with the snake below the cockpit. The snake and the pilot moved to the VF-14 *Tophatters* in 1981, flying modex AE 101, and ended up in the VF-101 *Grim Reapers*' squadron in 1982 with the rattlesnake on AD 102.

That same year (1982), another VF-101 F-14A, this one belonging to Cdr 'Moon' Vance, was photographed with artwork. His Tomcat, AD 101, was decorated with a dark-gray half-moon on the fin, and the famous Hot Rod 'Moon Equipped' logo and eyes on the aircraft nose. The *Grim Reapers* aircraft did not acquire more noteworthy art until much later in the Tomcats' career. As F-14 squadrons were disestablished during the 1990s, the Grim Reapers of VF-101, while at NAS Oceana, painted the lost squadrons' insignia and dates of service on the fin of one of their Tomcats, to keep each unit's memory alive. During this time VF-101 Tomcats carried the markings of VF-1, VF-33, VF-74, VF-84, VF-111, and others.

One of Alex 'Rattler' Rucker's F-8 Crusaders from VF-194; note the coiled rattlesnake artwork under the canopy. Mr Rucker was wingman for Lt Tony Nargi on 19 September 1968, when he shot down a Mig-21 over North Vietnam. This would be the last Crusader Mig kill of the Vietnam War. The above picture was taken after Lt Rucker had left VF-111 and joined VF-194. (*Don Spering A.I.R.*)

'Rattler' Rucker's VF-14 F-14A, modex AE 101 from the USS *Independence*, was photographed on 13 March 1982. This aircraft was stricken on 22 February 1995. (*Adelson via Jim Meehan*)

Above: F-14A-110-GR is the only known *Moon Equipped* Tomcat. 0–180mph in 2.8 seconds (with catapult assist) seems like a fair guess for this baby. Cdr 'Moon' Vance flew this F-14 as CO of VF-101. It was photographed in May 1982 on the ramp at NAS Oceana. (*Jim Meehan*)

Below: BuNo. 162689 is pictured at NAS Oceana in 1993. Along with the artwork, *Bombcat* has a black cheat line along its anti-glare area and black canopy frame. (*Jim Meehan*)

VF-41

With the possible exception of VF-111, which used the shark mouth to decorate many of their aircraft, VF-41 is probably the most decorated Tomcat squadron to date. The Black Aces started the trend of painting nose art on the skipper's plane in 1991, during Desert Storm. The roll of the Tomcat as a laser-guided attack bomber gave inspiration to create the artwork, and a variation of the famous twin-tailed Grumman Tomcat cartoon was used.

The first of these was *Bomb Cat*, BuNo. 162689, AJ 101, done in 1993. The slogan 'No Escort Required' was painted in small red letters next to the artwork, commemorating the first operational use of the F-14 as a bomb carrier. The two aircraft that followed this tradition were *Strike Cat*, BuNo. 160394, also AJ 101, in 1994, and *Tomcat FastFac*, BuNo. 162608, AJ 101 yet again, in 1999.

BuNo. 160394 carries the *Strikecat* art and was photographed on 17 September 1994. This aircraft was lost off the USS *Roosevelt* in May 1995. (*Jim Meehan*)

A close-up view of the twin tail Tomcat *Strikecat*. (*Jim Meehan*)

A twin-tailed Tomcat riding a smart bomb adorns the nose of BuNo. 162608. This F-14 flew forward air-control directing missions against targets in Yugoslavia during the 1999 NATO bombing campaign. In the *Tomcat FastFac* mission, the Black Aces flew ahead of the strike missions to locate the targets. (*Bill Tate*)

FLIR Cat, modex AA 213, was photographed on 29 April 1995. Note the differences in color and lettering style on each side of the nose. (*Kaminski*)

VF-103

VF-103 also used the Grumman Tomcat cartoon on one of their F-14Bs, modex AA 213, in 1995. *FLIR Cat* was the prototype for the LANTIRN equipped Tomcat. The LANTIRN system used FLIR, which stands for forward-looking infra-red, to deliver laser-guided ordnance. This replaced the bombing method VF-103 had used over Bosnia in 1992, in which targets were illuminated by FA-18s. Beginning in March 1995, *FLIR Cat* flew forty LANTIRN sorties and dropped one live laser-guided bomb. Modex AA-213 was assigned to VF-143 in late 1997. Christmas of 1999 saw a VF-103 *Jolly Rogers* F-14B decorated for the holidays. Modex AJ 201 had the traditional skull and bones modified with a Santa hat on the skull, and crossed candy canes in place of the bones. The same motif was used on modex AJ 103 for Christmas 2000.

OTHERS

VF-11 flew modex AE 110 with the legend *Blue Nose 88* on a blue-painted radome after participation in a 1988 North Atlantic exercise. F-14s of VF-11 were also decorated for the 2000 holidays.

In 1992, following the Tailhook convention crisis, VX-4's BuNo. 159853, an F-14A, featured their Playboy rabbit insignia with a tear running down its cheek as the controversial emblem was soon to be stricken from the unit's aircraft.

OPERATION DESERT STORM

The war against Iraq to free Kuwait involved a coalition of countries dedicated to working together as a military command. Nose art saw a revival on many types of aircraft and in many of these air forces. Britain's Royal Air Force had a great many of its Tornados, Buccaneers, Jaguars, and support aircraft painted with elaborate and sometimes almost obscene artwork. The United States Air Force produced pin-ups and airbrushed artwork on its A-10s, F-16s, B-52s, and tankers. The Navy and Marine Corps decorated many of its aircraft also; however, most of the art was removed before returning to the states.

A-7 CORSAIR II

The LTV A-7E Corsair II (or SLUF) flew its last combat missions in Desert Storm. VA-46 and VA-72 flew the A-7Es from the USS *Kennedy*. The SLUFs returned bearing elaborate scoreboards of their many missions, and one aircraft, modex AC 400 of VA-72, carried the large words *Desert Storm* across the tops of its wings.

A-6 INTRUDER OF VF-155

The A-6E Intruders of VF-155, the *Silver Foxes*, flew missions from the USS *Ranger*. VA-155 marked each aircraft's mission tally on the rudder and several rudders were named. *Cujo* was modex NE 400, *War Eagle* was modex NE 403, *Iraqi Widow Maker* was modex NE 407, and *Desperado* was modex NE 410.

F-14 TOMCATS

In 1991 Desert Storm saw a brief flurry of nose art activity in the Allied military aviation community, especially on its F-14s. Photos of VF-14's Tomcats flying over Kuwait show the Tophatters' CAG bird, modex AB 100, with *Go Navy-Beat Army* painted across the top wings, proving that spirits remained high and that even a war cannot eclipse the Army-Navy football game. Other photographs show some aircraft with artwork inspired by the war environment. The VF-24 Renegades had two such Tomcats: *Camel Smoker*, BuNo. 163409, and *Thief of Baghdad*, BuNo. 163411, both with appropriate cartoon art. VF-24 also flew briefly a Tomcat, NG 212, with the San Diego Chargers football team emblem on the fin. The VF-114 Aardvarks' CAG bird, modex NH 100, also displayed spirit by painting desert head gear on the F-14's orange aardvark and painting the name *Vark of Arabia* on the aircraft.

A Corsair II belonging to Attack Squadron 72 has the banner '*Desert Storm*' painted across its wing. (*US Navy*)

This VA-72 Corsair II did thirty missions (Camels Humps) over Kuwait and Iraq during Operation Desert Storm. (*John Kerr*)

OTHERS

Other Desert Storm artwork noted included EA-3B *Bart of Arabia* of VQ-2, with a Bart Simpson cartoon, and S-3B *The War Hoover*, modex AA 700 of VS-30 from the *Saratoga*.

AV-8B HARRIERS

A few of the Corps hardworking AV-8B Harriers were also personalized. *Venom* was painted on the VMA-231 squadron commander's aircraft, modex CG 01, along with a shark mouth. Another named AV-8B was *Angel* of VMA-331 with VL tail code and pin-up art.

A shark mouth adorns the nose of AV-8B BuNo. 163662 from VMA-231. This was 'Shark 01', the squadron CO's aircraft, which carried the name *Venom* and a record of fifty-four Desert Storm missions. The Arabic phrase above the mission marks means, *Free Kuwait*. Dave Brown photographed this aircraft at Cherry Point in 1991. (*Dave F. Brown*)

AIR WING 8 IN DESERT STORM

Carrier Air Wing Eight, CVW-8, went to the Gulf War aboard the USS *Theodore Roosevelt*, CVN-71. The Air Wing's aircraft included F-14As in VF-41 and VF-84, F/A-18As in VFA-15 and VFA-87, A-6Es in VA-65 and VA-36, EA-6Bs in VAQ-141, E-2Cs in VAW-124, S-3Bs in VS-24, and SH-3H helicopters in HS-9. The *Roosevelt* and its air wing were on station in the Gulf from 28 December 1990 until 28 June 1991. From the beginning of Desert Storm, 17 January 1991, Air Wing Eight was flying an assortment of combat missions against Iraq every day (or night as the case may have been). In fact, the *Roosevelt* was known as 'the night carrier' because most of its strikes were flown in the 0000 to 1400 hours timeframe. Several days into Desert Storm the Allies realized that the Iraqi Air Force was not a threat to Allied aircraft, and the Tomcats of VF-41 and VF-84 were sent on long missions deep into Iraq to prevent Iraqi aircraft from escaping to Iran. The S-3Bs of VS-24 flew bombing missions rather than their usual antisubmarine runs, and one Viking sank an Iraqi speedboat with two Mark 82 500-pound bombs.

The air wing was noted for its striking nose art, since almost every squadron commander's aircraft received a pin-up or similar artwork. Sadly, all were removed as the *Roosevelt* sailed home, with one exception—*Miss B. Havin* on E-2C BuNo. 161552 of VAW-124. This pin-up was covered in tape, sprayed with gray paint, and flown into NAS Norfolk on 26 June 1991. Upon arrival the paper was removed, and *Miss B. Havin* became the center of attention. An earlier photo of the same Hawkeye shows the name *Classic* and a different pin-up.

The VF-14's squadron commander's Tomcat, modex AJ 101, was decorated with a kneeling nude wearing a black spade tattoo on her rear, with the name *Queen of Spades*. VF-84's 201 bird, BuNo. 162692, had a standing nude wrapped in a Jolly Roger flag and the name *Cat Snatch Fever*. Both of these paintings were on the port nose of the Tomcats, but the VF-84 bird also sported a large pirate flag on its vertical fins, similar to those worn by the unit's F-4B Phantoms during the Vietnam War.

Two other squadron CO aircraft that had nose art were VA-65's A-6E, modex AJ 500, which had a large Garfield cartoon on its port nose and VS-24's S-3B, modex AJ 701, which had a reclining pin-up wrapped in the American flag next to a scrawny tomcat. A few other units had nose art represented on their planes as well. An Intruder of VA-36, modex AJ 536, carried the name *Heartless* and a drawing of a nude on a large red heart. *Heartless* was marked with twenty-seven mission symbols when it arrived at NAS Oceana on 26 June, but the artwork had disappeared. Also EA-6B, modex AJ 621, of VAQ-141 had a large painting of a scantily-clad girl riding a HARM missile, along with the name *Eve of Destruction*. Apparently, the only aircraft in Air Wing 8 that did not carry nose art or mission markings were the F/A-18 and SH-3H squadrons.

Queen of Spades, modex AJ 101, is pictured here on the deck of the USS *Roosevelt* during the Gulf War. (*National Archives*)

Miss B. Havin was a beautifully rendered pin-up done with an airbrush by one of the ship's company on board the USS *Roosevelt*. Fortunately, when one of the higher-ranking officers ordered all nose art to be removed from CVW-8 aircraft, VAW-124's enterprising maintenance personnel were able to comply with the order by covering over the questionable artwork with vinyl speed tape and painting it light gull-gray to match the aircraft's skin. This picture of the ground crew removing the tape was taken on the NAS Norfolk seaplane ram the day the CAG-8 returned home. (*Tate*)

F-14A, modex AJ 201, from the VF-84 Jolly Rogers, received the name *Cat Snatch Fever* and this attractive pin-up while flying from the USS *Roosevelt* during Desert Storm. It is reported that the name was originally *Cat Scratch Fever* but was probably abandoned for the more suggestive name. (*Cdr Rick Morgan via Brown*)

The *Theodore Roosevelt* in the summer of 1991 had a nose art derby were all CAG-8's aircraft were lined up on the flight deck for review. The lineup includes EA-6B, *Eve of Destruction*; A-6E, *Heartless*; A-6E, *The Big Stick*; F-14A, *Queen of Spades*; and E-2C *Miss B. Having*. The VF-84 Tomcat with a pin-up on the nose is across the deck from the others. Shortly after this event the art was removed before the aircraft returned to home port. (*Cdr Rick Morgan via John Kerr*)

An EA-6B Prowler of VAQ-141, modex AJ 621, carried two small missiles on the nose, representing two HARM launches during Operation Deliberate Force over Kosovo in 1995, as well as a gun-slinging hawk cartoon. It flew from the USS *Kennedy* and was photographed on 21 April 1996 at NAS Norfolk. (*Meehan*)

7

THE MODERN NAVY (1991–2001)

The period from 1991–2001 saw great changes in Naval Aviation. Two attack aircraft that had served the Navy well since the late '50s were retired from service. The Skyhawk and the Intruder left the Navy attack community, but not without a farewell splash of color and an artist tribute through nose art.

THE A-4M SKYHAWK

The CO of reserve squadron VMA-131 had a very colorful A-4M Skyhawk, QG 00, in 1994. This 'Diamondback' had yellow and black markings on the fuselage and fin unlike the rest of the squadron's aircraft. Above: On the Skyhawk's port side the name *Viper* and a cobra appear on the nose. A small drawing of a clamshell with the name 'Clam', which is the nickname of the aircraft's painter, appears on the port canopy rail. (*Don Spering A.I.R.*)

The starboard canopy rail has the CO's *Eagle* call sign with an eagle drawing.

The starboard fuselage bears an emblem that reads '*40 years of excellence*', denoting the Skyhawk's operational life. The aircraft was photographed on 7 August 1994 at NAS Willow Grove, just before the squadron gave up their beloved Skyhawks for F/A-18 Hornets. (*Don Spering A.I.R.*)

THE A-6E INTRUDER

The 1990s saw the last operational flight of one of the greatest carrier-based attack aircraft, the Grumman A-6 Intruder. Both the Intruder and its 'four-door' offspring, the EA-6B Prowler (which continues in service today), have seen a fair amount of nose art while in Navy and Marine service. The VA-95 Green Lizards, disestablished on 18 November 1995, retired their Intruders by inscribing *Lizard's Last Romp* and the lizard mascot on the nose of modex NH 501. VA-165 named their CO's last A-6E *Puff the Magic Dragon* in honor of an A-1H that flew with the squadron over Vietnam. But the honor of being the last unit to fly the Intruder fell to the Navy's oldest attack squadron, the *Sunday Punchers* of VA-75. Modex AA 501 had the old boxer emblem painted on the nose in December 1996 for its last launch from the USS *Enterprise*, CVN-65.

This picture is of the last active-duty Intruder at NAS Oceana, February 1997. (*Jim Meehan*)

The traditional boxer emblem of VA-75 was photographed at the squadron's disestablishment ceremony on 28 February 1997. Modex AA 501 made its last flight out of NAS Oceana on the rainy evening of 19 March 1997, bound for AMARC and storage. (*Meehan*)

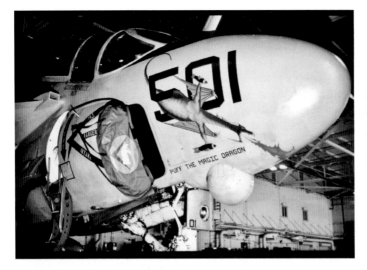

The elaborate artwork for *Puff the Magic Dragon* was rendered in 1996, as VA-65 took its last cruise on the USS *Nimitz* before being disestablished in September of that year. Modex NG 501 was painted in honor of an A-1J Skyraider with the same name, modex AK 204, which flew fifty-five combat missions from the USS *Intrepid* during the Viet Nam Conflict. (*Don Spering A.I.R.*)

One of VA-42's Intruders acquired the nickname 'trip nickel' and had three buffalo nickels painted on the nose in place of the modex numbers 555. It was photographed in July 1991 at NAS Oceana. (*Don Spering A.I.R.*)

8

THE WAR ON TERROR: VFA-115

The *Eagles of Navy* attack squadron VFA-115 is a unique unit as far as the history of naval aircraft nose art goes. This is the only squadron in recent times that has made a real effort to paint all their 'birds' with some form of artwork. All of the art has a patriotic tone and most of it pays tribute to the fallen heroes of the September 11 terrorist attack on the World Trade Center and the Pentagon. Each F/A-18E is painted with the names of the fifteen firefighters of Engine 54, *The Pride of Manhattan, Never Missed a Performance*, who were lost at the World Trade Center on September 11. In addition one aircraft is dedicated to the memory of Lt Cdr O. V. Tolbert who was lost on the same day at the Pentagon. Super Hornet NK 212 is entitled *Hijack This!!!* and memorializes the victims of the American and United Airlines flights which were hijacked by the terrorists on September 11.

VFA-115 received F/A-18E Super Hornets in March 2002. The *Super Bugs* gave the squadron a fighter aircraft that was 25 per cent larger than its predecessor, yet easier to maintain in that it had 42 per cent fewer structural parts. The new Hornets carried heavier payloads greater distances on more

Aircraft NK 201 is taxiing to launch on another mission in support of Operation Enduring Freedom; note the eagle's head nose art. (*US Navy photo by PH3 P. A. McDaniel*)

powerful engines than the F/A-18C. With this new aircraft the Navy also had a replacement for the KA-6D Intruder, which allowed the in-flight refueling of their own carrier attack aircraft. The *Eagles* would, after completing a 100-day transition period, receive a 'safe-for-flight' certification in the F/A-18E Super Hornet in May 2002. VAF-115 was the first squadron to fly the Super Hornet on an operational cruise in July 2002. On 11 September 2002 they arrived with Carrier Air Wing Fourteen (CVW-14) onboard the USS *Abraham Lincoln* (CVN-72) in the Indian Ocean. Two days later, two F/A-18E's from the unit flew the first Super Hornet combat mission in support of Operation Enduring Freedom over Afghanistan. While the CAS mission was nothing to write home about, it did signify a new period in Naval Aviation. On 6 November 2002, in support of Operation South Watch, VFA-115's F/A-18Es dropped four GPS-guided JDAM bombs on Iraqi SAM sites at Al Kut. These attacks were followed by two more strikes on 7 and 10 November. CVN-72 arrived in Fremantle, Australia, for holiday leave in December 2002, but by January 2003 they were ordered back to the Persian Gulf in anticipation of the war with Iraq. On 20 March 2003 they would participate in the first day of Operation Iraqi Freedom. After the start of hostilities, the Navy found that—due to a shortfall in air-to–air refueling assets—they needed to reconfigure four of the unit's F/A-18Es as tankers. These aircraft did increase loiter time for strike and CAS mission aircraft. Later in the conflict, four additional F/A-18E/F Super Hornets (two each from VFA-41 and VFA-14) were deployed to the *Lincoln* to assist VFA-115 in this task. On 14 April 2003 CVN-72, CVW-14, and VFA-115 were finally relieved to return to the States. After almost ten months away from home, traveling over 102,816 nautical miles, and helping CVW-14 drop 1.3 million pounds of ordnance on Iraq, the *Eagles* of VFA-115 returned to a hero's welcome and a well-deserved rest.

A Petty Officer paints artwork a VAQ-141 Prowler while passing the time on board CVN 71 USS *Theodore Roosevelt* during the crew's seven month long deployment. He is responsible for painting more than one of Carrier Air Wing Eight's aircraft. (*Rick Morgan via John Kerr*)

Two of the New York firemen who died at the World Trade Center during the 11 September 2001 attacks were remembered on VFA-115 Skipper's aircraft. During Operation Iraqi Freedom aircraft NK 201 flew at least six attack missions. (*US Navy photo by PH3 Michael S. Kelly*)

Aircraft NK 200, the 'CAG Bird,' with the FDNY Engine Company 54-4 Truck emblem on its nose, prepares to launch on a tanker mission over Iraq, 25 March 2003. This aircraft flew the squadron's first strike mission over Afghanistan back in September 2002. (*US Navy photo by PH3 Phillip A. McDaniel*)

23 March 2004: a 'Super Bug' of VFA-115 lands aboard CVN-74 John C. Stennis. The squadron is doing carrier work-ups and training and preparing to go back to war. Note the FDNY emblem is still being worn on aircraft NK 200; however, all the other planes in the unit had their nose art removed after their return from Operation Iraqi Freedom. (*US Navy photo by PHAN Erik C. Naville*)

Aircraft NK 212 flew at least four bombing missions over Afghanistan; but, as can be seen, she will be flying a strike support mission, tanking other fighters over Iraq. In the insert note, 212's nose art is a tribute to the fallen heroes of American Flights 11 and 77 and United Flights 175 and 93. (*US Navy photo by PH3 Michael S. Kelly and PH3 Phillip A. McDaniel*)

Aircraft NK 210 at rest on the deck of the *Abe Lincoln* after a long day over Iraq. The artwork on the nose of this aircraft combines the emblem of the FDNY and CVN 72. (*US Navy photo by PH3 Tyler Clements and PH3 Michael S. Kelly*)

FRANKEN-PROWLER

In February 2001 the Naval Air Depot at Jacksonville, Florida, began work on two former test-bed EA-6B Prowlers, combining them into one new EA-6B. Aircraft BuNo. 158542 and 158547 had been in the desert of Arizona at the AMARC facility at Davis Monahan AFB since 28 September 1994. NADEP accomplished this by joining the aft fuselage of 158547 with the forward fuselage of aircraft 158542 and various parts from Prowler 156482. They were joined together through a newly-manufactured wing center section. This assembly was joined together with the addition of new engines, wiring, flight controls, avionics, and weapon systems, which included night vision capability. In September of 2004, when the aircraft was delivered to VAQ-141, the Navy received a new up-to-date EA-6B Prowler at a significant savings, compared to the cost for a new aircraft.

This evolution which involved the piecing together of body parts from three different aircraft reminds one of Mary Shelley's *Dr. Frankenstein*. Just as this fictional doctor took body parts from the graveyard and created the monster Frankenstein, NADEP Jacksonville took three Prowlers from the bone yard in Arizona and fabricated a Franken-Prowler. With a call sign like *Franken-Prowler*, someone in the Navy thought the occasion should be commemorated with appropriate nose art.

Right: After 11 September 2001 the world changed, and with it life in America and the US Navy. The United States and its military found itself in the War on Terror. This soon developed into a war on two fronts, in Afghanistan and Iraq. As this war continued, the wear and tear on the machines of the Navy and Marines began to show. The airframes of the aircraft were aging and approaching the limits of their designed strength. With these aircraft becoming time-expired the Navy had to find ways of procuring new equipment. With the economy in flux and Congress trying to limit the military's spending the Department of the Navy had to come up with a creative way of procuring like-new aircraft to replace war weary airframes.

Below: The *Franken-Prowler* art consisted of a stylized logo of the Frankenstein monster on the nose cap and on both sides of the vertical stabilizer. In addition to this, the renderings of two large bolts on both sides of the forward fuselage electronic bays were added. This artwork represents the bolts used in attaching the head of the fictional monster to his reconstructed body. (*USAF via John Kerr and Bill Tate*)

Bolt

Frankin Art

VAQ-141's Prowler on patrol over Afghanistan is refueled by a USAF KC-135R on 15 December 2008. (*USAF*)

The EA-6B Prowler, assigned to the *Shadowhawks* of Electronic Attack Squadron 141, (VAQ-141), was allotted to Carrier Air Wing Eight (CVW-8), currently embarked aboard USS *Theodore Roosevelt* (CVN 71). Note the large bolt artwork prominently displayed on the starboard electronics-bay access door. The *Theodore Roosevelt* and Carrier Air Wing (CVW) 8 were conducting operations in the US 5th Fleet area of responsibility. (*US Navy Photo by Mass Communication Specialist 3rd Class Jonathan Snyder*)

FRANKEN-TIGERS

The second Navy aircraft to go through combining different airframes and parts into a newly-built aircraft was the F-5F, dual-seat version of the F-5 Tiger II, a twin-engine tactical fighter commonly used for training and adversary combat-tactics training. These Tiger IIs are used in the aggressor role to simulate the capabilities of Soviet Block fighter aircraft. Many of the Navy F-5s had been around since the late 1960s, and the airframes were getting a little long in the tooth. The US Navy decided to replace these aging aircraft with low-hour surplus F-5Ns acquired from the Swiss Air Force. In 2005 the F-5 Acquisition-Re-capitalization Program was in place to replace the present high-time Navy F-5Es with low-time F-5Ns. This allowed the US Navy/USMC to operate the newer F-5N aircraft into Fiscal Year (FY) 2015. The Naval Reserve also wanted to replace its two-seat F-5F Tiger II trainers, so the Reserve Command turned to NAVAIRSYSCOM to design and build a new composite airframe to replace the aging F-5F adversary aircraft. The problem was solved by simply taking a two-seat cockpit section and a tail section from an older Navy F-5F and bolting them onto a newer center section from an ex-Swiss Air Force F-5N Tiger II. NAVAIRSYSCOM dubbed these aircraft the *Franken-Tigers*. Three of these airframes were delivered by Northrop Grumman, St Augustine, Florida, to the US Navy/USMC by December 2008. Only one of the three F-5F *Franken-Tigers* carries nose art, and that is *Franken-Tiger*s, BuNo. 810834, of VFC-111, stationed NAS Key West, FL.

The *Sundowners* of VFC-111 adopted the unit badge and the squadron history and traditions of the former VF-111 *Sundowners*. VF-111 was disestablished in 1995, at the end of the Cold War, when the Navy had a reduction in force. An old Sundowner's tradition was to apply a shark mouth on all the units' aircraft. The *Sundowner* of the new squadron, VFC-111, followed its predecessor's tradition and also painted shark-mouth nose art on their aircraft. (*Bill Tate*)

The *Franken-Tiger* F-5F of the *Sundowners'* attended the 2011 *Sun N Fun* fly-in in Lakeland, FL were they not only displayed the squadron's traditional shark-mouth design but also the *Rising Sun* tail marks. This tail design is a holdover from the Second World War. (*Bill Tate*)

VFA-15 VALIONS

The fighter/attack squadrons of Carrier Air Wing 8 (CVW-8) returned to NAS Oceana on 7 December 2011, after a seven-month combat cruise on USS *George H. W. Bush* (CVN-77) in support of Operation Enduring Freedom. During this cruise, the *Valions* of VFA-15 painted their CAG jet, F-18C 164236 AJ 300, to mark the 100th anniversary of Naval Aviation and the 69th year of VFA-15 excellence in attack missions. The spine and inner fins of the F-18C are painted black. The inner fin on the right carries the emblem of CVN-77, and the left inner fin carries the CVW-8 emblem. The spine-mounted speed brake is painted as the American flag.

The *Lions* of Torpedo Squadron 4 (VT-4) were established on 1 January 1942 as a component of Air Wing 4, aboard the USS *Ranger* (CV-4). VT-4 began operations with the Douglas TBD Devastator and soon transitioned to the Grumman TBM Avenger. Ranger and its air wing supported the invasion of North Africa in 1942, and later operated in the Norwegian Sea against German shipping and installations in Norway. VT-4 deployed to the Pacific theater in 1944.

VT-4 became VA-15 in 1948, and flew Douglas A-1 Skyraiders and Douglas A-4 Skyhawks on combat missions over Vietnam in the 1960's. The *Valions* transitioned to the Vought A-7 Corsair II in 1969, and to the F/A-18A Hornet in 1986.

An F/A-18C Hornet assigned to Strike Fighter Squadron (VFA) 15 lands aboard the aircraft carrier USS *George H. W. Bush* (CVN 77). *George H. W. Bush*, the Navy's newest aircraft carrier, is deployed as a part of the US 5th Fleet. The fleet's area of responsibility on its first operational deployment is conducting maritime security operations and support missions for Operations Enduring Freedom and New Dawn. (*US Navy photo by Mass Communication Specialist 3rd Class Jeffrey M. Richardson/Released*)

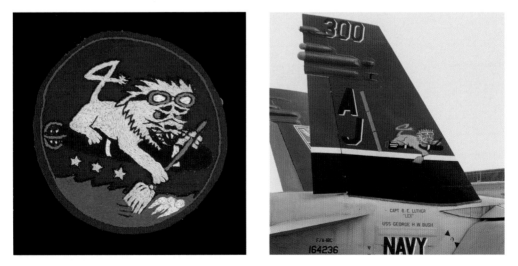

The original Second World War squadron insignia consisted of a cartoon lion wearing goggles and riding a torpedo while 'sweeping the seas' with a broom. (*Courtesy of the Nation Museum of Naval Aviation*)

This insignia was reproduced on the right fin of AJ 300. The left fin carries the current squadron insignia—a more lifelike lion, riding a laser-guided bomb. (*Jim Meehan*)

21 September 2011, Sailors maneuver an F/A-18C Hornet assigned to Strike Fighter Squadron 15, VFA-15, on the flight deck of the aircraft carrier USS *George H. W. Bush* (CVN 77). Note the pilot's wife's name, *Cathy*, and the plane captain's hand prints on the forward radome. (*US Navy photo by Mass Communication Specialist 3rd Class Billy Ho/Released*)

Above left: As an acknowledgement to the Second Word War tradition of aircraft nose art, each of the *Valions* jets carries the name of a pilot's spouse on the nose. Most of the jets carried mission marks on the nose—a silhouette of an LGB indicating a bombing mission and bullet markers for strafing missions. This is AJ 300 *Cathy* as it appears on 7 December 2011, after the squadron returns to NAS Oceana, and now the aircraft has one bomb and two strafing mission marks. (*Jim Meehan*)

Above right: Other typical Valions' F-18Cs were 164661, AJ 305 *Andrea*...

Right: And 164671, AJ 307 *Shannon*. (*Jim Meehan*)

NOSE ART LISTED BY AIRCRAFT TYPE

Type	Artwork	Name	Squadron	Modex	BuNo.
A-1A	Mission marks	Tiger 7	VA-702	A 507	
A-1A	Cow girl sitting on horseback (chalk outline)	Miss Hayward	VA-923	D 5__	
A-1D	A pelican on the left crew door	Arab Airlines–See Japan	VA-115, CVA-33 Kearsarge	A 502	
A-1D	Girl's silhouette	Hefty Betty	VA-923	D 504	122737
A-1D	Mission marks and mule	US Mule	VC-33	SS 803	126985
A-1D	Pin-up	Miss Mary Jane	VF-194	B 401	126905
A-1D	Pin-up with rebel flag	Little Miss Rita	VF-194	B 417	126921
A-1H	Arab on camel	Sayonara Kitty Hawk	VA-115	NH 501	137552
A-1H	An aircraft, a cricket, and a bird mission marks	Crickets	VA-115 USS Hancock	NF 504	137612
A-1H	A mail bag	Air Mail	VA-152	NL 208	137502
A-1H	Mission marks	Miss Pussy Galore	VA-165	AK 209	134577
A-1H	A cartoon dog w/ club	None	VA-196, USS Bon Homme Richard	NM 601	139702
A-1H	Mission marks	Paper Tiger II	VA-25	NE 572	135297
A-1J	Tonkin Gulf Yacht Club	Baby	VA-145	AK 501	142033
A-1J	Mission marks	Shush Boomer	VA-165	AK 210	135272
A-1J	Mission marks (fifty-five)	Puff the Magic Dragon	VA-165	AK 204	142059
A-3B	Roadrunner	None	WEAPONS TEST		142246
A-4A	Running kangaroo on side	Scooter	VA-36	AC 400	142227
A-4B	Mission marks	Tonkin Gulf Yacht Club	VA-95	AK 03	142783
A-4C	Twenty-seven mission marks	Fanny Hill	H&MS-15	YV 81	147681
A-4C	Thirty mission marks	Mamie Stover	H&MS-15	YV 83	147829
A-4C	Mission marks	Polly Adler	H&MS-15	YV 82	147809
A-4C	Mission marks	The Ko Sisters	H&MS-15	YV 84	148464
A-4C	A black cat	None	VA-172	AB 310	142827
A-4C	Twenty-seven mission marks	Fanny Hill	VA-22	YV 81	147681
A-4C	Old bearded caricature	Whiskers	VA-34		145141
A-4C	Top hat, gloves, cane	Party Babe	VA-34	AA 300	148483
A-4C	Ninety-one mission marks	The Ram	VA-66	AK 301	145122
A-4C	175 mission marks	Fanny Hill	VA-94	NF 401	147681
A-4E	Snoopy on dog house	None	CV-31 Bon Homme Richard		
A-4E	None	Lady Jessie	VA-164	AH 406	152048
A-4E	None	Lady Jessie	VA-164	AH 407	151180
A-4E	Twenty mission marks	The Suzy Parmer	VA-23	No. 335	
A-4E	Skull	Chicken Man	VMA-211	CF 3	149983
A-4E	Small kangaroo holding a flag	None	VMA-211	CF 16	149653
A-4E	Minute man	None	VMA-322	QR 00	151125
A-4E	Bee w/crown	King Bee	VMA-331	VL 1	151177
A-4E	Black knight	Black Mac	VMA-331	VL 6	150016
A-4E	Crutch and polo mallet	?	VMA-331	AJ 501	151102
A-4E	Pirate w/peg leg	None	VMA-331		
A-4F	Elephant and VC and mission mark	Bingo King	VA-164	NP 402	155022
A-4F	None	Lady Jessie	VA-164	NP 401	155018

Type	Artwork	Name	Squadron	Modex	BuNo.
A-4F	None	Lady Jessie	VA-164	NP 401	155022
A-4F	None	Lady Jessie	VA-164	NP 401	155029
A-4F	R. Crumb's 'Keep on Truckin'	None	VA-212	NP 311	155047?
A-4M	coiled snake/eagle and Scooter Pin-up on drop tank	Viper	VMA-131	QG 00	160024
A-6A	Andy Capp comic character	Cheers	VA-175	NE 503	156997
A-6A	Mission marks	Mixed Emotions	VMA(AW)-224	NL	155655
A-6E	Mission marks and no Saddam	None	VA-115/185	NF	161107
A-6E	Kill marks on rudder	The Beast	VA-155	NE 412	152916
A-6E	Mission marks	Cujo	VA-155	NE 400	152916
A-6E	Mission marks	Desperado	VA-155	NE 410	149946
A-6E	Mission marks	Iraqi Widow Maker	VA-155	NE 407	155595
A-6E	Mission marks	War Eagle	VA-155	NE 403	159314
A-6E	Flying dragoon	Puff the Magic Dragon	VA-165	NG 501	155600
A-6E	Pin-up and mission marks	Heart Less	VA-36	AJ 536	155589
A-6E	Pickle barrels	None	VA-42	AD 573	162202
A-6E	Three nickels	Triple Nickels	VA-42	AD 555	162211
A-6E	Three nickels	None	VA-42	AD 555	161675
A-6E	Garfield	The Big Stick	VA-65	AJ 500	162179
A-6E	Boxer	The Last Intruder	VA-75	AA 501	164383
A-6E	Lizard	Lizard's Last Romp	VA-95	NH 501	161669
A-6E	A cartoon tiger w/ bomb	None	VMA(AW)-224		
A-7A	A pin-up	None	VA-72	NL 502	154135
A-7B	A pair of dice	None	NATC Lakehurst	NAEC373	154373
A-7B	A pair of dice	Four O Seven	VA-72	AB 407	154375
AD-5W	Caricature of an insect	Bogey Baiters	VA-72	No. 783	
AH-1J	Shadow of girl	Kentucky Gal	HMA-773	No. 410	157801
AH-1J	Small cobra 'S'	Scarface	HMA-773	No. 407	157785
AH-1J	Twenty-seven mission marks	None	HML-367	VT 477?	
AH-1W	A nude girl on a missile	None	HMLA-167	TV 44	
AH-1W	A volcano and a mermaid	None	HMLA-167, 22nd MEU (SOC) LHA-3 Kearsarge	EM 31	162533
AH-1W	Girl in bikini with sign, Baghdad Or Bust	Spring Break 2003	HMLA-269		
AH-1W	Pin-up with guns and ammo	Lookin' for some Action!	HMLA-269	SN 21	
AH-1W	Pumpkin head w/ chain saw w/ four heads @ his feet	Off With Their Heads	HMLA-269	No. 40	
AH-1W	Skull the shape of a spade	None	HMLA-269	SN 24	
AH-1W	Skull the shape of a spade	None	HMLA-269	SN 28	
AH-1W	Skull the shape of a spade	None	HMLA-269		
AH-1W	Uncle Sam and Saddam Hussein cartoon	It's Time For Your Punishment	HMLA-269, 24th MEU, LHA 4 Nassau	HF 19	152823
AH-1W	Anime drawing	Skid Kidz Rule	HMLA-269, 24th MEU, LHA 4 Nassau	EG 36	160825
AH-1W	Cartoon drawing of angry rooster	None	HMLA-269, 24th MEU, LHA 4 Nassau	EG ?	
AH-1W	Cartoon drawing pin-up	Sweet Cheeks	HMLA-269, 24th MEU, LHA 4 Nassau	EG 34	
AH-1W	Pin-up Zombie and skull	Christine	HMLA-269, USS Saipan LPA-2	HF 06	160815
AH-1W	Angel pin-up	Easy on the Eyes- Hard on the Soul	HMLA-269, USS Saipan LPA-2	HF 07	
AH-1W	Pin-up	Bond Girl	HMLA-771, 24th MEU	YM 41	169___
AH-1W	A pin-up in a red dress	None	HMLA-775	WR 43	34
AH-1W	Pin-up and a pink heart	None	HMM-162?		
AH-1W	Beckinsale character fr. Movie Underworld w/ US flag in background	None	HMM-261	EM 30	165317
AH-1W	A large cobra snake painted down the side	None			

Type	Artwork	Name	Squadron	Modex	BuNo.
AH-1W	Art work on nose hood	None	HMM-261	EM 30	160744
AH-1W	A pin-up on a rocket pod	None	VMM-263, 22nd MEU	EG 30	161019
AH-1W	Art work on nose hood	None	VMM-263, 22nd MEU	EG 32	163950
AH-1W	Artwork on hood w/ white ball	None	VMM-263, 22nd MEU	EG 35	162546
AH-1W	A ghost	None		No. 30	
AH-1W	A rhino's head	Rhinos Revenge??		No. 27	163924
AH-1W	Black knight on horse	None			
AH-1W	The Grim Reaper	Fear the Reaper			
AH-1Z	Pin-up in front of burning city	None	HMLA-167, 22nd MEU (SOC)?		
AH-1Z	Pin-up w/gun and bottle	On Call 24/7	HMLA-167, 22nd MEU (SOC)?		
AH-1Z	Two pin-ups in bikinis	None	HMLA-167, 22nd MEU (SOC)?	TV 32?	
AH-1Z	Pin-up w/sword and shield	GT 66, Cap. Martini- We Will Never Forget	HMLA-369		
AH-1Z	Alien predator creature	None	HMM-162	No. 22	160817?
AH-1Z	Alien predator creature	None	HMM-162, 26th MEU	YS 30	160817?
AH-1Z	A nude girl on a missile	None	HMM-162, 26th MEU, USS Kersarge LHD-3	YS 31	
AJ-2	Gas pump on cloud	We Give Green Stamps	VC-6	NF 3	
AJ-2	Shell emblem	Use our Gas or go to Shell	VC-6	NF 13	134069
AJ-2P	Mean hairy hog	None	VJ-61	PB 6	129185
AJ-2P	Pin-up	None	VJ-61	PB 7	130423
AP-2H	Mission marks	Deuces Wild	VAH-21	SL 2	148353
AP-2H	Mission marks	Iron Butterfly	VAH-21	SL 4	145902
AP-2H	Mission marks	Napalm Nellie	VAH-21	SL 3	148337
AQM-3Q	Mission marks	Flying Submarine		Q15	
AS332 Puma	Pin-up	?	NAVSEALIFT COMM, USS Richard E. Byrd	P-1	N9OR
AS332 Puma	Pin-up	Shore Leave	NAVSEALIFT COMM, USS Richard E. Byrd	P-4	N330KW
AV-8B	Antelope head on the tail and a Shark Mouth	None	HMM-163 USS Peleliu, Operation Restore Hope	YP 51	163880
AV-8B	Elephant head on tail and a Shark Mouth	None	HMM-163 USS Peleliu, Operation Restore Hope	YP 52	163879
AV-8B	Panther head on the tail and a Shark Mouth	None	HMM-163 USS Peleliu, Operation Restore Hope	YP 53	163866
AV-8B	Rhino head on tail and a Shark Mouth	None	HMM-163 USS Peleliu, Operation Restore Hope	YP 50	163870
AV-8B	Zebra head on tail and a Shark Mouth	None	HMM-163 USS Peleliu, Operation Restore Hope	YP 55	163178
AV-8B	A horse w/sunglasses on nose	Mr. Ed	HMM-264 (Reinforced)	EH 04	
AV-8B	MOH ribbon	Capt. Elrod Hammering Hank	VMA-211, USS Tarawa	CF 50	
AV-8B	Bulldog w/wings on tail and mission marks	The Great American Bulldogs	VMA-223	WP 01	165354
AV-8B	Fifty-four missions/shark mouth	Venom	VMA-231	CG 01	163662
AV-8B	Pin-up with wings	Angel	VMA-331	VL	162722
BD-2	Daisy Mae	Daisy Mae	VJ-2 NAS Pax. River	2-X-14	7039
BD-2	Cartoon caricature	Lil' Abner	VMJ- Paris Island		7040
C-117	Fleagle on roller skates	Gooney Bird	NAV Arctic ResLab	N722NR	17156
C-117D	Snoopy	Peanut Airlines	Cam Rhan Bay	No. 087	390877
C-117D	Elephant	Bouncing Bertha	NAVSP Danang,		
C-121J	A blue hound dog	Old Blue from Point Mugu	PMTC		131643
C-121J	Cartoon dog on nose gear door	None	VQ-1	No. 659	131659
C-121J	Phoenix bird	Phoenix 6	VXE-6	JD 6	131624
C-121J	Winged horse	Pegasus 7	VXE-6	JD 7	131644
C-121J	Eagle/lighting/globe	None	VXN-8		131622
C-121J	Eagle/lighting/globe	None	VXN-8		131641
C-130T	Old Man Winter	None	VR-53	AX 998	164998

Type	Artwork	Name	Squadron	Modex	BuNo.
C-1A	Snoopy	None	CVA-31 *Bon Homme Richard*	022	146022
C-1A	Bird on rudder	*Sick Eagle*	CVA-34 USS *Oriskany*		136760
C-1A	A banner	*Midway Magic*	CVA-41 *Midway*	600	146038
C-1A	A pair of dice	*Easy Way Airlines*	CVA-43 USS *Midway*	No. OOO	146035
C-1A	Little canine on nose	*Charles the 1st?*	CVA-43 USS *Midway*	No. 039	146039
C-1A	A tailhook in the clouds	*The Happy Hooker*	CVA-59 USS *Forrestal*	No. 59	136761
C-1A	Liberty bell	*Miss Belle*	CVA-62 USS *Independence*, VRC-40	No. 62	146044
C-1A	A falcon w/ a Chinese man on his head	None	CVA-63 *Kitty Hawk*	OOO	
C-1A	A smiley face	None	CVA-63 USS *Kitty Hawk*		146053
C-1A	Three nuts	*Triple Nuts*	CVA-64 USS *Constellation*		146021
C-1A	Flags	*Nuclear Task Force One*	CVN-65 USS *Enterprise*		
C-1A	Dog on engine cowling	None	CVS-31 USS *Bon Homme Richard*	No. 782	136782
C-1A	Blue Casper cartoon ghost	*Blue Ghost*	CVT-16 USS *Lexington*	No. 754	136754
C-2A	Snoopy Cartoon	None	VR-24	JM 123	
C-2A	Flames on the nose	None	VRC-30	RW 23	
C-2A	Flames on the nose	None	VRC-30, Det-3	NH 23	
C-2A	Raising Sun and 50th Anniversary Scheme	*Logistics Excellents Since 1960*	VRC-40	JK 50	162144
C-47	Penguin emblem	*Project Highjump*	Operation High Jump		
C-47A	Betty Boop cartoon	?	VR-4, 5, 11		39091
C-47J	A big bird on aft fuselage	None		251	17251
C-54D	An alligator on snow shoes	*Eloise*	NAS Argentia	No. 489	56489
C-54P	The Playboy 'Granny'	*Me Retire Never*	NARTU, NAF Washington, DC	6A 865	50865
C-54Q	The Playboy 'Granny'	*Me Retire Never*	NARTU, NAF Washington, DC	6A 490	56490
C-54Q	Two penguin	None	VXE-6	JD 5	56528
CH-34C	Snoopy on dog house aft fuselage	*H&MS-17 Non Lifers*	H&MS-17		
CH-37C	A hand	None	HMH-461	CJ 113	
CH-37C	A pig with wings	*The Flying Pig II*	HMH-461	CJ 10?	
CH-37C	A ruptured duck	None	HMH-461		
CH-37C	A Tasmanian Devil	None	HMH-461	CJ 10?	
CH-37C	Cat in a champagne glass	*The Champagne Flight-Potts a Puck*	HMH-461	CJ 10?	
CH-46	Playboy logo	None	HC-6	HW 21	153341
CH-46	Pin-up warrior on saber tooth tiger	*Heavy Metal Mistress*	USMC LHA-2 *Saipan*		
CH-46A	Dominos 'Avoid the Noid' cartoon character	None	HC-5 Det-1 USS *Guam 1991*	RB 04	150271
CH-46A	A cowboy in sombrero	None	HC-5, Det. 2	RB 02	150938
CH-46A	A blue pin-up silhouette	*Princess*	HMM-262		
CH-46A	A happy dog	??	HMM-262	ET 1	
CH-46A	A pregnant Lucy fr. Charlie Brown comics	*Damn You Jim J*	HMM-262		
CH-46A	A shamrock	None	HMM-262	ET 21	
CH-46A	Bugs Bunny	None	HMM-265		
CH-46A	Rabbit	*The Rape'n Rabbit*	HMM-265	EP 12	
CH-46A	Two cherries	*Double Nuts*	HMM-265		
CH-46A	Thirty-five mission marks	*The Putney Swamp*	HMM-362	YK 21	
CH-46A	Thirty-eight mission marks	*The Greatful Dead*	HMM-362	YK 21	
CH-46D	Tony the Tiger	None	HC-11	VR 70	
CH-46D	A male character lifting a bar bell	*Bad Iron*	HC-11 Det. 7	VR 74	152553
CH-46D	A rainbow on the tail	*R_____C*	HC-3 Det. 103	SA 31	154826
CH-46D	A vulture	None	HC-6	HW 14	152567
CH-46D	Cobra snake	*Sultans of Swing*	HC-6		154028

Type	Artwork	Name	Squadron	Modex	BuNo.
CH-46D	Greek theater masks	The Sorrow & The Rage 9-11-2001	HC-6	HW 62	153699
CH-46D	Helo logo	Air Savannah	HC-6	HW 04	152555
CH-46D	Skull and crossed bones	Old Milwaukee	HC-6	HW 14	154032
CH-46D	A Viking in helmet	None	HC-6	HW 17	154824
CH-46D	Tiger head and flames on sponson	Detroit Flying Tigers	HC-6 Det. 3	No. 17	
CH-46D	A helo, palm tree, and a sea monster	None	HC-6?		
CH-46D	Planters Peanut on forward rotor housing	Salty	HC-8, USS Kearsarge	BR 16	151950
CH-46D	Cobra snake	Patrick & Murray	HMM-161		
CH-46D	Small red cartoon man	Dead Bone	HMM-165		
CH-46D	An alien head on side	None	HMM-166	YX 606	154825
CH-46D	A skull in a cowboy hat	??	HMM-261	EM 06	
CH-46D	NY Yankees baseball emblem	NY Yankees	HMM-261	EM 07	
CH-46D	A pigmy warrior	Jungle Bunny?	HMM-364	YK 21	
CH-46E	A African warrior w/ shield and twenty-nine kills	None	HC-11 Det. 5/ USS Camden	VR 63	150957
CH-46E	American flag (large)	None	HC-11 Det. 5/ USS Rainer	VR 64	152493
CH-46E	American flag (small)	None	HC-11 Det. 5/ USS Rainer	VR-65	153319
CH-46E	Hot rod flames	HC-11 Air Hog DET 1	HC-3 Det 104	SA 40	154000
CH-46E	Big shooting star on tail	Mars Star	HC-3 Det-106	SA 12	154832
CH-46E	Hotel California artwork on bottom and volcanoes on fuselage	Hotel California & Golden Arches Airlines	HC-8 Team 6	BR 56	153339
CH-46E	Crossed tools and skeleton art on fwd dog house	ST_____	HMM-?	No. 04	156424
CH-46E	Skull and crossed rotors	None	HMM-161	YR 05	156465
CH-46E	An animal w/ MG	?	HMM-161	YR 55	
CH-46E	A shield and mission marks	HMM-161 The First-55 Years of Winning the Nations Battles	HMM-161	YR 06	
CH-46E	Pin-up on Maltese Cross	None	HMM-162	YS 11	153958
CH-46E	A bomb eight ball character	??	HMM-162	YS 12	
CH-46E	A cartoon dog and a purple pig	Hoorayy	HMM-162	YS 01	
CH-46E	A frog	?	HMM-162	YS 04	
CH-46E	A jester's skull	The Reckoning	HMM-162	YS 13	156467
CH-46E	A Mexican bandito	Peace _____ ?	HMM-162	YS 07	153395
CH-46E	A ninja baby w/ a gun and RPG	None	HMM-162	YS 00	157713
CH-46E	A phoenix bird symbol	The Peace Maker	HMM-162	YS 05	
CH-46E	A question mark	None	HMM-162	YS 03	
CH-46E	A smiley face	None	HMM-162	YS 00	157713
CH-46E	A wolf's head	Boeing Racing	HMM-162	YS 10	
CH-46E	Helo drag racer	?	HMM-162	YS 01	154034
CH-46E	Kevlar armor door art	None	HMM-162	YS 06	
CH-46E	Pin-up on motorcycle	None	HMM-162	YS 05	
CH-46E	Skull on red/white/blue banner	Aged to Perfection	HMM-162	YS 1	154034
CH-46E	Portrait of a lady	None	HMM-162	YS 14	153402
CH-46E	Bikini clad pin-up	None	HMM-162	YS 14	153983
CH-46E	Green frown face	Gal Friday??	HMM-162 IFOR	YS 00?	153402
CH-46E	Pin-up in brown shorts	C------THE------?	HMM-162, 26th MEU		157655
CH-46E	Pin-up on flag	BOO??	HMM-162?		
CH-46E	A dancing cow w/ skirt and sunglasses	Super Phrog Airlift??	HMM-163	YP 01	
CH-46E	A frog	Short Bus	HMM-163		
CH-46E	A loop	I am Jack's Battlephrog	HMM-163	YP 04	
CH-46E	A smiley face		HMM-163	YP 12	
CH-46E	Bevis and Butthead	Now Touring Uh, Hu, Gh, Cool	HMM-163		156429

Type	Artwork	Name	Squadron	Modex	BuNo.
CH-46E	Darth Vader	Imperial Battle Force	HMM-163	YP 03	153956
CH-46E	Foghorn Leghorn rooster	None	HMM-163	YP 13	156459
CH-46E	Large breasted red-head pin-up	Lot of Jean?	HMM-163	YP 07	153377
CH-46E	Marilyn pin-up	Bombs Away	HMM-163	YP 00	156434
CH-46E	Martini glasses and party scene	Pukin' Tr____ - All In	HMM-163	YP 13	
CH-46E	Two angry boys peeing on Terrorist	Terrorist	HMM-163		
CH-46E	University of Wisconsin badger	Wisconsin	HMM-163		
CH-46E	A character of girl w/ MG	None	HMM-163	YP 05	156427
CH-46E	A pin-up on a Red Bed on 4 of Clubs	None	HMM-163	YP 04	157662
CH-46E	Skulls on a Red armor plate	None	HMM-163	YP ?	
CH-46E	A fleur-de-lis	Big Easy	HMM-163, 13th MEU	YP 15	157702
CH-46E	A dark cloud over a green field	None	HMM-165	YW 02	155311
CH-46E	A frog, ace of spades, and pin-ups	Lady Ace Double Nuts	HMM-165	YW 00	154023
CH-46E	A landscape	None	HMM-165	YW 00	154023
CH-46E	A native figure sitting	?	HMM-165	YW 1-2	157704
CH-46E	A Tasmanian Devil	None	HMM-165	YW 12	156457
CH-46E	Boba Fett from Star Wars	Bounty Hunter	HMM-165	YW 12	
CH-46E	Cartoon characters in the desert	None	HMM-165		
CH-46E	Fantasy knight/armor plate	Wild?	HMM-165		
CH-46E	Kevlar armor door art	None	HMM-165	YW 06	154851
CH-46E	Pin-up	Lady Ace 04	HMM-165	YW 04	153346
CH-46E	Pin-up on a red Spad	Aircraft 10	HMM-165	YW 10	
CH-46E	Pin-up on frog w/ top hat	None	HMM-165	YW 10	154853
CH-46E	Pin-up w/ ace of spades	Lady Ace 03	HMM-165	YW 03	154027
CH-46E	Pin-up w/ ace of spades	Lady Ace 07	HMM-165	YW 07	153969
CH-46E	Skull on ace of spades	None	HMM-165		
CH-46E	Pin-up on a blue Spad	Lady Luck	HMM-165, Al Asad		
CH-46E	Pin-up on the Ace of Spades	Lady Ace 12	HMM-165, Al Asad	YW 12	156457
CH-46E	Pin-up w/ Grim Reaper	Lady Ac 14	HMM-165, Al Asad	YW 14	
CH-46E	Pin-up wrapped in a US flag (black and white)	None	HMM-165, Al Asad		
CH-46E	Two pin-ups and a Transformer	Lady Ace 01	HMM-165, Al Asad	YW 01	155309
CH-46E	Two pin-ups w/ 50 Cals. On a black Spad	The Deuce- Because Two are better than One	HMM-165, Al Asad	YW 02	157703
CH-46E	Pin-up in a thong	Thunderclap	HMM-165, USS Boxer	YW 11	
CH-46E	Pin-up w/ a Marine hat	Miss Behavin'	HMM-165, USS Boxer	YW 05	157661
CH-46E	Porky Pig w/ 50 Cal. MG	That's All Folks- The War Pig	HMM-165, USS Boxer	YW?	
CH-46E	A Frog w/ M-16 and Afghanis	Gone Fishin' in the Gulf	HMM-166	YX 09	152574
CH-46E	A moose w/ MG on tail	None	HMM-166	YX 00	155311
CH-46E	Pin-up in flames	None	HMM-166	YX 05	157701
CH-46E	Cow girl pin-up	?	HMM-166, USS Wasp	YS 8	156476
CH-46E	A cartoon helo w/ sniper rifles	Reaking Destruction Since 1964	HMM-261	EM 02	156469
CH-46E	A dancing skeleton	None	HMM-261		
CH-46E	A devil	Death Angel II	HMM-261	EM 05	155307
CH-46E	A flying pink pig	None	HMM-261	EM 06	
CH-46E	A green alien swordsman	None	HMM-261	EM 03	154009
CH-46E	A green goblin	None	HMM-261	EM 12	157721
CH-46E	A hillbilly character	Hillbilly	HMM-261	EM 06	153402
CH-46E	A kid w/ a banana	Plane Ramrod–Cherry Carry	HMM-261	EM 05	157665
CH-46E	A red hot rod	Snoot and Hollywood's Little Deuce Coupe	HMM-261		

Type	Artwork	Name	Squadron	Modex	BuNo.
CH-46E	A steers skull and crossed 50 Cal MG	None	HMM-261	EM 00	153330
CH-46E	A steers skull w/ wings	None	HMM-261	EM 12	157721
CH-46E	A witch	??	HMM-261	EM 11	156464
CH-46E	An animal w/ a ball	None	HMM-261	EM 06	157726
CH-46E	An eagle w/ a US Flag	None	HMM-261	EM 02	156469
CH-46E	Dark bird	None	HMM-261	EM 04	153849
CH-46E	Four leaf clover	None	HMM-261	EM 04	157716
CH-46E	Green frog	None	HMM-261	EM 01	
CH-46E	Green frog	??	HMM-261	EM 01	
CH-46E	Muscular Uncle Sam w/ bombs and bullets	*Cry Havoc and Let Slip the Phrogs or War*	HMM-261	EM 14	153368
CH-46E	NC State emblem	*Slippery Sally II-HMM-261 Returns to Iraq*	HMM-261	EM 07	156470
CH-46E	NC State emblem	*?*	HMM-261	EM 07	154037
CH-46E	Pin-up w/ 50 Cal. on shoulder on a red armor plate	*Chunky Chelsea*	HMM-261	EM 10	154037
CH-46E	Pin-up w/ knife	None	HMM-261	EM	
CH-46E	Red grim reaper	None	HMM-261	EM 13	157690
CH-46E	SC State emblem the palmetto palm	None	HMM-261	EM 11	155308
CH-46E	Snoopy and Woodstock w/ wrench	*Too Cool*	HMM-261	EM 11	154851
CH-46E	The Grim Reaper	*Heather Jean*	HMM-261	EM 03	157660
CH-46E	Yosemite Sam	None	HMM-261	EM 14	154816
CH-46E	Eagle head wrapped in POW flag	*POW/MIA*	HMM-261?		
CH-46E	A flaming skull from Hell Raiser	*Climb Aboard*	HMM-261, 22nd MEU (SOC)	EM 11	
CH-46E	A flaming robot w/ demons door armor	None	HMM-261, 22nd MEU (SOC)?		
CH-46E	A bandit in a flying saucer	None	HMM-262	ET 10	
CH-46E	A skull and crossed cutlasses	None	HMM-262	ET 15	154844
CH-46E	A Tiger head	None	HMM-262	ET 07	157722
CH-46E	A winged creature	None	HMM-262	ET 1	156462
CH-46E	Little red hen	*Chicken Hawk*	HMM-262	ET 12	156437
CH-46E	NASCAR Logos and racing emblems	None	HMM-262	ET 08	157669
CH-46E	Pin-up in sailor suit	*We Got Your Back*	HMM-262	ET 16	
CH-46E	Tiger eye and stripes on side and front	*Here Comes The Pain*	HMM-262	ET 00	153365
CH-46E	Yosemite Sam	None	HMM-262	ET 7	156419
CH-46E	Pin-up w/ a bomb	*??*	HMM-262 USS Harpers Ferry LSD 49	ET 08	
CH-46E	A black frog	*Eazy Wind*	HMM-263	EG 02	153872
CH-46E	A buck hunter symbol	*?*	HMM-263	EG 05	156473
CH-46E	A Crow over a dead forest	*Eazy Wind*	HMM-263	EG 12	157667
CH-46E	A dog's head	None	HMM-263	EG 4	153981
CH-46E	A jester	*Jester??*	HMM-263	EG 12	157667
CH-46E	A pin-up cow girl	*Caroline*	HMM-263	EG 04	
CH-46E	An eagle w/ three white stars	*Freedom*	HMM-263	EG 12	157667
CH-46E	Atomic bomb mushroom	None	HMM-263	EG 2?	
CH-46E	Chopper emblem	*Live to Fly the Chopper*	HMM-263	EG 14	153999
CH-46E	Cow girl pin-up and purple heart	None	HMM-263	EG 13	156418
CH-46E	Dark Batman	None	HMM-263		
CH-46E	Dragon slayer	*Slayer*	HMM-263	EG?	
CH-46E	Eagle w/flag and Twin Towers	*Dottie*	HMM-263	EG 05	156473
CH-46E	Helo on a cloud	*American Dream*	HMM-263	EG 5	157651
CH-46E	Pin-up		HMM-263	EG?	
CH-46E	Pin-up	None	HMM-263	EG 14	153999

Type	Artwork	Name	Squadron	Modex	BuNo.
CH-46E	Swan wings	Swan Song	HMM-263	EG 2	153372
CH-46E	Winged face/ speed bird and Port Authority Police badge	Eazy Wind	HMM-263	EG 02	153872
CH-46E	Pin-up on MG w/POW flag	Smilin' Through II	HMM-263, 24th MEU	EG?	
CH-46E	Warrior girl and demon	Hostile Intent	HMM-263, USS Wasp	EG 15	156476
CH-46E	A frog and cross	None	HMM-264	EH 07	157673
CH-46E	A shield, banners, and WOT ribbons	??	HMM-264	EH 13	154038
CH-46E	An angel playing a flute	None	HMM-264	EH 05	154851
CH-46E	Bullet head	Bullet Hero / The Bullet	HMM-264		157656
CH-46E	Dark figure in street between buildings	None	HMM-264	EH 11	157690
CH-46E	Dark figure w/ 911 Pentagon emblem	None	HMM-264	EH 11	157678
CH-46E	Death Angel	None	HMM-264	EH 11	157678
CH-46E	Freddy Kruger art	Saddams Nightmare	HMM-264	EH 07	156477
CH-46E	Lady Liberty w/ flag and 911 Pentagon emblem	None	HMM-264	EH 02	157687
CH-46E	NY City sky line	None	HMM-264	EH 01	157690
CH-46E	US Flag and Liberty Torch	None	HMM-264	EH 06	156456
CH-46E	a girl with a pair of dice and a 9/11 symbol	Lady Luck Old No. 7	HMM-264 398th AEG, Liberia USMC	EH 07	
CH-46E	an angry leprechaun and a 9/11 symbol	Feeling Lucky	HMM-264 398th AEG, Liberia USMC	EH 05	157656
CH-46E	a globe and a skeleton in a shroud	Last Ride Ead	HMM-264, 26th MEU, USS Iwo Jima LHD-7	EH 10	
CH-46E	Three Bob the Builder figures	Joe ___	HMM-265	EH 07	
CH-46E	A cow diagram	None	HMM-265	EP 04	154034
CH-46E	A warrior	?	HMM-265	EP 15	155313
CH-46E	Angry dogs head w/ fangs	None	HMM-265	EP 01	
CH-46E	Angry dogs head w/ fangs	None	HMM-265	EP 05	156446
CH-46E	Black bottle of booze	None	HMM-265	EP 07	157714
CH-46E	Caterpillar Logo	Cat-Al's Destruction	HMM-265	EP 06	
CH-46E	Darth Vader	?	HMM-265	EP 04	
CH-46E	Green frog w/ black top hat	None	HMM-265	EP 05	156458
CH-46E	Pin-up blonde w/ white mini skirt	None	HMM-265	EP _4	
CH-46E	Skull w/ crossed bones	None	HMM-265	EP 00	153365
CH-46E	Sponge Bob Square Pants	None	HMM-265	EP 07	
CH-46E	Two black knights	None	HMM-265	EP 04	
CH-46E	A cartoon Phrog about to go over a cliff	None	HMM-265	EP 05	156442
CH-46E	A cartoon turtle	Pagong	HMM-265	EP 00	
CH-46E	A left hand	South Paw Connection	HMM-265		
CH-46E	A skull and crossed daggers	Battle Hog	HMM-265	EP 03	154020
CH-46E	A Spartan warrior	265 Prepare for Glory	HMM-265	EP 00	
CH-46E	A winged creature	The Guardian	HMM-265		
CH-46E	A winged skull	Dirty Dozen	HMM-265	EP 01?	
CH-46E	Crossed Texas and American flags over Texas	Texas Touch	HMM-265		
CH-46E	General Bart Simpson	War is Hell	HMM-265		
CH-46E	Pin-up	Saguaro Sweet Heart	HMM-265		
CH-46E	The Grim Reaper	Vinceve Ast Mort	HMM-265	EP 10	
CH-46E	University of Kentucky mascot wildcat	Kentucky Wildcat	HMM-265		
CH-46E	A Dragon and a boy	None	HMM-265 (REIN) LPD-2 USS Essex	EP 06	153366
CH-46E	A Spartan warrior	265 Prepare for Glory	HMM-265, LHD-2, USS Essex	EP 10	
CH-46E	The Grim Reaper	Vinceve Ast Mort	HMM-265, LHD-2, USS Essex	EP 00	156442
CH-46E	A pin-up w/ gun belt< leather flight helmet and a grenade	Easy Come, Easy Go	HMM-266	ES 07	154020
CH-46E	A school girl pin-up	Sweet Sixteen Untouched and ready for Action	HMM-266		

Type	Artwork	Name	Squadron	Modex	BuNo.
CH-46E	Bart Simpson	Eat My Shorts Al Qaeda	HMM-266	ES 00	153318
CH-46E	Pin-up, frog, and a pair of dice	Doing it Phroggy Style	HMM-266	ES 15	154009
CH-46E	A crewman riding astride a Sea Knight	Riding Dirty	HMM-268	YQ 01?	
CH-46E	A wing skull w/ knife	Bad to the Bone	HMM-268	YQ	
CH-46E	Artwork	??	HMM-268	YQ 00	152574
CH-46E	James Dean	Chill out	HMM-268	YQ 12	156446
CH-46E	Joker's accomplice and girlfriend Harley Quinn from Batman comics	Harley Quinn	HMM-268	YQ 12	154805
CH-46E	Pin-up on flag	Bad Kitty	HMM-268		
CH-46E	Snoopy on a red dog house	Red Baron	HMM-268	YQ 02	153350
CH-46E	Pin-up w/ 50 Cal. MG with US flag	None	HMM-364	PF 12	
CH-46E	A cartoon character	?	HMM-364	YM 02	
CH-46E	A cartoon character (mouse?)	None	HMM-365	YM 06	155306
CH-46E	A Gremlin	None	HMM-365	YM 04	
CH-46E	A redhead pin-up	Shootin' Blanks	HMM-365		
CH-46E	An Eagle sharpening his claws w/ a file and a American Flag	Come and Get It	HMM-365	YM 02	
CH-46E	Camel cigarettes camel character	Keepin' 'em Sharp	HMM-365		
CH-46E	Pin-up in blue dress	Smooth Character	HMM-365	YM 15	
CH-46E	Skull w/ crossed MGs	Big Dolly Hauler	HMM-365	YM?	
CH-46E	Dominos 'Avoid the Noid' cartoon character w/bomb and Rebel flag	Forsaken	HMM-365		
CH-46E	Pin-up	None	HMM-365 USS Guam	YM 15	
CH-46E	Warrior princess on a horse	Big Willy Airlines	HMM-365, 26th MEU (SO) Afghanistan		
CH-46E	A frog holding a 50 Cal. MG by nose and a frog w/ top hat and cane on tail	Get Some	HMM-365, Kandahar, Afg.		
CH-46E	Kevlar armor door art	??	HMM-764	ML 426	154815
CH-46E	A dark barbarian standing on skulls	The Weak Shall Inherit... Nothing	HMM-764	ML 430	155308
CH-46E	A frog	Froggingroovin'	HMM-774	MQ 435	154801
CH-46E	A frog holding a 50 Cal. MG	None	HMM-774	MQ 408	158462
CH-46E	A poem or verse	Their Horses are Swifter... to Devour	HMM-774	MQ 427	156461
CH-46E	An angel carrying another angel	None	HMM-774	MQ 435	154801
CH-46E	Black and white artwork	None	HMM-774	MQ 432	154829
CH-46E	Eagle and flag	War Eagles	HMM-774	MQ 430	155310
CH-46E	Hooters Owl eating a hamburger	Hooters- Melbourne FLA. More than a Mouthful!	HMM-774	MQ 407	154000
CH-46E	Kevlar armor door art	?	HMM-774	MQ 423	156443
CH-46E	Kevlar armor door art	?	HMM-774	MQ 431	154014
CH-46E	Speedy Gonzales w/ 50 Cal. MG	None	HMM-774	MQ 434	156433
CH-46E	A circle w/ US Flag and two eagles flying	None	USMC	No. 40	
CH-46E	A frog in a cowboy hat	None	USMC	No. 11	
CH-46E	Demon pin-up w/ bat wings	Demon Child	USMC	No. 26	
CH-46E	Pin-up in Stars and Stripes bikini w/ US flag and POW flag	Viva's Valentine	USMC		
CH-46E	Pin-up in red dress and pink hearts	The Mongoose / Gale	USMC Iraq, 2007		
CH-46F	Mongoose	None	HMM-263	EG 2	156472
CH-46F	A snarling dog	None	HMM-264	EH 13	
CH-46H	Eagle w/ flag draped wings	The Phoenix	HC-11	VR 51	
CH-46H	A phoenix bird symbol	Black Jack you Lose	HMM-261	EM 05	153369
CH-53	Skull clown	None	USMC		
CH-53A	Dog and fire plug and clown face	?	USMC	No. 34	
CH-53D	Art work on forward RH ebay	None	HMH-363	YZ 75	
CH-53D	Cartoon charter w/ 50 Cal. MG	Big Johnson 50 Cal. Might Short E... T...	HMH-363	YZ	

Type	Artwork	Name	Squadron	Modex	BuNo.
CH-53D	Crouching beast	Junya	HMH-363	YZ 15	
CH-53D	Block head artwork on nose	Charlie's Block Heads	HMH-462	YH 12	
CH-53D	Fire breathing skull with dagger through it	463rd Bombers	HMH-463	YH	
CH-53D	Maltese Cross	K? Shitters??	HMH-463	YH 12	157168
CH-53D	Pin-up on a Green bomb	Heavy Lifters	HMH-463	YH 11.5	156656
CH-53D	Playboy Granny cartoon	None	HMH-463	YH 6	157751
CH-53D	Snoopy and Woodstock	None	HMH-463		
CH-53D	The Blob monster	The Green Slime	HMH-463		
CH-53D	Ayatollah head in the cross hairs	None	HMH-463, Iranian Hostage Crisis		
CH-53D	Hulk Comic	The Incredible Hulk	NAS Pax River		
CH-53D	Aircrew character	Cornfed	USMC		
CH-53E	Black cat on fuel tank	Black Cats	HC-1	No. 743	
CH-53E	A dinosaur with a star and MAG emblem	Doing what we do Best- Carry the Gas	HHM-461	CJ 09	
CH-53E	Art work on door	S____ Dragon	HMH-361		
CH-53E	Art work on door	None	HMH-361	YN 54	
CH-53E	Blonde pin-up w/ 50 Cal MG	None	HMH-361	YN _8	
CH-53E	Pin-up	Choppers Inc.	HMH-361	YN 69	
CH-53E	Pin-up in a tiger suit	Amber	HMH-361	YN 21	
CH-53E	Pin-up in blue bathing suit	None	HMH-361	YN 24	
CH-53E	Pin-up in blue bathing suit	None	HMH-361		
CH-53E	The Grim Reaper	None	HMH-361	YN 06	157742
CH-53E	Marine in Dress Blues charging into battle	Vulgar Display of Power	HMH-363	YZ 12	
CH-53E	A pin-up in red polka dots	High Maintenance	HMH-461	CJ 20	163062
CH-53E	A pin-up in red polka dots	High Maintenance	HMH-461	CJ 13	162518
CH-53E	A spotted dog and fire hydrant	Spot Baby	HMH-461	CJ 01	
CH-53E	Calvin and Hobbs cartoon	None	HMH-461		
CH-53E	Pin-up	In the Mood	HMH-461		
CH-53E	Pin-up straddles a 50 Cal./ mount	V??	HMH-461	CJ 13	
CH-53E	Punk smoking a cigarette	Sonic Youth Goo	HMH-461		
CH-53E	The Blues Brothers	?	HMH-461		
CH-53E	9-11 New York sky line w/ grenade or bomb art	We Never Forget	HMH-461, 22nd MEU, HMM-261 (REIN)	CJ 06	161995
CH-53E	9-11 New York skyline w/ pin-up	Payback can be a Real Pain in the...	HMH-461, 22nd MEU, HMM-261 (REIN)	EM 22	162521
CH-53E	A pig's face	Thunder Pig	HMH-462	EM 21	
CH-53E	A charging Navy Ram	None	HMH-464	EN 08	161533
CH-53E	An Ace of Spades with a skull	Let's Roll	HMH-464	EN 21	163063
CH-53E	Art work on door	None	HMH-464	EN 26	
CH-53E	Bulldog	The Citadel	HMH-464	EN 00	161180
CH-53E	Calvin and Hobbs cartoon	Natural Born Killers	HMH-464	EN 16	
CH-53E	Darth Vader	?	HMH-464	EN 03	
CH-53E	Eagle and flag over NYC skyline	None	HMH-464	EN 00	
CH-53E	Jasmine pin-up w/ cross 50 Cal.	Don't Mess with Jasmine	HMH-464	EN 11	162001
CH-53E	Marine in battle dress	?	HMH-464	EN 15	
CH-53E	Marine in Dress Blues charging into battle	Vulgar Display of Power	HMH-464	EN 06	
CH-53E	Skeleton with machine gun	None	HMH-464	EN 08	161533
CH-53E	Skull and crossed bones	None	HMH-464	EN 10	
CH-53E	Spy vs. Spy characters	Feeling Lucky	HMH-464	EN 05	
CH-53E	The Navy ram mascot	None	HMH-464	EN 06	161533
CH-53E	Transformer logo door	None	HMH-464	CJ 22	

Type	Artwork	Name	Squadron	Modex	BuNo.
CH-53E	Well-endowed redhead pin-up	Lucy Quipment	HMH-464	EN 01	
CH-53E	'St L' emblem on door Warhorse on drop tank	West Coast Choppers	HMH-465	YJ 67	
CH-53E	Art work on door	None	HMH-465		
CH-53E	Big red lips	It's my O'Keary____	HMH-466	YK 51	
CH-53E	Five faces in the camouflage paint	None	HMH-466	YK 65	
CH-53E	Large pin-up in camouflage	None	HMH-466	YK 70	
CH-53E	Large pin-up, Foghorn Leghorn, and Texas painted in camouflage	The Kickin' Chicken	HMH-466, HMH-WEST	No. 53	164361
CH-53E	Pin-up on forward e-bay	?	HMH-772		
CH-53E	An elf with a gun and wings	None	HMH-772	EG 24	
CH-53E	Mean pig with wings	Sky Pig	HMM-162 (REIN) LHA-4 USS Nassau	YS 26	
CH-53E	Whiskey bottle label	The Marines #53 Proof	HMH-165	YW 22	
CH-53E	Red head waitress w/ beer	None	HMM-165, 31st MEU	YW 63	
CH-53E	A dancing skeleton	Somewhere between Haven and Hell	HMM-261	EM 22	162491
CH-53E	Marine in Dress Blues charging into battle	Vulgar Display of Power	HMM-262	No. 24	
CH-53E	Snow White and Dopey	None	HMM-262	No. 43	
CH-53E	The Statue of Liberty, Twin Towers, w/ US Flag in bkgd. Door art	Iron Butterfly	HMM-263 24th MEU	No. 40	163060
CH-53E	Univ. Tenn. Emblem	Brock Landers	HMM-263 24th MEU		161989
CH-53E	Yellow jacket	None	HMM-264	EH 25	
CH-53E	Art work on door	Lady Lucy	HMM-264	EH 20	
CH-53E	Betty Boop cartoon	None	HMM-264	EH 23	
CH-53E	Pin-up w/ helmet, ammo belt, vest and rifle	Deuce Deuce	HMM-264	EH 22	
CH-53E	UPS and Texaco Logos	Haulin' Ass	HMM-264 398th AEG, Liberia USMC	EH 23	
CH-53E	Pin-up sitting on Aircrew Wings	Wide Open?	HMM-264, 26th MEU(SOC)	EP 22	161388
CH-53E	Outhouse and a dog?	None	HMM-265	YM 22	
CH-53E	The Joker	Did someone say Djibootie & Wish you were here 100 Proof	HMH-365, MCAS Jacksonville, NC		
CH-53E	Pirate girl standing on a chest	Bad Karma	SFOR-Opertn. PHOENIX GAUNTLET, Congo	No. 41	
CH-53E	Bettie Page pin-up	None	USMC	No. 24	
CH-53E	A dragon or horse	UG_____	USMC	No. 20	
CH-53E	Art work on door	No Brew	USMC	No. 04	
CH-53E	Cartoon redneck boy	None	USMC	No. 22	
CH-53E	Red Japanese symbol	None	USMC	No. 108	
CH-53E	Superman emblem on door	None	USMC	No. 24	
CH-53E	Superman emblem on fwd dog house	None	USMC	No. 07	
CH-53E	Uncle Sam in gas mask	None		No. 23	
CH-53E	A pin-up in a cape	?		No. 25	
CH-53E	A pin-up sitting on a mail bag	Mail Bag			
CH-53E	An angry leprechaun	?			
CH-53E	Beckinsale character fr. Movie *Underworld* w/ US flag in background	None			
CH-53E	Cartoon character	What the Deuce			
CH-53E	Pin-up w/ M-60 MG	Weapons Free			
CH-53E	The Baby from Roger Rabbit	Man-Child			
CH-60S	Giant eight ball and chain painted along the fuselage	Eightballers	HSC-8	NG 0	165765
CH-60S	Giant eight ball and chain painted along the fuselage and large eight ball on nose	Eightballers	HSC-8	NG 8	
Curtiss H-12	A ram knocking the 'L' out of something	L-uk-tur?	Pensacola Squadron IV	No. 67	
Curtiss R-type	Barney Google & his horse	Spark Plug	First Yale Unit?, Huntington Beach, L.I., NY		A-767
DB-26J	A sailfish	Village of Wickford	VU-2	JE 3	77165

Type	Artwork	Name	Squadron	Modex	BuNo.
E-2C	Drug bust score board	*Nadine*	USCG CGAW		159112
E-2C	Eagle w/ US Flag on tail	None	VAW-113	NK 600	165648
E-2C	A Teenage Mutant Turtle	*Snapper Control*	VAW-115	NF 600	165301
E-2C	Red head pin-up w/ shark mouth on engines	None	VAW-117	NH 600	165649
E-2C	American flag covers the whole nose	None	VAW-123	AB 601	
E-2C	American flag covers the whole nose	None	VAW-123, CVN-65 *Enterprise*	AB 600	163693
E-2C	Bear claw down the side of the aircraft	None	VAW-124	AJ 600	165300
E-2C	Pin-up	*Classic*	VAW-124	AJ 601	161552
E-2C	Pin-up	*Miss B. Havin'*	VAW-124	AJ 601	161552
E-2C	Mission marks from drug bust		VAW-77	AF 600	164483
EA-1E	Cartoon		VAW-12	AK 723	135219
EA-1F	Snoopy profile on nose	None	NATC NAS Pax. River		132443
EA-1F	Snoopy profile on nose	None	NATC NAS Pax. River		132532
EA-1F	Cancelled post mark	*From USS JFK to Smithsonian Inst.*	VAQ-33	AB 752	132506
EA-3B	Pin-up silhouette	None	VQ-1	NF 005	146457
EA-3B	Rabbit w/ eight ball	None	VQ-1	PR 06	142671
EA-3B	Gun out of a seven on nose number	None	VQ-1 Det 64	PR 007	146452
EA-3B	Shamu killer whale	*Killer Whales*	VQ-2	JQ 010	144852
EA-3B	Shark's mouth/ Shamu killer whale	*Killer Whales*	VQ-2	No. 004	146454
EA-6B	Large green Dragoon on tail	None	VAQ-130	AC 500	162937
EA-6B	A Spartan Warrior	*Molon Lade*	VAQ-131	NE 500	163525
EA-6B	American Indian artwork of hailstones, lighting bolts, stars, & mission marks	None	VAQ-131	NE 502	
EA-6B	Flames around the intakes	None	VAQ-132	AA 500	163404
EA-6B	A redhead pin-up on a Black Raven	None	VAQ-135	NH 500	163399
EA-6B	Pin-up in a sailors outfit and Raven Eyes on nose	*Madeline*	VAQ-135	NH 500	158544
EA-6B	Remington's Mounted Warrior, 'The End of the Trail'		VAQ-135	NH 502	163522
EA-6B	A large snarling panther head	None	VAQ-136	NF 500	160707
EA-6B	A panther on a AGM missile	None	VAQ-136	NF 620.5	161883
EA-6B	A pin-up holding a Rook	*Rookie*	VAQ-137	AB 500	163527
EA-6B	A pin-up holding a Rook	*Rookie*	VAQ-137	AB 500	162936
EA-6B	A pin-up w/ CVN-65 Emblem	*Ready on Arrival*	VAQ-137	AB 501	163047
EA-6B	A pin-up jester or joker	*Radar Love*	VAQ-137	AB 502	163522
EA-6B	A bee w/ HARM missile	None	VAQ-138	NG 624	163523
EA-6B	Sabre tooth tiger and claws on tail	None	VAQ-139	NK 500	161245
EA-6B	Sabre tooth tiger and claws on tail	None	VAQ-139	NK 500	163527
EA-6B	Tail hook	*Top Hook*	VAQ-139	NK 620	
EA-6B	Old lady cartoon	*Grammaw*	VAQ-139, USS *Reagan*	NK 6??	
EA-6B	A lighting eagle on tail	None	VAQ-140	AG 40	158039
EA-6B	Large US flag on tail	None	VAQ-140	AG 500	163046
EA-6B	Chicken with gun and two kills	None	VAQ-141	AJ 621	163526
EA-6B	Darth Vader chicken	None	VAQ-141	AJ 626	
EA-6B	Frankenstein cartoon	*Franken-Prowler*	VAQ-141	AJ 500	158542
EA-6B	Frankenstein cartoon	*Franken-Prowler*	VAQ-141	AJ 502	158542
EA-6B	Missile art	None	VAQ-141	AJ 500	161350
EA-6B	Pin-up on a HARM	*Eve of Destruction / Deception Lass*	VAQ-141	AJ 621	163527
EA-6B	Frankenstein cartoon and large bolts on the side of the nose	*Franken-Prowler*	VAQ-141, CVN-71 *Roosevelt* 2008	AJ 503	158542
EA-6B	Darth Vader on tail	None	VAQ-209	AF 500	161883

Type	Artwork	Name	Squadron	Modex	BuNo.
EA-6B	World Trade Center/ Pentagon mural	9-11, NYPD, FDNY, Flight 93	VAQ-209	AF 500	158029
EA-6B	Purple Heart and metals	None	VMAQ-1	CB 01	161242
EA-6B	Seattle Mariners Logo on nose cone	None		No. 02	
EA-6B	Six mission marks	Gumby		AC 500	
EC-121K	Fruit and Connie Siolette	Sicilian Citrus Express	AEWBARRONPAC	No. 313	141313
EC-121K	Roadrunner	El Paisano	FASRON 102/VXN-8		126513
EC-121K	Clipper ship	?	VW-11	MJ 941	145941
EC-121K	Clipper ship	Bamboo Clipper	VW-11	MJ 293	141293
EC-121K	Clipper ship	Flying Cloud	VW-11	MJ 292?	141292?
EC-121K	Clipper ship	Flying Scud	VW-11	No. 299	141299
EC-121K	Clipper ship	Quick Step	VW-11	MJ 309	141309
EC-121K	Clipper ship	Sovereign of the Seas	VW-11	MJ 330	141330
EC-121K	Clipper ship	Staghound	VW-11	MJ 332?	141332?
EC-121K	Clipper ship	Superior / Surprise (3/60)	VW-11	MJ 305	141305
EC-121K	Clipper ship	Trade Wind	VW-11	MJ 308	141308
EC-121K	Clipper ship	West Wind	VW-11	MJ	
EC-121K	Clipper ship	Witch of the Wave	VW-11	MJ 327	141327
EC-121K	Clipper ship	Cutty Sark	VW-11 1963	MJ 939	145939
EC-121K	A dog on nose gear door	The Malta Dog & Brunheild	VW-2	XD 9	131389
EC-121K	Clipper ship	Thor	VW-2	No. 8	135761
EC-121K	Clipper ship	Tyr	VW-2	XD 7	135746
EC-121P	Clipper ship	Golden Light	VW-11	MJ 320	141320
EC-121P	Clipper ship	Surprise	VW-11	MJ 312	141312
EC-121P	Clipper ship	Trade Wind	VW-11	MJ 936	145936
EC-121P	Clipper ship	Velox	VW-11	MJ 326	141326
EC-121P	Clipper ship	Cutty Sark	VW-11 1965	MJ 937	145937
EC-130E	Roadrunner	Pasquotank Roadrunners	USCG		1414
EC-130Q	Surfer on surf board	4 Sale ---- Cheap	VQ-3		156173
EC-130Q	The Simpson Family on starboard nose	Gone with the Wind	VQ-3		156173
EC-130Q	Golf green 12th hole	Southwest Tour '90	VQ-4		156172
EC-130Q	Snoopy w/ golf clubs	True Tacamo Warriors	VQ-4		156172
EC-54U	A frowning face in the Modex 00	The Leper Colony	VXE-6	No. 00	159348
EKA-3B	Three leaf clover	B ____ Clover	USCG	9147	9147
EP-3	Two jets silhouettes	Save	VAQ-130	AH 616	147648
EP-3E	Bud character	Coors	VQ-2	No. 25	
EP-3E	Pin-up in leather jacket	Amber MXMXMXM	VQ-1	RP 33	
EP-3E	A bull	None	VQ-2	JQ 21	149668
EP-3E	Bat & mission marks	Evelyn	VQ-2	JQ 26	157320
EP-3E	Desert sheik	Storm	VQ-2	No. 26	157320
ERA-3B	Pac Man cartoon	None	VAQ-33	GD 101	144827
F-14A	Eight ball on tail	None	Pax River	No. 8	157987
F-14A	Eyes on nose/crescent moon on tail	Moon Equipped	VF-101	AD 101	161134
F-14A	Rattlesnake	None	VF-101	AD 102	161135
F-14A	Tomcat on LGB	FLIR Cat	VF-103	AA 213	161608
F-14A	A blue nose	Blue Nose 88	VF-11	AE 110	161869
F-14A	Shark's mouth and pin-up	Miss Molly	VF-111	NL 200	161621
F-14A	Shark's mouth and Superman motif	None	VF-111	NL 201	
F-14A	Orange Aardvark on nose	Vark of Arabia	VF-114	NH 100	160660

Type	Artwork	Name	Squadron	Modex	BuNo.
F-14A	Rattlesnake	None	VF-14	AE 101	160899
F-14A	Rattlesnake	None	VF-142	AE 204	159453
F-14A	A red rose bud	Tina Rose	VF-154	NF 102	
F-14A	Bill the Cat cartoon	Oop, Ack, Baby!	VF-154	NK 104	161618
F-14A	25th Anniversary Of Tomcat	The Cat is Back	VF-2	NE 101	159630
F-14A	Bill the Cat cartoon	Oop, Ack, Baby!	VF-21	NK 205	161601
F-14A	A pistol	High Noon	VF-213	NH 206	
F-14A	Arab on camel chased by F-14s	Camel Smoker	VF-24	No. 210	163409
F-14A	Bettie Page pin-up	Queen of Spades	VF-41	AJ 101	162689
F-14A	Tomcat	Bombcat No Escort Required	VF-41	AJ 101	162689
F-14A	Tomcat	Strikecat	VF-41	AJ 101	160394
F-14A	Tomcat on LGB with gun	Tomcat Fast FAC	VF-41	AJ 101	162608
F-14A	Pin-up	Cat Snatch Fever	VF-84	AJ 201	162692
F-14A+	Tomcat with bomb	Thief of Baghdad	VF-24	No. 212	163411
F-14B	A women's silhouette on a nickel	Kate's Nickel	VF-103	AA 103	161435
F-14B	Bones emblem and four bomb marks.	None	VF-103	AA 103	161435
F-14B	A yellow rose/ two mission marks	San Antonio Rose	VF-103, CAG-17	AA 100	162918
F-14B	Red Ripper hog w/ green Irish hat and shamrocks on tail	None	VF-11	AA 107	161437
F-14B	Tomcat and puking dog	Last Ride 1975-2005	VF-143	AG 101	
F-14B	Tomcat and puking dog	Last Ride 1975-2005	VF-143	AG 102	162921
F-14B	Forty-three mission marks. and space shuttle	STS107 / Deus Et Patria	VF-32	AC 107	163224
F-14B	Mission marks	Desert Fox	VF-32	AC 100	162916
F-14D	Tomcat on a AIM-54C missile	Thanks for the Ride 1980-2005	VF-11	AG 200	163227
F-14D	OEF/OIF and twenty-four mission marks	None	VF-213	AJ 104	159628
F-14D	OEF/OIF and thirty-one mission marks	None	VF-213	AJ 100	164602
F-14D	OEF/OIF and nine mission marks	None	VF-213	AJ 103	163899
F-14D	OEF/OIF and twenty-three mission marks	None	VF-213	AJ 105	161163
F-14D	OEF/OIF and twenty-three mission marks	None	VF-213	AJ 106	163893
F-14D	Nineteen mission marks + one MG	Ms. Heidi	VF-31	NK 106	164343
F-14D	Bore sight reflector ring and MIG	Tomcats and Targets	VF-31	AJ 106	164343
F-14D	Campaign medal	I Gave so others could Fly	VF-31	NK 105	159610
F-14D	Pin-up	Sweet Little Miss	VF-31	AJ 110	164346
F-14D	Pin-up w/ six shooter	My Lil' Sixshooter	VF-31	AJ 107	163902
F-18A	Don't tread on me flag/ twenty mission marks	None	VFA-201	AJ 200	162904
F-18A	Mardi Gras art work on speed brake	None	VFA-204	AF 401	163135
F-18A	? Mission marks.	Galant Fox 1930	VFA-97	NH 201	163143
F-18A	? Mission marks.	Secretariat 1973	VFA-97	NH 200	163098
F-18A	Navy ram and Army knight 'Go Navy-Beat Army/mission marks.	Affirmed 1978	VFA-97	NH 210	163106
F-18A	A deck of cards/ SC Flag on air brake	Joe's Jokers	VMFA-115	VE 200	1629047
F-18A	US flag art on speed brake	None	VMFA-115	AC 200	163133
F-18A	US flag art on speed brake	None	VMFA-115	VE 201	163133
F-18A+	'Jazz' speed break	None	VFA-204	AF 400	163135
F-18A+	Twelve mission marks	Ultimate Warrior	VFA-87	AJ 410	
F-18A+	Twelve mission marks	Ultimate Warrior	VFA-87	AJ 410	163105
F-18A+	Four mission marks and artwork on speed brake	Fleet D-Fender	VFA-87	AJ 400	162886
F-18C	Nine mission marks.	Tonight... We Ride	VFA-105	AC 400	164246
F-18C	NYPD badge	None	VFA-106	AD 400	163457
F-18C	Chief fouled anchor and memorial reef	None	VFA-113	No. 300	

Type	Artwork	Name	Squadron	Modex	BuNo.
F-18C	Blue flames on nose, and Moose head art	Rosa	VFA-146	NG 300	163777
F-18C	Red, white, and blue flag in flames	None	VFA-146	NG 300	163777
F-18C	Five mission marks	Caesar Augustus	VFA-15	AJ 305	164661
F-18C	One mission mark	Lester	VFA-15	AJ 306	164258
F-18C	One mission mark	Raptor	VFA-15	AJ 300	164627
F-18C	Two mission marks	La Navaja	VFA-15	AJ 314	164657
F-18C	Two mission marks	The Dude Chuck Norris	VFA-15	AJ 310	164673
F-18C	Sixteen mission marks	In Memory of Flight 11 American Airlines	VFA-151	NE 312	164740
F-18C	Don't Tread On Me flag on speed brake	None	VFA-201	AF 200	
F-18C	Mardi Gras artwork on speed brake	None	VFA-204	AF 400	
F-18C	Three mission marks	Avery's Aviator	VFA-83	AA 302	165215
F-18C	Anchor/ ?mission marks	Chief	VFA-83	AA 301	165212
F-18C	Map of Afghanistan	Ram on	VFA-83	AG 307	
F-18C	OIF Markings/Dime Flight and mission marks	None	VFA-83	AA 300	164201
F-18C	Ten mission marks.	Buster Stuff	VFA-83, CVW-7, USS Eisenhower	AG 303	164244
F-18C	Four mission marks.	Modest Maiden	VFA-83, CVW-7, USS Eisenhower	AG 306	164225
F-18C	Eight mission marks.	Miss Camille	VFA-83, CVW-7, USS Eisenhower	AG 301	164214
F-18C	map of Middle East OIF/OEF op area, and scores	Ram Rod	VFA-83, CVW-7, USS Eisenhower	AG 300	164201
F-18C	One mission mark	Mean Jeanne	VFA-83, CVW-7, USS Eisenhower	AG 311	164240
F-18C	Three mission marks	Miss Vay	VFA-83, CVW-7, USS Eisenhower	AG 302	164210
F-18C	Two mission marks	St. Pauli Girl	VFA-83, CVW-7, USS Eisenhower	AG 307	
F-18C	FDNY emblem and eagle	None	VFA-86	AB 414	164978
F-18C	Seventeen mission marks OID/ twenty-four mission marks OEF	Ultimate Warrior	VFA-87	AJ 411	164669
F-18C	The Navy ram mascot	None	VX-9	XE 100	
F-18C	? Mission marks.	William Freeman	VMFA(AW)-121	VK 06	
F-18D	Seventy-four mission marks	Joe Foss	VMFA(AW)-121	VK 01	165413
F-18D	Four mission marks	Kenneth Ford	VMFA(AW)-121	VK 05	165411
F-18D	Ten mission marks	William Marontate	VMFA(AW)-121	VK 11	164652
F-18D	Three mission marks	Cecil Doyle	VMFA(AW)-121	VK 04	165867
F-18D	Three mission marks	Donald Yost??	VMFA(AW)-121	VK 10	
F-18D	Pin-up on speed brake	None	VMFA(AW)-224	WK 00	164886
F-18D	Death Dealer ace of spades card on speed brake	Death Dealer	VMFA(AW)-225	CE 01	
F-18D	A deck of cards/ map of Iraq	Dealer	VMFA(AW)-332	EA 00	164967
F-18E	Absolute bottle with Osama body tag	Absolute Justice	VFA-115, CVW-14, USS Lincoln	NK 203	165784
F-18E	An eagle and flag motif+ memorial for FDNY+ five mission marks.	?	VFA-115, CVW-14, USS Lincoln	NK 201	165782
F-18E	Crest of fallen FDNY Engine Cy./ four mission marks	Never Forget	VFA-115, CVW-14, USS Lincoln	NK 210	165789
F-18E	F-18 Hornet/ memorial to 911 hijacked airliners+ four mission mk.	Hijack This!!!	VFA-115, CVW-14, USS Lincoln	NK 212	165791
F-18E	FDNY 'Pride of Midtown' Engine 54 badge	None	VFA-115, CVW-14, USS Lincoln	NK 200	166859
F-18E	FDNY 'Pride of Midtown' Engine 54 badge+ thirteen mission marks.	Will Not Be Forgotten	VFA-115, CVW-14, USS Lincoln	NK 200	165781
F-18E	lady with flag on eagle + thirty-nine mission marks	Justice 4 All	VFA-115, CVW-14, USS Lincoln	NK 214	165792
F-18E	Red, white, blue eagle	?	VFA-115, CVW-14, USS Lincoln	NK 202	165783
F-18E	Statue of Liberty + two mission marks	We Will Never Forget	VFA-115, CVW-14, USS Lincoln	NK 204	165785
F-18E	Uncle Sam	We're Coming for You	VFA-115, CVW-14, USS Lincoln	NK 211	165790
F-18E	WTC names and forty-six mission marks	None	VFA-115, CVW-14, USS Lincoln	NK 206	165787
F-18E	A flaming eagle w/ US Flag on tail	None	VFA-137	NE 200	165899
F-18E	Paw and claw marks down the side of the fuselage and vertical stab	None	VFA-143	AG 100	166608
F-18E	A skull in a Chief's Hat w/ crossed cutlasses and mission marks	114 Years of CPO Leadership	VFA-143, CVW-7, USS Eisenhower	AG 114	166599
F-18E	Four mission marks and artwork on speed brake	Party One	VFA-87	AJ 400	

Type	Artwork	Name	Squadron	Modex	BuNo.
F-18F	CMC pennant and six mission marks	Easy Day Jeff	VFA-103	AG 200	166620
F-18F	Four mission marks	Fly 3 Big Bob	VFA-103	AG 201	166621
F-18F	A skull and cross bones in a Chief's Hat	114 Years of CPO Leadership	VFA-211	AB 114	165807
F2H-2P	2 die equaling 7 (Seven)	None	VC-61 Det. B	PP 7	
F2H-2P	Eight ball	None	VC-61 Det. B	PP 8	
F2H-2P	Ray-O-Vac nine lives cat logo	None	VC-61 Det. B	PP 9	
F-4B	MIG kill	The Mig Killer	VF-161	NF 105	153915
F-4B	MIG kill	Mad Dog	VF-51	NL 113	149457
F-4B	Pin-up	Blondie	VMF-542		
F-4B	Omega tail marking of NAS No. 899 Squadron	None	VMFA-531	AA 207	151477
F-4B	Spy character on splitter plate	None	VMFAT-101	SB 00	149421
F4B-3	Big black Maltese Cross		VF-1, CV-3 Saratoga	1-F-2	
F4D-1	Pin-up	Sexy Six	VF-74	AF 106	139113
F4D-1	Alfred E. Newman	What Me Worry	VMF(AW)-114	AB 208	134964
F4F/FM-2	Three kills	Mah Baby	VC-10	B 6	
F4F/FM-2	Kill marks	Baldy	VC-7		?155875
F4F-3	Indian head as in Lafayette Esqd.	None	Guadalcanal	No. 8	
F4F-4	Red head pin-up	Impatient Virgin	VMF-112	No. 29	
F4F-4	Captain Marvel and Jap monkey on tail	Ringer	VMF-221	No. 77	12094
F4F-4	Lil Abner cartoon(Hairless Joe)	Melvin's Massacre	VMF-221/121	No. 17	
F4F-4	Art work	My Lovia??		No. 92	
F-4J	Yosemite Sam on nose gear door	None	PMTC	AJ 101	155563
F-4J	Mouse head	Mickey Krause Club	VF-101	AJ 110	153900
F-4J	Mouse head	Mickey Krause Club	VF-101	AA 100	153808
F-4J	Spook' on nose gear door	Mig Eater	VF-11	NK 212	157308
F-4J	A spook character and Mig kill	The Rat	VF-142		?155875
F-4J	Andy Capp comic character	Labella	VF-31	AC 103	155513
F-4J	Bud character on nose gear door	Bud Man	VF-31	AJ 211	153784
F-4J	Music eighth note	Sound of Philly Bro DB	VF-74	AA 201	153777
F-4J	Spook on tail	First in Phantoms	VF-74	AJ 203	153900
F-4J	Two fish	None	VF-74	SH 36	152230
F-4N	Outhouse	Topgun	VMFAT-101	MG 04	157261
F-4S	Day-glow pin-up	ACM DET Key West	VMFA-321	MG 06	156980
F-4S	Day-glow pin-up	ACM DET Key West	VMFA-321	MG 06	155580
F-4S	Hell's Angel under palm tree	ACM DET Key West	VMFA-321	MG 000	153904
F-4S	Phantom character and pin-up	Phabulous Phantoms 1973-1991	VMFA-323	NK 100	150480
F-4S	Large rattle snake on rudder	None	VFB-10	No. 29	92132
F4U	Three kills	Frisco Kid	VMF-122		
F4U	Wolf head	Stinky	VMF-214	No. 883	??883
F4U/FG-1	Kill marks	Lady Carol W.	VMF-512, USS Gilbert Islands	FE 62	82842
F4U/FG-1D	Nude pin-up	Hard Hearted Hanna	VF-17	No. 9 & No. 33	48772?
F4U-1	Five kills	Lonesome Polecat	VMF-115	No. 11	
F4U-1	Indian chief	The Sioux Chef	VMF-213	No. 38	
F4U-1	A pair of dice	Defabe	VMF-213	No. 10	
F4U-1	Devil's head	Lucifer	VMF-213	No. 20	
F4U-1	Disney character/ eight kills	Gus's Gopher	VMF-213		No. 02351
F4U-1	Eagle and two kills	None			

Type	Artwork	Name	Squadron	Modex	BuNo.
F4U-1	Eight ball	Dangerous Dan/ Eight Ball	VMF-213	No. 8	
F4U-1	Kill marks	Daphne C.	VMF-213	No. 13	No. 03829
F4U-1	Six kills	Daphne C.	VMF-213	No. 15	No. 02350
F4U-1	Three kills	Daphne C.	VMF-213	No. 7	No. 02350?
F4U-1	Two kills		VMF-213/124	No. 13	No. 02350?
F4U-1	Kill marks	Martha	VMF-214	No. 883	??883
F4U-1	Pin-up	Marine's Dream	VMF-214	No. 576	No. 02576
F4U-1	Five kill marks	Jinny	VMF-215	No. 34	
F4U-1A	Four kills	Big Hog	VF-17	No. 1	17649
F4U-1A	Hawaiian pin-up (tail)	None	VF-17	No.?	17677
F4U-1A	Pin-up (tail)	None	VF-17	No. 28	
F4U-1A	Two kills/sign	LA City Limits	VF-17	No. 7 & No. 34	17932
F4U-1A	Pin-up	Ring Dang Doo	VMF-217	No. 033	50033?
F4U-1A	Pin-up	Ring Dang Doo	VMF-217	No. 185	50033?
F4U-1A	SEABEE's emblem	None	VMF-222	No. 98	
F4U-1A	Pin-up	Heavenly Body	VMF-321	No. 842	
F4U-1A	Pin-up	Katy Did	VMF-422		
F4U-1A	Pin-up, Vargas' cowgirl	None	VMF-422		
F4U-1D	Pin-up	None	Iwo Jima	No. 8	
F4U-1D	Skull and crossbones & three kills	Penny	VBF-83	No. 205	
F4U-1D	Pin-up and shark mouth on drop tank	Flak Bait	VMF-? Ie Shima	No. 600	
F4U-1D	Milt Caniff's Dragon Lady	None	VMF-122, CA Div. 24?	No. 86	
F4U-1D	Dragon	Reluctant	VMF-213	No. 831	
F4U-1D	Kill marks	Lucybelle	VMF-214		
F4U-1D	Pin-up	Luscious Lil-Nan	VMF-321		
F4U-1D	Sign post	Milwaukee City Limits	VMF-322		
F4U-1D	Elephant on l/g door	None	VMF-323, in1945		
F4U-1D	Caricature	Ichy??	VMF-351		
F4U-1D	A Frenchman w/ sword chopping off a Japanese head	Touché!	VMF-422	FF 61	
F4U-1D	A hog	Thundering Hog	VMF-422		
F4U-1D	Pin-up	Thundering Hog II	VMF-422	No. 20	
F4U-1D	Three-and-a-half meat balls	Palpitain Paulie	VMF-441	No. 422	
F4U-1D	Pin-up	Daisy June	VMF-511	1 m 82	
F4U-2	Four aces and mission marks	Grand Slam	VMF-512, USS Gilbert Islands	No. 22	82732
F4U-4	Kill mark and squadron emblem	Midnight Cocktails	VMF(N)-532	No. 212	
F4U-4	Eleven kill marks	Big Hog Mk. II CAG	CAG-74	CAG	
F4U-4	Squadron emblem/scores	Little Lady	VF-113	V 301	
F4U-4	Scores/map of Korea	Korea	VF-192	B 208	
F4U-4	Mission marks	Bobbie D	VF-713	H 211	
F4U-4	Mission marks	Gaye	VF-713	H 210	
F4U-4	Ten mission marks	Sex Machine	VF-713	H 202	
F4U-4	Mission marks	??	VF-74, USS Bon Homme Richard CVA-31	L 409	
F4U-4	Thirty-five mission marks	Babe	VF-74, USS Bon Homme Richard CVA-31	L 408	
F4U-4	Squadron emblem/scores	Baby Leonora	VF-783	D 201	81849
F4U-4	Squadron emblem/scores	Ginger II	VF-783	D 206	81956
F4U-4	Squadron emblem/scores	Peggy	VF-783	D 202	81991
F4U-4	Sixteen mission marks	Dot	VF-791	A 211	81712

Type	Artwork	Name	Squadron	Modex	BuNo.
F4U-4	Squadron emblem/scores	Yvonne III	VF-791	A 207	82084
F4U-4	??	Bakersfield Sheriff	VF-871	B 303	97230
F4U-4	??	Baldy's Baby	VF-871	B 301	
F4U-4	??	Bob's Job	VF-871	B 308	
F4U-4	??	Mac's Hack	VF-871	B 304	
F4U-4	??	Ray's Roost	VF-871	B 307	81057
F4U-4	??	The Princess	VF-871	B 316	
F4U-4	??	Wolf's Witch	VF-871	B 315	
F4U-4	Bird's nest/ scores	Louie's Love Nest	VF-871	B 302	
F4U-4	Corsair and donkey	After Your Ass	VF-871	B 305	
F4U-4	Lightning bolts	Speedy Gomez	VF-871	D 3XX	
F4U-4	Pin-up	Hot to Go	VF-871	B 313	
F4U-4	Pin-up	Lorie	VF-871	B 310?	
F4U-4	Pin-up	Passionate Shirley	VF-871	B 306	
F4U-4	Pin-up	Peg O' My Heart	VF-871	B 309	
F4U-4	Pin-up under a palm	Rebel's Delight	VF-871	B 312	97053
F4U-4	Small car/ scores	Memories	VF-871	B 311	
F4U-4	Squadron emblem/scores	Don's Hopped up Model A	VF-874	B 310	
F4U-4	116 mission marks	June	VF-884	D 401	
F4U-4	Thirty-five mission marks	Sweet Sue	VF-884	A 413	80788
F4U-4	Fifty-six mission marks	Bon Lee	VF-884	A 414	81530
F4U-4	Mission marks	Sweet Sue	VF-884	A 403	82027
F4U-4	Mission marks	?	VF-884	A 409	
F4U-4	Mission marks	Judy IV?	VF-884	A 406	
F4U-5N	Mission marks	Sleepless Knight	VC-3	NP 6	122186
F4U-5N	Mission marks	Vortex	VC-3	NP 1	
F4U-5N	Mission marks	Yokosuka Queen	VC-3	NP 24	124442
F4U-5N	Sun burst and art	Jody??	VC-3	NP 4	
F4U-5NL	Thirty-five mission/five kills/girl in skirt	Annie-Mo	VC-3	NP 21	124453
F4U-5NL	Mission marks	Annie-Mo	VC-3	NP 21	124???
F-5N	Rattlesnake	None	VF-9M	9 * 2	A-7397
F6C-4	Felix the Cat skating / on the tail	None	USS Essex	No. 24	
F6F-3	Two meat balls	Sha-BOOM	VF-15		
F6F-3	Six kills	Frumious Bandersnatch	VF-33	No. 13	25813
F6F-3	Five kills	My Own Joan II	VF-38		
F6F-3	One kill	Ruth-Less	VF-51		
F6F-3	A pair of dice	Little Joe	VF-6	X 3	
F6F-3	Bull's head/nine kills	Gadget	VF-6	No. 19	40467
F6F-3	two dice 'Seven/eleven' and Three kills	None		No. 32	40467
F6F-3	Kill marks	Hawk		No. 17	41476
F6F-3	Kill marks	Hawk		No. 17	66237
F6F-5	Lily and kill marks	Hangar Lily	CAG-19	No. 99	
F6F-5	Twenty-four kills	Minsi III	VF-15	CAG	94203
F6F-5	Kill marks	Minsi II	VF-15		
F6F-5	Kill marks	Minsi III	VF-15?	No. 14	70143
F6F-5	Esquire pin-up	Comet	VF-781	L 69	72684
F6F-5	Skull and crossbones and nine kills	Death 'n' Destruction	VF-83	No. 115	72534

Type	Artwork	Name	Squadron	Modex	BuNo.
F6F-5K	Eighteen hash marks	18th Nolo	VU-3K	No. 502	
F6F-5N	Scotty dog playing drum	Blues in the Night	VF-83	F (N)?	
F6F-5N	Pin-up in bikini reclining and kill marks?	None	VMF(N)-541	F(N) 59	
F6F-5N	Pin-up in sun bonnet (seated)	None	VMF(N)-541	F(N) 64	
F6F-5N	Pin-up standing w/ long flowing hair	None	VMF(N)-541	F(N) 84	
F6F-5N	Two-and-a-half kills	Chief Wahoo	VMF(N)-542	F(N) 76	78669
F6F-5N	A big fifth of whiskey/ large red heart	Black Death/ Millie Lou	VMF(N)-542	F(N) 78	
F6F-5N	Pin-up in negligee (standing)	1 o'clock Jump	VMF-512, USS Gilbert Islands	No. 29	77690
F6F-5P	A cat holding a camera	Survey	VMF(N)-513	WF 24	
F7F-3N	Mission marks	Linda			
F-8C	flames and flaming eyes on nose	None	VF-84	AG 201	145559
F-8C	Flames and flaming eyes on nose	None	VF-84	AG 210	
F-8C	Flames and flaming eyes on nose	None	VF-84	AG 208	146948
F-8E	Cartoon cat	None	VF-191	NM 00	
F-8H	MIG kills	Thunder	VFP-63		147916
F-8J	A cat or dog leaping (panther)	None	VF-194	NM 203	
F-8J	Boot w/ wings	None	VF-194	NM 206	150328
F-8J	Rattlesnake	None	VF-194	NM 205	149220
F-8J	Rattlesnake	Rattler	VF-211	NP 110	150347
F-8J	John Deere logo on tail	None	VF-24	NP 200	149201
F-8J	Peg leg pirate	Bulldog?	VF-24	NP 201	150311
F-8J	Pirate Goofy	Pirate	VF-24	NP 207	150670
F-8J	Pogo' alligator	Gator	VF-24	NP 213	
F-8J	Thunder cloud	Thunder	VF-24	NP 203	149145
F-8J	Yosemite Sam	None	VF-24	NP 211	150883
F-8K	Rattlesnake	Rattler	VF-111	AK 10?	146951
F9F-2	A knight on a horse	The Knight??	VF-151	H 314	
F9F-2	Art work on nose	??	VF-151	H 301	
F9F-2	Cowboy w/ hat	Ramblin' Rebel	VF-72, USS Bon Homme Richard CVA-31	L 209	
F9F-2	Mission marks	Paper Doll	VF-781	D 121	123702
F9F-2	Mission marks	Kathusaletm	VF-781	D 119	123669
F9F-2B	Mission marks	Octane Sniffer	VF-191	B 104	123633
F9F-2B	456 mission marks	Jet Cats	VMF-311	WL 2	123451
F9F-2B	Three pronged flame symbol	?	VC-61		123595
F9F-2P	Life logo and mission marks	Life	VC-61	PP 155	
F9F-2P	Lightning bolts	AWK	VC-61	PP 12	
F9F-2P	Mission marks	Look	VC-61	PP 154	123510
F9F-2P	Mission marks	Look	VC-61	PP 54	123536
F9F-2P	Mission marks	Peepin' Tom	VC-61	PP 70	
F9F-2P	Mission marks	Pic	VC-61	PP 153	123708
F9F-2P	Mission marks	Honey Bunny	VC-61 Det. E	PP 40	
F9F-2P	Mission marks	Pic II	VC-61 Det. N Bon Homme Richard CVA-31	PP 46	
F9F-5	Mission marks	Jr	VF-153	H 307	
F9F-5	Mission marks	Jr	VF-153	H 308	125437
F9F-5	Mission marks	Jr	VF-153	H 313	126230
F9F-5	Dark cloud	BLPFSTK	VF-71	L 106	
F9F-5	A bird??	Big Dick	VF-72	L 211	127180
F9F-5P	2 die equaling 7 (Seven)	None	VC-61 Det. B	PP 7	

Type	Artwork	Name	Squadron	Modex	BuNo.
F9F-5P	Eight ball	None	VC-61 Det. B	PP 8	
F9F-5P	Ray-O-Vac nine lives cat logo	None	VC-61 Det. B	PP 9	
F9F-6P	A rooster	None	VC-61	PP 7	134458
F9F-8	Fox cartoon	None	VFP-61	PP 87	141726
FG-1	Pin-up	None	VMF-114	No. 056	
FG-1A	Pin-up	Virgin Jackie	VMF-222	No. 993	13993
FG-1D	Hula girl pin-up	None	censored maybe VMF-321	No. 056	
FG-1D	Red bloomers	Maggie's Drawers	CV-9 Essex CAG-83: VBF-83?	No. 191	
FG-1D	Pin-up	Skipper's Orchid	HQSS-22	No. 99	
FG-1D	A menu	Chow Hound	VFB-83		
FG-1D	Ace of hearts	None	VMF-122	No. 643	
FG-1D	Pin-up	Miss-Conduct	VMF-422	No. 28	76481
FG-1D	Pin-up	Twin Acres	VMF-422	No. 22	
FG-1D	Cossack character in Corsair	The Mad Cossack	VMF-512, USS Gilbert Islands	No. 26	
FG-1D	Cossack character in Corsair	The Mad Cossack	VMF-512, USS Gilbert Islands	No. 11	
FG-1D	Meat cleaver	Brooklyn Butcher	VMF-512, USS Gilbert Islands	No. 21	
FG-1D	Single finger in could	Semper Fi	VMF-512, USS Gilbert Islands	No. 25	
FM-2	Two pin-ups	Smokey's Lucky Witch	VC-10	B 27	
FM-2	Pin-up	The Reluctant Maiden	VC-14	D 9	
FM-2	Nine kills	Baldy	VC-27		
HC-130J	Lil' Martian and cartoon C-130	HC-130J Project Office To the 21st Century and Beyond	USCG Elizabeth City	USCG 2004	
HC-130J	Lil' Martian and cartoon C-130	HC130-J Project Office To the 21st Century and Beyond	USCG Elizabeth City	USCG 2005	
HC-130J	Yosemite Sam		USCG Sacramento	USCG 1705	
HH-2D	A smiley face		HSL-30	HT 73	
HH-46A	Angry boy on forward dog house and tail	None	HC-11	VR 71	150954
HH-46A	Angry boy on forward dog house	Det 5, USA	HC-11 Det 5	VR 73	150954
HH-46A	Mission marks/ No camels	Club Bohica	HC-5	RB 10	150962
HH-46A	Mutant Ninja Turtles	Heroes on a Clamshell	HC-5	RB 06	
HH-46A	A rodent in flight suit and mae west	Water Rats	NAS Pax River		150947
HH-46D	A flying frog	Your Pad or Mine	HC-5 Det.1	RB 03	
HH-46D	A mouse on a piece of cheese	None	HC-5 Det.3	RB 07	150947
HH-46D	A stick man and oil well derrick?	None	HC-6	HW 75	151953
HH-52A	Cartoons and map	Polar Star	USCG		1383
HH-52A	Yosemite Sam	Whirlybird Cowboy	USCG		
HH-53D	Mouse head	None	NAS Pax River		158683
HH-60H	A pair of dice	None	HS-6, CVW-11 CVN-68 *Nimitz*	NH 4	165256
HH-65A	A shark on the side	Jaws 90	USCG *Cutter Boutwell*	No. 90	6590
HNS-1	Inuit and penguin	Labrador Special	USCG		39045
HO3S-1	Pin-up	Angel	HU-1	UP 25	
HO3S-1	A pair of dice	Lucky Lady			
J2F	Donald Duck on nose	None	VMF-Samoa		
J4F-2	Porpoise	Petulant Porpoise	EDO	E 175	32976
JM-1	Pin-up on nose		NAS Banana River, Fl.	MJ 15	66690
JM-1	A Seabee	Miss 28th Seabee	US NAVY		
JM-1	Fake mission marks and sub kills	Tornado from Hell	VJ-15 NAF Bermuda	15-B-8	41-35586
JM-1	Flying donkey w/ broom	The Red Ass	VMJ-3	No. 3	90507
JM-1	Little boy	Little Butch		No. 2	
KA-3B	Three leaf clover	Luck of the Irish	VAH-10	AP 613	138974

Type	Artwork	Name	Squadron	Modex	BuNo.
KA-3B	Andy Capp comic character	*Killer Whale*	VAH-13	NF 031	142659
KA-3B	Snoopy w/ gas hoses and dynamite	None	VAH-4	ZB 899	142660
KA-3B	Snoopy w/ gas hoses and dynamite	None	VAH-4	ZB898	142656
KA-3B	Large lips on tail cone	*Deep Throat II*	VAQ-130	TR 70	138953
KA-6D	Large eagle head on nose	None			151809
KC-130F	Refuel hose	*Hose Monster*	VR-22		148895
KC-130J	Skull and cross bones	None	VMGR-352	QB 765	166765
LC-117D	Penguin	*Lou Byrd II*	VXE-6	JD 7	17188
LC-117D	Penguin	*Wilshie Duit*	VXE-6	JD 10/7	99853
LC-130F	Penguin	*Penguin Express*	VXE-6	JD 19	148319
LC-130F	Penguin at the Pole	*The Crown*	VXE-6	JD 21	148321
LC-130F	Penguin at the Pole	*The Emperor*	VXE-6	JD 20	148320
LC-130F	Penguin at the Pole	*The King*	VXE-6	JD 19	148319
LC-130F	Phoenix bird	*Phoenix*	VXE-6	XD 03	148321
LC-130F	Puckers' Pete the penguin	*Pete*	VXE-6	XD 06	148320
LC-130R	Betty Boop cartoon	*Betty/ Pride of McMurdo*	VXE-6	XD 07	148319
LC-130R	Map of NZ w/ zaps from RAAF	*AO-TEA-ROA*	VXE-6	JD 17	155917
LC-130R	Penguin	None	VXE-6	XD 1	159130
LC-130R	Penguin	None	VXE-6	XD 1	160741
LC-130R	Penguin	None	VXE-6	XD 5	159129
LC-130R	Penguin on map of Antarctica	*Chilly/ Spirit of Willy Field*	VXE-6	XD 04	159130
LC-47H	Hawaiian Island and sunrise scene	??	Operation Deep Freeze		17197
LC-47H	Penguin in yellow jumper	*Mail- ?*	Operation High Jump	TT 17?	
LC-47H	Ski jump cartoon	None	Operation Skijump II		
LC-47H	Goose w/ long neck	*Mutha Goose*	VXE-6	JD 4/14	17221
LC-47H	Green tiki	*Yankee Tiki Au Te Hau*	VXE-6	JD 14	17221
LC-47H	Kiwi on skis	*Kool Kiwi*	VXE-6	JD 14	17221
LC-47H	Penguin	*Takahe*	VXE-6	XD 7	17163
LH-34D	A cartoon helicopter	??	VX-6	JD 27	144662
LP-2H	Kiwi on nose and kangaroo on Jet pod	*City of Auckland*	VXE-6	JD 1	140437
LP-2J	Penguin plus nine barber poles	*_____ Pete*	VXE-6	JD 2	140436
Mchi. M-5	Skull and crossbones	None	263rd Squadriglia NAF Porto Corsini	No. 31	M7293
Mchi. M-5	Winged goat	*Jeff*	263rd Squadriglia NAF Porto Corsini	No. 32	M13021
Mchi. M-5	Winged goat	*Mutt 2ⁿᵈ*	263rd Squadriglia NAF Porto Corsini	No. 36?	
MH-60R	A desert/ tan hawk speed bird on the tail		HSM-41	TS 13	
MH-60R	Large blue seahawk on tail	None	HSM-41	TS 00	166402
MH-60R	Skeleton of a Raptor on tail	*Raptor*	HSM-71	No. 710	166520
MH-60S	A hand of cards	*Deuce's Wild!*	HC-11 Det. 2	VR 66	166307
MH-60S	Dice and a hand of cards	*Deuce's Wild!*	HC-11 Det. 2	VR 62	
MH-60S	A seahawk on the tail	None	HC-3	SA 00	165746
MH-60S	A dog's head on a pirate flag	*Dirty Dawgs*	HC-6	HW 63	165772
MH-60S	A Golden Falcon speed bird on tail	*Golden Falcons*	HSC-12	NE 0	167832
MH-60S	CONA markings rotor head Penguin art	*Blue Deuce*	HSC-2	HU 02	166294
MH-60S	A beach scene w/ surf boards	*Endless Summer Tour*	HSC-21	VR 74	166319
MH-60S	Jolly Roger flag	None	HSC-22	AM 00	166294
MH-60S	Large schematic diagram on the side and four drug bust Mission marks	None	HSC-22, USS *Freedom* LCS-1	AM 11	167818
MH-60S	A cowboy playing poker	*All In*	HSC-23	WC 40	166298

Type	Artwork	Name	Squadron	Modex	BuNo.
MH-60S	Blue Transformer Logo	None	HSC-23	WC 51	165766
MH-60S	Large deck of cards on a blue tail	None	HSC-23	WC 41	165776
MH-60S	Red Transformer Logo	None	HSC-23	WC 50	
MH-60S	Two knights and palm trees on tail	Island Knights	HSC-25	RB 00	166356
MH-60S	A toucan	Two Can Do It	HSC-26	HW 72	165778
MH-60S	Rooster caricature	Dirty Birds	HSC-26	HW 65	165748
MH-60S	Casper The Ghost	Ghostriders RS Det. 7	HSC-28	No. 41	166322
MH-60S	Neptune throwing dice	High Rollers	HSC-85	No. 07	165743
MV-22	Small penguin on tail	Chilly Willy 24	HX-21, NAS Pax River, MD		165383
N2T-1	Smiling cat face	None	USMC?	No. 6	A2466
N-9H	Young gosling	None	Training Sq. Two 1918		132443
NA-1E	Snoopy	None	WEP Test NATC, Pax River, MD		142630
NA-3B	A boxing kangaroo	?	NATF NAS Lakehurst	NATF 01	
NC-121J	Eagle/lighting/globe	None	VXN-8	JB 627	131627
NC-121J	Eagle/lighting/globe	None	VXN-8	JB 655	131655
NC-121J	Eagle/lighting/globe	None	VXN-8		128444
NC-121K	Fox on ice block	The Arctic Fox	VXN-8	JB 325	141325
NC-121K	Roadrunner	El Paisano	VXN-8		131659
NC-121K	Roadrunner	Paisano Dos	VXN-8		145925
NC-121K	Wiley Coyote	El Coyote	VXN-8	JB 924	145924
NC-54R	Kiwi on skis	Kiwi Special	VXN-8 Project Magnet	JB 396	90396
NKC-135A	Yosemite Sam on shark	None	EW Test		56-03596
NOP-2E	Snoopy	Wolof	NADC		128397
NP-3D	Skating fox	The Arctic Fox	VXN-8	No. 03	154587
OL-8	Winged seal	Sitka	Alaskan Survey		A-8076
OP-2E	Dragon	The Green Dragon	VO-67		
OP-2E	Dragon	The Green Garuda	VO-67	MR 9	131525
OS2U-1	A white bird under the canopy	None	VCS-1D1, 1st Naval Dist.		
OS2U-1	A lady baker w/ pie	Sweetiepie	VS-1D13, Adak, Alaska		
OS2U-3	Snake	Blue Racer			
OV-10	Snoopy	Here it Comes Charlie	VAL-4		
OV-10A	Giant bumblebee	None	H&MS-24		155480
OV-10A	Grimacing face on nose	None	VMO-1	ER 209	155443
OY-1	art on fuselage	Barbara Ann II	USMC Saipan		60507
OY-1	Pin-up	Lady Satan	VMO-4, Iwo Jima		No. 02766
P-2E	Playboy logo	Jacks Rabbits	VP-661	LV 2	128371
P-2E	Snoopy	Robbie's Rowdies	VP-661	LV 3	128345
P-2H	Hurricane symbol	None	VW-3	PM 1	124892
P-2H	Inuit art?	None	VXE-6	JD 2	
P-2H	Polar bear	Arctic Basin II	Weapons Test, NAS Pax. River		
P2V-1	Turtle on pedal prop	The Turtle	Flight Test	No. 082	89082
P2V-2	Ghost	The Thing	FASRON 112		
P2V-2N	Ski jump cartoon	Willie Jump Jump	Operation Skijump II	TT 16	
P2V-2N	Penguin	Amen	VXE-6	XD 4	122466
P-3B	A reef art	?	VP-10	LD 3	152745
P-3B	Trident pendent and mission marks.	None	VX-1	JA 1	152744
P-3C	Orion character	Orion Update	NADC PAX		158928
P-3C	A Bermuda bird	None	VP-16		

Type	Artwork	Name	Squadron	Modex	BuNo.
P-3C	Orion character	500th P-3 Orion	VP-26	LK 1	161011
P-3C	Grey shield and banner	65 Years of Grey Knight Excellence	VP-46	No. 315	
P-3C	Orion character	400th Orion	VP-5	LA	158926
P-3C	Mission marks	King Cobra	VP-60	LS 1	
P-3C	Cartoon character w/ mission marks.	None	VP-8	LC 327	157327
P-5A	Dennis the Menace	None	VP-48	SF 5	127698
PB2Y-3	Jimmy Durante cartoon	None	USS *Hamlin* (AV-15)	CC 62	
PB2Y-3	Nude pin-up	Hot body	VP-13	13-27	7127
PB4Y-	Sleepy time pin-up	None		X	
PB4Y-1	Nude	Nite Hop	FAW-7	No. 2	
PB4Y-1	Outlaw pin-up	None	FAW-7	No. 6	
PB4Y-1	Pin-up	Brooklyn Bombshell	FAW-7	B-8	
PB4Y-1	Pin-up	Lazy May-Z	FAW-7	No. 10	
PB4Y-1	Pin-up	Sea Hag	FAW-7	B-8 H	
PB4Y-1	Pin-up	Wild Her	FAW-7	No. 8	
PB4Y-1	Pin-up/mission marks/2 sub kills	Piccadilly Pam	FAW-7 UK	B 12	63916
PB4Y-1	The flight crew on a cloud	Thundercloud	FAW-7 UK	B-3 Q	
PB4Y-1	Fosdick cartoon/m. marks sub kill	Fearless Fosdick	FAW-7 VB-110	B 5	32233
PB4Y-1	King Sol caricature	King Sol's Royal Jesters	HEDRON 2, FAW-5 or VPB-113	No. 4	
PB4Y-1	Pin-up in sailor hat and tie	Navy's Gravy	Tinian	No. 292	65292
PB4Y-1	Pin-up	None	VB-103 or 109	No. 40	32040
PB4Y-1	Pin-up	Mark's Farts	VB-104		38761
PB4Y-1	Pin-up	Vulnerable Virgin	VB-104	No. 77	32077
PB4Y-1	Pin-up	Whit's Shits	VB-104		32081
PB4Y-1	Thirty mission marks	Cover Girl	VB-105	B-14	38948
PB4Y-1	Thirty mission marks and cover girl pin-up	Cover Girl	VB-105	B-14	38948
PB4Y-1	Cow	Sky Cow	VB-109	No. 21	32121
PB4Y-1	Fox riding a Liberator	Helldorado	VB-109	No. 37	32137
PB4Y-1	Pin-up	Come Get It	VB-109	No. 68	32068
PB4Y-1	Pin-up	Mission Belle	VB-109	No. 112	32112
PB4Y-1	Pin-up	No Foolin'	VB-109	No. 18	32118
PB4Y-1	Pin-up	Sugar Queen	VB-109	No. 41	32241
PB4Y-1	Pin-up	Urge Me	VB-109		32145
PB4Y-1	Pin-up Ring Master	Flying Circus	VB-109	No. 48	32148
PB4Y-1	Winged chamber pot	Thunder Mug/ Olde 8 Ball'	VB-109	No. 08	32108
PB4Y-1	Pin-up	Climaboard	VB-109/122/123	No. 40	32140
PB4Y-1	Cartoon character	Available Jones	VB-109/VD-1/VD-4	No. 49	32149
PB4Y-1	Pin-up in wagon	Satan's Wagon	VD-1	No. 82	
PB4Y-1	A little devil w/ halo and wings	Hell's Angel	VD-1 and VPB-102	No. 95	31995
PB4Y-1	Patriot/ minuteman	Spirit of 76	VD-1/VPB-102	No. 76	31976
PB4Y-1	Mission marks	Calamity Jane	VD-3	No. 96	
PB4Y-1	Pin-up sitting	Sleepy Time Gal	VD-4	No. 22	32122
PB4Y-1	Pin-up	Slick Chick	VD-5		
PB4Y-1	Pin-up	Dangerous Lady	VD-5 OR VPB-111?	No. 58?	
PB4Y-1	Nude with a bottle of Miller High Life beer and three kill marks	Miller's High Life	VPB-101	No. 280	32280
PB4Y-1	Wolves and girl	Comair Wolfpac II	VPB-101/FAW-10 loan VPB-104	No. 276	32276
PB4Y-1	Caricature	Demon Dilbert	VPB-102	No. 64	
PB4Y-1	Crewman caricature	No Strain II	VPB-102	No. 93	38783

Type	Artwork	Name	Squadron	Modex	BuNo.
PB4Y-1	Dog and fire hydrant	The Lady	VPB-102	P 483	90483
PB4Y-1	Pin-up	Boss Burton's Nitemare	VPB-102	No. 843	38843
PB4Y-1	Pin-up	Impatient Virgin	VPB-102	No. 920	38920
PB4Y-1	Pin-up (unfinished)	None	VPB-102	No. _19	38819?
PB4Y-1	Pin-up w/ bomb and mission marks	Lt Stillmans' Fightin' Lady	VPB-102	965	38965
PB4Y-1	Pin-up with umbrella	Beachcomber (The Lone Wolf) Murray	VPB-102	No. _3	38943
PB4Y-1	Small pin-up	None	VPB-102		
PB4Y-1	Nurse pin-up and mission marks	Lil' Effie	VPB-102?	No. 843	38843
PB4Y-1	Cartoon bird	The Kee Bird	VPB-103	B-15	32028
PB4Y-1	Large bomb	Berlin Express	VPB-103	B-13 N	32014
PB4Y-1	WAAF wasp	None	VPB-103	B-7	
PB4Y-1	Ninety mission marks	Piccadilly Pam	VPB-103/114	B-12 M	90474
PB4Y-1	Donald Duck w/ flag	Donald's Ducks	VPB-104	No. 74	32074
PB4Y-1	Kilroy drawing	None	VPB-104	No. 809	38809
PB4Y-1	Nude pin-up	None	VPB-104	No. 814	38814
PB4Y-1	Pin-up	Frumious Bandersnatch	VPB-104		38774
PB4Y-1	Pin-up and three meat balls	Unapproachable	VPB-104/115/120	No. 8_	32080
PB4Y-1	One kill mark and thirty-two mission marks	Six's Avenger	VPB-105	B-4 R	38751
PB4Y-1	A banana and one kill mark and thirty mission marks	The Green Banana	VPB-105	B-1 'O'	63944
PB4Y-1	Cool zoot suit dude, one kill mark and fifty mission marks	The Solid Character	VPB-105	B-2 P	
PB4Y-1	Jimmy Durante cartoon	Umbriago II	VPB-105	B-13	
PB4Y-1	Pin-up	Mitzi-Bishi	VPB-106	No. 091	_091
PB4Y-1	Pin-up and kill marks	Bales' Baby	VPB-106 and VPB-115	No. 243	32243
PB4Y-1	Pin-up, Beryl Wallace	Chick's Chick	VPB-106 and VPB-115		32238
PB4Y-1	Bomb and sub	Subduer	VPB-107	No. 5 & 10	32057
PB4Y-1	Brazilian pin-up	Macahyba Maiden/ Madam	VPB-107	No. 4	32055
PB4Y-1	Jose Carioca: Disney caricature	Passarola	VPB-107	No. 3	32056
PB4Y-1	Mallard duck	Urabu	VPB-107	No. 12	32065
PB4Y-1	Pin-up	Heavenly Body	VPB-107	No. 1	
PB4Y-1	Pin-up	Sea Beasts / Torrid Toots	VPB-107	No. 6	
PB4Y-1	Sailor running	Brown Bagger's Retreat	VPB-107	No. 7	65385
PB4Y-1	Skeleton riding on a depth charge	Gallopin' Ghost of the Braz. Coast	VPB-107	No. 11	32052
PB4Y-1	Southern Cross constellation and cross	Southern Cross	VPB-107		
PB4Y-1	Two bombs & dice	Little Joe	VPB-108/VD-3/VPB-122/123	No. 4	32098
PB4Y-1	Pin-up	Sugar	VPB-109	No. 98	32148
PB4Y-1	Clown in clouds w/bomb	Flying Circus II	VPB-111	No. 745	38745
PB4Y-1	Pin-up	Shady Lady	VPB-111	No. 853	38853
PB4Y-1	Pin-up on a bomb	Low Blow	VPB-111	No. 386	38836
PB4Y-1	Pin-up under palm tree	Little Snatch	VPB-111	No. 747	38747
PB4Y-1	Pin-up	Big Dick too hot to Handle	VPB-111	No. 892	38892
PB4Y-1	Pin-up	Lady Luck	VPB-111	No. 733	38733
PB4Y-1	Pin-up	Modest Miss	VPB-111	No. 906	38906
PB4Y-1	Pin-up	Reputation Cloudy	VPB-111	No. _3	38913
PB4Y-1	Pin-up	Rugged Beloved	VPB-111		
PB4Y-1	Pin-up	Doc's Delight	VPB-111 and VPB-117/106	No. 746	38746
PB4Y-1	A pin-up holding four aces	Little Bill's Lucky Lady	VPB-115	No. 215	32215
PB4Y-1	Drunk hill-billy w/ moonshine	Loose Livin'	VPB-115	No. 304	32304
PB4Y-1	Pin-up	Baby Shirley	VPB-115	No. 50	32150

Type	Artwork	Name	Squadron	Modex	BuNo.
PB4Y-1	Pin-up	Hell's Belle	VPB-115	No. 25	32225
PB4Y-1	Pin-up	So Sorry	VPB-115	No. 69	32169
PB4Y-1	Pin-up	None	VPB-115	No. 20	32220?
PB4Y-1	Pin-up	None	VPB-115	No. 68	32168
PB4Y-1	Pin-up and three meat balls	Snuffy's Mischief Maker	VPB-115	No. 82	32182
PB4Y-1	Pin-up/ sign post	Tokyo-USA	VPB-115		
PB4Y-1	Pin-up/six meat balls	Mischief Maker III	VPB-115	No. 74	32274
PB4Y-1	Alley cat fr. Smokey Stover comic	Willie's Wildcat II	VPB-116		38845
PB4Y-1	Cave man with club	Bush Shaker	VPB-116		38844
PB4Y-1	Daise Mae and three meat balls	Dazy May?	VPB-116	No. 734	38734
PB4Y-1	Girl riding bomb	Ridin' High	VPB-116		38779
PB4Y-1	Mountain lion	Willie's Wildcat	VPB-116		32310
PB4Y-1	Ostrich bird cartoon w/long beak	Worrybird	VPB-116	R 960	38960
PB4Y-1	Pin-up	Anchor's Away	VPB-116		90483
PB4Y-1	Pin-up	Call House Madam	VPB-116	No. _2	90482
PB4Y-1	Pin-up	Red's Playmate	VPB-116		38777
PB4Y-1	Pin-up	Stateside Structure	VPB-116		38755
PB4Y-1	Pin-up	The Snooper	VPB-116		__50
PB4Y-1	Pin-up	Tin Yan Ty Foon	VPB-116		38800
PB4Y-1	Pin-up and ship kills	Easy Maid	VPB-116	R 923	38923
PB4Y-1	Pin-up	Sleepytime Gal	VPB-116/VD-5	No. 977	38977
PB4Y-1	Pin-up	Dirty Gerty	VPB-117	No. 757	38757
PB4Y-1	Pin-up	Ready Willing and Able	VPB-117	No. _9	38759
PB4Y-1	Pin-up	Slidin' Home	VPB-117	No. 901	38901
PB4Y-1	Pin-up	The Lewd Nude	VPB-117	No. 741	38741
PB4Y-1	Pin-up on bomb	Daring Dame	VPB-117	No. 740	38740
PB4Y-1	Pin-up w/bee	The Stinger	VPB-117	No. _42	38742
PB4Y-1	Uncle Sam	So Solly	VPB-117	No. _36	38736
PB4Y-1	Pin-up	Pop's Cannon Ball	VPB-117	No. 735	38735
PB4Y-1	Character and outhouse	Uncle Tom's Cabin	VPB-117 @ Tacloban, P.I.	No. 737	38737
PB4Y-1	Mermaid	Neptune's Virgin	VPB-117/104	No. _1	38761
PB4Y-1	Bulldog and mission marks	Bull of the Woods (Bulldog)			31987
PB4Y-1	Cow girl pin-up	Persuader		No. 9?	
PB4Y-1	Nude sitting	?			40
PB4Y-1	Pin-up in undies	Sleezy Beast			
PB4Y-1	A gorilla holding a nude pin-up	The Beast	VPB-106	No. 085	32085
PB4Y-1	Donald Duck w/ umbrella and mission marks	Stoop an' Drop It	VPB-106	No. 075	32075
PB4Y-1P	A pot belly sailor in whites	Fats	VD-1	No. 07?	
PB4Y-1P	A question mark	Why, Where, When	VD-1	No. 29	
PB4Y-1P	An eagle w/ camera and green apples	Little Green Apples	VD-1	No. 67	32067
PB4Y-1P	Lemon and twenty-five mission marks	The Lemon	VD-1		38764
PB4Y-1P	Pin-up	Bosom Buddy	VD-1	No. 28	
PB4Y-1P	Pin-up	The Kamikaze Miss	VD-1	No. 24	
PB4Y-1P	Pin-up	Touche!	VD-1	No. 25	
PB4Y-1P	Pin-up	Wild Cherry II	VD-1	No. 27	
PB4Y-1P	Pin-up in sailor suit	Tourist	VD-1	No. 23	
PB4Y-1P	Pin-up	Rovin' Redhead	VD-1 and VD-5 1946	No. 22	65299
PB4Y-1P	A dog	Devil Dog	VD-3	No. 5	

Type	Artwork	Name	Squadron	Modex	BuNo.
PB4Y-1P	Pin-up	Cover Girl	VD-4	No. ?	321xx
PB4Y-1P	Pin-up	Over Exposed	VD-4	No. 19	32119
PB4Y-1P	Pin-up on flying carpet	Flying Carpet	VD-4	No. ?	321xx
PB4Y-1P	Witch w/ cauldron	Witch Craft	VD-4	No. 43	32143
PB4Y-1P	Pin-up	Blue Belle	VD-5		
PB4Y-1P	Pin-up	Dick's Dixie	VD-5 or VPB-115/117	No. 298	65298
PB4Y-2	Pin-up on bomb	Bouncin' Betty	NARU New York	R	66311
PB4Y-2	Names of ports of call	Mon Cheri	NARU Niagara	H 207	59631
PB4Y-2	Pin-up	Angel in Di-Skies	NAS Kaneohe Bay		
PB4Y-2	Pin-up	Impatient Lady	Tinian	No. 480	
PB4Y-2	Pin-up	Torchey Lena	VP-109 post war	X	59337
PB4Y-2	A hand of cards	Wild Deuce	VP-28	CF 2	
PB4Y-2	Girl getting out of car	Joy Rider	VPB-106	X 370	59370
PB4Y-2	Indian girl	Indian Made	VPB-106		59586
PB4Y-2	Indian girl and scores	Redwing	VPB-106	X 505	59505
PB4Y-2	Pin-up	Blue Diamond	VPB-106	X 396	59396
PB4Y-2	Pin-up	I'll Get By	VPB-106		
PB4Y-2	Pin-up	Our Baby	VPB-106	X 525	59525
PB4Y-2	Pin-up	Tarfu	VPB-106	X 433	59433
PB4Y-2	Pin-up	The Superchief	VPB-106	X 563	59563
PB4Y-2	Pin-up on both sides	Umbriago	VPB-106	X 390	59390
PB4Y-2	Pin-up/tiger head/five meat balls	Tiger Lady	VPB-106	X 384	59384
PB4Y-2	Shark's mouth and hillbilly	Baldy, Tortilla Flat	VPB-106 and VPB-197	X 398	59398
PB4Y-2	Pin-up and die	Lucky-Leven	VPB-106/ HEDRON 14-2	X 3	59397
PB4Y-2	Nude	Els Notcho	VPB-108	Z 460	59460
PB4Y-2	Nude running/ panther	Hippin Kitten II	VPB-108	Z 480	59480
PB4Y-2	Pin-up	Accentuate the Positive	VPB-108	No. 441	59441
PB4Y-2	Pin-up	Anchors Away	VPB-108		59483
PB4Y-2	Pin-up	Lady Luck II	VPB-108	No. 446	59446
PB4Y-2	Pin-up	Lady Luck III	VPB-108	Z 459	59459
PB4Y-2	Pin-up w/bomb	Super Snooper	VPB-108	No. 498	59498
PB4Y-2	Pin-up in nightie	La Cherie	VPB-108 and VPB-121	No. 489	59489
PB4Y-2	Cartoon giant	Lambaster	VPB-109	No. 528	59528
PB4Y-2	Goat with bombs	Hogan's Goat	VPB-109	V 515	59515
PB4Y-2	Nude	Blind Bomber	VPB-109	No. 514	59514
PB4Y-2	Pin-up	Bachelor's Delight	VPB-109	V 521	59521
PB4Y-2	Pin-up	Miss Lotta Tail/Handy Andy & Poison Ivy gun turr.	VPB-109	V 522	59522
PB4Y-2	Pin-up in cape	Shanghai Lil	VPB-109		
PB4Y-2	Pin-up	Green Cherries	VPB-109	V 502	59502
PB4Y-2	Pin-up reclining on pillow	Punkie	VPB-109	No. 501	59501
PB4Y-2	A mature pin-up	Stanley?	VPB-111	R 786	59786
PB4Y-2	Chinese pin-up	Big Snow Propaganda	VPB-116		
PB4Y-2	Mermaid	Water Spy	VPB-116		59682
PB4Y-2	Milt Caniff's Dragon Lady	Cover Girl	VPB-116	No. 760	59760
PB4Y-2	Pin-up	Peace Feeler	VPB-116	R 755	59755
PB4Y-2	Pin-up and six kills	Miss Sea-Ducer	VPB-116	R 582	59582
PB4Y-2	Flat chested nude in panties	Pirate Queen	VPB-118	No. 404	59404
PB4Y-2	Flying pin-up	Vulnerable Virgin	VPB-118	No. 449	59449

Type	Artwork	Name	Squadron	Modex	BuNo.
PB4Y-2	Girl in long dress	Summer Storm	VPB-118	No. 380	59380
PB4Y-2	Nude	Modest O' Miss II	VPB-118	No. 448	59448
PB4Y-2	Nude	Modest O' Miss	VPB-118	No. 402	59402
PB4Y-2	Nude pin-up	Miss Behavin'	VPB-118	No. 392	59392
PB4Y-2	Nude pin-up	Miss Behavin' II	VPB-118		59470
PB4Y-2	Pin-up	Miss You (1)	VPB-118		59381
PB4Y-2	Pin-up	Sleepy Time Gal	VPB-118	R 470	59470
PB4Y-2	Pin-up	Twitchy Bitch	VPB-118	No. 430	59430
PB4Y-2	Pin-up in orange grass skirt	Miss Lottatail	VPB-118	No. 410	59410
PB4Y-2	Pin-up on top hat	Mark's Farts II	VPB-118	No. 405	59405
PB4Y-2	Pin-up on top hat	Miss Natch	VPB-118	No. 405	59405
PB4Y-2	Pin-up with torch	Navy's Torchy Tess	VPB-118	No. 383	59383
PB4Y-2	Swan diving nude	The Soaring Fin	VPB-118	No. 388	59388
PB4Y-2	Pin-up on pillow	Miss You (Dee) (2)	VPB-118	No. 432	59432
PB4Y-2	Fat nude diving	Flying Tail?	VPB-118 and VPB-197?	No. 379	59379
PB4Y-2	A hobo in patched up clothes and a bomb	Holt's Patches	VPB-118/106	W 413	59413
PB4Y-2	Mission and kill marks	None	VPB-119	W 403	59403
PB4Y-2	Pin-up	Red-Hot Riden-Hood III	VPB-119		
PB4Y-2	Eleven aerial kills	The Mad Frenchman	VPB-121	R 566	59566
PB4Y-2	Bugs Bunny	Buccaneer Bunny	VPB-121	Y 478	59478
PB4Y-2	Cartoon girl	Louisiana Lil	VPB-121	Y 475	59475
PB4Y-2	Indian girl running	Tail Chaser	VPB-121	Y 491	59491
PB4Y-2	Nine little hill billy or dwarves	Ol' Blunderbuss	VPB-121	Y 564	59564
PB4Y-2	Pin-up	Abroad for Action	VPB-121	Y 450	59450
PB4Y-2	Pin-up	Come 'n' Get It	VPB-121		59409
PB4Y-2	Pin-up	Lotta Tayle	VPB-121	Y 484	59484
PB4Y-2	Pin-up in sailor hat and necktie	Naval Body	VPB-121	Y 406	59406
PB4Y-2	Pirate girl	Pirate Princess	VPB-121	Y 492	59492
PB4Y-2	Pin-up	Miss Milovin	VPB-121 / VPB-116/ VP(HL)-12	R 617	59617
PB4Y-2	A pin-up with ball and chain	Pistol Packin' Mama III	VPB-121?	Z 56	5956_
PB4Y-2	Kilroy drawing	Where are you at?	VPB-123	No. ?35 or ?85	
PB4Y-2	Pin-up	Nobody Else's Butt	VPB-123	X 520	59520
PB4Y-2	Pin-up	Vagrant Virago	VPB-123	X 487	59487
PB4Y-2	Pin-up in sailor hat and necktie	La Cherrie	VPB-123	No. 382	59382
PB4Y-2	Pin-up on pillow	Lady of Leisure	VPB-123		59438
PB4Y-2	Pin-up w/ umbrella	Typhoon	VPB-123	No. _48	59548
PB4Y-2	Pirate girl with skull	Pirate Princess	VPB-123	X 476	59476
PB4Y-2	Pin-up w/ ball and chain	Jackson's Jail	VPB-123 and VP(HL) ATU-12	X 510	59510
PB4Y-2	Hillbilly character	Supreme Zu Zu	VPB-124		59_
PB4Y-2	Pin-up	Miss Pandemonium	VPB-124		59_
PB4Y-2	Pin-up w/chastity belt and key	Gear Down and Locked	VPB-124		59519
PB4Y-2	Pin-up and kill marks	Pastime	VPB-124 and VPB-121	X 504	59504
PB4Y-2	Pin-up sitting	No Strain III	VPB-124/ NAS Kaneohe Bay		59540
PB4Y-2	Cow girl pin-up	The Outlaw		No. _40	
PB4Y-2	Pin-up	Out of Bounds			
PBJ-1D	A flaming demon	None	VMB-611	MB 3	

Type	Artwork	Name	Squadron	Modex	BuNo.
PBJ-1J	Dog's head	Lassie	VMB-433		35144?
PBJ-3	Pin-up	The States or Bust	VMB-433	V2	64949
PBM	Pin-up	Miss Happybottom	VPB-32		
PBM-3C	Cartoon character resembling Al Capp's Shmoo and dark cloud	??	USCG	S 6582	6582
PBM-3C	Two sub kills	Nickle Boat	VP-74	74-P-5	48144
PBM-3D	A tortes on tail (shell back)	Boomerang	VPB-16		48198
PBM-5	Pin-up	Vicious Virgin	VH-6		
PBM-5	Bugs Bunny	Belle Bottom	VP-731	SF 2	85146
PBM-5	Eight ball	Never Hoppen Twice	VP-731	SF 8	85148?
PBM-5	Eight ball	Never Hoppen	VP-731	SF 8	84748
PBM-5	Goofy	Puddle Jumper	VP-731	SF 6	
PBM-5	Hobo cartoon	Ramp Tramp	VP-731	SF 3	84675
PBM-5	Woody Woodpecker	Zowie	VP-731	SF 7	
PBM-5	A desert scene	The Mirage of Willcox Dry Lake	VPB-22?	S 22B	
PBM-5	Pin-up	Dinah Might	VPB-27	E 2/ E 019	59019
PBM-5	Graffiti	Carol Ann 3		J12 Y	
PBM-5	Pin-up	Belle of the Pacific		E 8	
PBM-5E	Nude in white outline on nose				
PBM-5S2	A pair of dice	Fighting Crew 10	VP-74	SF 3	84713
PBM-5S2	Shield	Shin Pai Nai	VP-731	SF 9?	84735
PBY	Black cat and dog	Leann Lena	VP-53 Green Island		
PBY-5	Raft mission marks	Donnie Girl	VP-91		
PBY-5	Raft mission marks	Ruthie	VP-91		
PBY-5	Pin-up and mission marks/two meatballs	Pistol Packin' Mama	VP-11		
PBY-5	Pin-up and mission marks/two meatball	None	VP-11	No. 30	
PBY-5	A large white horse w/ long blonde main	None	VP-72	No. 07	
PBY-5A	Flags	Lady Ann	HEDRON FAW-3		
PBY-5A	Flags	Shady Lady	HEDRON FAW-3		
PBY-5A	Mission marks and etc.	Amoozin' but Confoozin'	NAS JAX	No. 43	34043?
PBY-5A	Pin-up	Miss-Able	NAS Kaneohe Bay		??4
PBY-5A	Pin-up	Miss-Take	NAS Kaneohe Bay		
PBY-5A	Falcon art work	Aluminum Falcon	VP-61	No. 59	48426
PBY-5A	Mission marks and five kills	Nite Life	VP-81	No. 45	
PBY-5A	Mission marks and kills	Jerry Gee	VP-81	No. 07	
PBY-5A	Mummy in wheel chair	McKees Insane Assiam	VP-81	No. 30	
PBY-5A	Pin-up	None	VP-91 Kaneohe Bay		34
PBY-5A	Pin-up	Sleepy Time Gal	VPB-71	E 68	46517
PBY-6A	Pin-up	Homesick Angel	NAS Kaneohe Bay		46680
PM-2	Popeye and Wimpy	Santa Claus Special	Coco Solo, Panama CZ, 1937		
PV-1	Cartoon sailor	Kid Vega	Burbank factory	No. 25	
PV-1	Disney caricature	?	Burbank factory	No. 47	
PV-1	Donald Duck	Not-Just Mid-way! It'll be all the way!	Burbank factory		
PV-1	Donald Duck	Super Race Huh! Look at the Score Tojo: Navy-97 – Japs-0	Burbank factory		
PV-1	Donald Duck	Way to go _____ Joe	Burbank factory		
PV-1	Mickey Mouse in snow	We can take care of 'em up here	Burbank factory		
PV-1	Donald Duck w/bomb	Go Get 'em Pal	FAW-4 HEDRON, NAS Attu, AK	No. 19	

Paint Locker Magic

Type	Artwork	Name	Squadron	Modex	BuNo.
PV-1	Donald Duck	None	VB-136, NAS Adak, AK	No. 3	
PV-1	Three kills and musical notes	Chloe	VMF(N)-531	No. 53	33253
PV-1	eight ball	Eight Ball	VMF(N)-531		
PV-1	Kill marks and pin-up	Coral Princess/ Target for Tonight	VMF(N)-531	No. 51	33251?
PV-1	Three white stick figures	None	VP-150	No. 895	xx895
PV-1	Pin-up with rattlesnake	Gotcha Rattled	VPB-128		
PV-1	Pretty girl and boxing gloves	Punch and Judy	VPB-131		
PV-1	Thumper	Thumper	VPB-132	132-B-1	
PV-1	Octopus on top	Sea Deuce	VPB-132	No. 2	
PV-1	Octopus on top	None	VPB-133	No. 991	34991
PV-1	Pin-up	I'll Get By	VPB-133		
PV-1	Pin-up on fence	Going My Own Way	VPB-133		49599
PV-1	Octopus on top, three figures by rear door	Hewego	VPB-133 or maybe VPB-150	No. 1	
PV-1	Cartoon of tank hitting a tree full of Japanese	Looks like we hit the Jap-Pot	VPB-135	No. 2	48909
PV-1	Pluto	?	VPB-135	No. 22	
PV-1	WAVE caricature and mission marks	It's from that Sailor I Knitted a Sweater for last Spring	VPB-135		48891
PV-1	Mickey Mouse cartoon	Hang I Can Beat a Routen Japs MYS	VPB-135	X 12	
PV-1	Mission marks	Baby Bing	VPB-136		
PV-1	Smiling bomb cartoon	Right in Tojo's Face	VPB-136	X 4	
PV-1	Cartoon character on bomb	?	VPB-136, FAW-4	X 5	
PV-1	Donald Duck w/ cloths off	?	VPB-138		
PV-1	Cartoon cowboy	They don't make Them any Tougher than Us	VPB-139	No. 32	34640
PV-1	Mickey Mouse head	None	VPB-139	No. 31	34641
PV-1	Pin-up	?	VPB-139	No. 30	
PV-1	Pin-up	Miss Us Flak	VPB-142	No. 436	?33436
PV-1	Pin-up	Jimmy Junior	VPB-144		34877
PV-1	Pin-up	Pistol Packin' Mama	VPB-144		34805
PV-1	Pin-up	Senorita Ventura	VPB-144	No. 730	34730
PV-1	Scores and Bugs Bunny	Shoot-You'er Faded	VPB-144	No. 741	34741
PV-1	Nude pin-up	Patches	VPB-148	No. 727	
PV-1	Bugs Bunny	We're Tokyo Bound Doc			
PV-1	Daise Duck	We're all Behind you Sailor			
PV-1	Donald Duck-n-a box	Surprise____ Tojo		No. 20	
PV-1	Mickey Mouse cartoon	1000th are we Proud			
PV-1	Mickey Mouse cartoon	That's the finish for that Sub Pilo			
PV-1	Mickey Mouse cartoon	We'll Soon do the Laughing			
PV-1	Mickey Mouse cartoon	We've got their number but We can			
PV-1	Pin-up	Blonde Blitz		No. 5	
PV-1	Stork carrying bombs	Crosby can wait, I was Drafted			
PV-2	A pin-up on aft fuselage	None	VPB-139	No. 32	
QF-4N	Caricature	None	NWST Mugu	NWAC422	152277
QF-4N	Roadrunner	GEWP GEWP	NWST Mugu	No. 143	152970
QF-4N	Roadrunner	GEWP GEWP	NWST Mugu	NWAC 40	150465
QF-4N	Roadrunner and fourteen mission marks	GEWP GEWP	NWST Mugu	EWAT 140	150465
QF-4N	Sidewinder mission marks and color tail art	Spuds	VX-30	No. 122	148360
QF-86H	Three missile mission marks	Ol' Slippery	NMC Point Mugu, CA	No. 31	53-1381
QF-86H	Snoopy on dog house being chased by a Sidewinder Missile	None	NWC China Lake, CA	O-31314	53-1314
RSC-1	Baggage tag on nose	TAG	TAG, NAS Honolulu	No. 51	

Type	Artwork	Name	Squadron	Modex	BuNo.
R5C-1	Baggage tag on nose	*The Victory Line*	TAG, NAS Honolulu	No. 66	
R5C-1	A cartoon ghost on nose	*Blithe Spirit*			
RA-3B	Bart Simpson	*Bart of Arabia*	VQ-2	JQ 006	
RA-5C	Indian head	*Head Savage*	RVAH-5	No. __ 601	
RA-5C	Ubangi on tail	None	RVAH-5	NE	149307
RF-4B	A Phantom Spook on tail	None	VMFP-3	RF 17	153102
RF-4B	Cartoon character on nose	*Spirit of America*	VMFP-3	EF 10	153101
RF-8A	Fourteen camera mission marks.	*The Hanio Hawkeye*	VFP-63 Det. 43	PP 989	
RF-8G	A flying turtle and an arresting wire	*Stapps Snappers*	VFP-	No. 911	
RF-8G	A small character under Castro's hat	*Larry's Legion*	VFP-62	AJ 913	145645
RF-8G	Droopy w/ a camera on a Carrier	None	VFP-62	AF 927	146872
RF-8G	Huge bee	None	VFP-62	AB 913	145624
RF-8G	Question mark and spy	None	VFP-62		
RF-8G	Speedy duck w/camera	None	VFP-62	AB 914	145622
RF-8G	Yogi Bear	None	VFP-62	No. 906	
RF-8G	Yogi Bear	None	VFP-62	No. 929	
RF-8G	Snoopy w/ fangs	None	VFP-62 Det. 6	No. 913	
RF-8G	Playboy bunny	None	VFP-63	NM 644	146827
RF-8G	Wiz cartoon character	None	VFP-63	AB 601	146863
RH-53D	No mine symbol	*Who you gonna call Mine Busters*	HM-14		
RP-3A	Skating fox	*The Arctic Fox*	VXN-8		150500
RP-3A	Wiley Coyote	*El Coyote*	VXN-8		149667
RP-3C	Wiley Coyote	*El Coyote*	VXN-8	No. 01	153443
RP-3D	Roadrunner	*Paisano Tres*	VXN-8	No. 02	158227
RQ-2B	Bart Simpson	*Bartman—Eat my shorts Saddam*	2nd RPV Platoon,		
S-2E	Duck dropping eggs	None	Strike Test Pax River MD		133061
S-2E	Snoopy on dog house aft fuselage	None	VS-3?	No. 13	151654
S-3A	CAG emblem on cargo pod	*Topcats We'er No. 1*	VS-30	AG 700	
S-3B	Pin-up on nose and Bugs Bunny on tail; farewell markings	*1945-2005 Torpedo Bomber Squadron Two One*	VS-21	NF 710	160604
S-3B	Fla DMV tag on the rear tail cone	*Gassman*	VS-24	AJ 706	160602
S-3B	Fla DMV tag on the rear tail cone	*Retir'n @ 30*	VS-24	AJ 704	159732
S-3B	Pin-up w/ a black tom cat	*Eyes of the Storm*	VS-24	AJ 701	159743
S-3B	Superman emblem on fwd fuselage	None	VS-29	NL 703	160597
S-3B	Red shield w/ skull and crossed hammers	*Defending Freedom to the Very Last Day*	VS-30	AA 700	
S-3B	Magic lamp w/smoke	*Aladdin*	VS-32	AB 700	159419
S-3B	Pin-up	*World Famous Maulers*	VS-32	AB 701	159751
S-3B	Blue Wolf surveillance upgrade. Mark	None	VS-35	NK 707	159387
S-3B	fox cartoon on tail	*Navy 1*	VS-35	NK 700	160124
S-3B	Santa Claus on nose after midair	None	VS-35	NK 700	
SB2C	Kilroy face	*Baby III*	VMB-? Banshees	No. 702	
SB2C-3	Donald Duck	*Rugged*	VB-80, CV-19 USS Hancock	No. 1	
SB2C-4E	Cartoon characters	*The Hannah Special*	VB-6, CV-19 USS Hancock	U 14	
SBD-3	Green Sinclair dinosaur	None	VS-41	41-S-13	6624
SBD-3	Eight ball	None		No. 2	
SBD-4	Goose or duck drawing	*Sister*	VMSB-233	No. 16	6783
SBD-5	Mission marks (114)	*Queenie*	USMC	No. 713	
SC-1	Pop bottle?	*Soda H2O*	NAF Mustin Fld, Philadelphia	No. 2	
SH-2D	A pin-up of Marilyn	*Beware Det. 7*	HSL-33		

Type	Artwork	Name	Squadron	Modex	BuNo.
SH-2F	Comic book super hero	Just Call Me Fifi!	DET-1		
SH-2F	A collage of the Seasprite	Bulldogs Det. IV	HSL-32	HV 141	149744
SH-2F	A helo, frigate, and sub	None	HSL-32	HV 136	149030
SH-2F	Bull	Ragin' Bulls	HSL-32	HV 135	151321
SH-2F	Character	Zulu Invader	HSL-32	HV 134	150163
SH-2F	Helo/ skeleton	Ocean Scanners	HSL-32	HV 133	161642
SH-2F	Sub kills	Fifi	HSL-32	HV 134	150163
SH-2F	Woody woodpecker w/ rebel flag	None	HSL-32		
SH-2F	A Triceratops	Dinosaur The Last of a Dying Breed	HSL-32 DET. 2		
SH-2F	A cartoon Seasprite w/ cowboy hat and bandanna	Outlaws	HSL-32 DET. 2, USS Capodann		
SH-2F	Seasprite skull and cross bones	Bas to the Boneyard	HSL-32 Det. 3		
SH-2F	Trident striking sub and five kills	Valery	HSL-32 Det. Five, USS Valdez	HV 137	152203
SH-2F	skull over flames w/ a red berra and nude on drop tank	Det. Seven	HSL-32, Det. 7	HV 135	151321
SH-2F	A pin-up riding a Seasprite w/ a shark mouth	Wicked Wanda Med-Red HSL-32 Det. 8	HSL-32, USS Truett		162577
SH-2F	A world globe	HSL-33 Det. 9	HSL-33		
SH-2F	Tomb stones and skulls	HSL-33 1973-1994	HSL-33		
SH-2F	Map of Central America	Tour Farewell Sold out	HSL-33/ USS G. Philip		150179
SH-2F	A hawk w/ a rotor head attacking a periscope	Sub Stompers	HSL-34	HS 234	
SH-2F	A wolf w/ green hat	Det. 5 Wolfpack	HSL-34	HS	149024
SH-2F	An eagle	??	HSL-34	HX 237	149773
SH-2F	Beaver	Subhunter Det. Three	HSL-34	HS 230	149748
SH-2F	Checked ace of spades	Your Ace in the Hole	HSL-34 FF-1085 DET. 4	HX 230	161656
SH-2F	A rat in a green flight suit	Desert Rats	HSL-34 Det. 5		
SH-2F	A bottle of booze	Boggs Bandits Beatin' the Odds	HSL-34 Det. 7		
SH-2F	A cage full of rats	HSL-34 Det. 8 The Labrats!	HSL-34 Det. 8 USS Iwo Jima		
SH-2F	A running wolf	None	HSL-34, CG-47 Ticonderoga	HX 243	
SH-2F	A women's red lips	Ginger	HSL-35	TG 41	
SH-2F	A pin-up on a fur rug	The Furtrappers	HSL-35 Det. 5		
SH-2F	Helo w/ batwings	Night Flyers-Lost Boys	HSL-35 Det. 5	TG 43	150140
SH-2F	Map of Orient	Orient Express 40/ Westpac 92	HSL-35/ USS John A. Moore	TG 40	161904
SH-2F	Eight ball	None	HSL-36	HY 09	150154
SH-2F	A pin-up on a barrel over a map of the Persian Gulf	Rhumb Runners you buy we Fly	HSL-36 Det. 2		
SH-2F	Unknown	Det.???	HSL-37 USS Rathburne	TH 57	149780
SH-2F	A cartoon of a Seasprite	Det. One	HSL-74 Det. 1	NW 44	149__72
SH-2F	A Trojan Warrior	Magic Lantern Kaman Panama City	HSL-94		
SH-2F	A Trojan Warrior	Unitas XXXVI Titians	HSL-94		
SH-2F	An artic sunrise	Northern Lights	HSL-94	NW 22	161644
SH-2F	Large Titan w/ a long lance	None	HSL-94	NW 20	163214
SH-2F	Eagle over ship at sea	The Last Great Act	HSL-?	No. 20	
SH-2G	A flaming gopher w/ a M-60 mg	HSL-32 Gopfers Det. 1	HSL-32	HV 145	162583
SH-2G	A beast with mg in ring of fire	Taming the Beast in the Middle East	HSL-32 Det. Five, USS Valdez	TF 10	150614
SH-2G	Bart Simpson sitting on a mine w/ a M-60	We'er Det. 8 _____ Our Mission _____	HSL-33	TF 17	162576
SH-2G	Japanese rising sun art		HSL-33		
SH-2G	Little devil on torpedo	Daredevils	HSL-35 Det. 7		161913
SH-2G	Skull and sword through it	Penetration Guaranteed	HSL-36	HY 343	151311
SH-2G	Pin-up	None	HSL-37	TH 55	150157
SH-2G	Lucy character	None	HSL-37	TH 57	
SH-2G	A nude riding bare back on a polar bear	Bare Riders	HSL-37 Det. 6	TH ?55?	

Type	Artwork	Name	Squadron	Modex	BuNo.
SH-2G	Pin-up silhouette	Det. 3's MIA Tai Express-Aloha	HSL-84 Det. 3		
SH-2G	A cartoon of a Seasprite bombing a Sub	Baltops 96	HSL-94		
SH-3H	Cartoon duck 'Donald'	Desert Duck	HC-2, USS Nimitz	AJ	151523
SH-3H	Cartoon duck 'Heuy', Louie, or Dewey	None	HC-2, USS Nimitz	AJ 733	148999
SH-3H	Five Apollo spacecraft recovery marks and UDT Team No. 13 Frog	None	HS-4	NT 66	152711
SH-3H	Five Apollo spacecraft recovery marks and UDT Team No. 13 Frog??	None	HS-4	NT 66	148045
SH-3H	Black and white dog	Ol' Shep	HS-7, Saratoga, Aug 1980	No. 730	148052
SH-3H	Snoopy	Snoopy	HS-7, Saratoga, Aug 1980	No. 733	152104
SH-3H	Camel	Dawdling Dromedary	NAS Pax River		
SH-3H	USS Fife emblem	USS Fife DD-991 Successum Merere Conemur	DD-991, USS Fife		
SH-60B	A skull	None	HS-14	NF 623	164447
SH-60B	An eagle and Mt. Fuji on back fuselage	None	HS-14	NF 610	164460
SH-60B	Statue of Liberty + two mission marks	None	HS-4	HC 6	165117
SH-60B	Flames	None	HS-6		
SH-60B	Giant tomahawk and Indian head	None	HS-6	NH 610	
SH-60B	A pin-up sitting on a eight ball	The Blow Must Go	HS-8	No. 455	
SH-60B	A Transformer logo	None	HSL-42	HM 436	163908
SH-60B	Medieval knight	Overlord CG-60 Normandy	HSL-42	HN 434	162132
SH-60B	Skeleton w/ six shooter	Wanted Outlaws	HSL-42		
SH-60B	Skull and crossed bones	None	HSL-42 Det. 5	HN 426	162347
SH-60B	Art work on sono door	?	HSL-43	TT 23	162341
SH-60B	Tiger striped tail	?	HSL-43	TT 20	162339
SH-60B	A red donkey superimposed over a map of the Persian Gulf	USS Antietam Donkey Rollers	HSL-43 Det.5		
SH-60B	A monkey on a green 'X'	Trackers FFG-46 Rentz HSL-43 Det. 6 Fear the Monkey	HSL-43 Det.6		
SH-60B	A fighting roster	Thunder-Rockin' Out	HSL-43 Det.7		
SH-60B	Red furry monster	FFG-8 USS McInerney?	HSL-44	No. 36	
SH-60B	Skeleton Grim Reaper	World Tour	HSL-44	HP 453	162347
SH-60B	South Park cartoon characters	Hell Raisers CG-61	HSL-44 Det. 4	HP 4_	
SH-60B	A desert nomad	The Nomads	HSL-45	TZ 47	165707
SH-60B	A skull	Kartell Khurshers-Det. III-FLG-41	HSL-45	TZ 57	164178
SH-60B	A skull and bandana	Rowdy Rogues	HSL-46, Det 3	TT 461	
SH-60B	A bulldog smoking a cigar	HSL-46 Det. 8 Bulldogs USS Winston S. Churchill DDG-81	HSL-46, Det 8		
SH-60B	A hawk and flag on tail	Saber Hawks	HSL-47	TY 65	162997
SH-60B	A tan hawk speed bird on tail		HSL-47	NE 65	
SH-60B	Homer Simpson	HSL-47 Det. 6 Do IT The _____	HSL-47	TY 71	
SH-60B	A large snake draped around the tail	Viper Maintenance	HSL-48	HR 500	
SH-60B	Cobra snake	Det. One	HSL-48	HR 510	163905
SH-60B	Wally Gator character	??	HSL-48	HR 500	
SH-60B	Cobra snake	There Can Be Only One	HSL-48, Det. 1	HR?	
SH-60B	A OK symbol hand w/ ship in it	Jake	HSL-49	No. 101	
SH-60B	A rising sun cartoon w/ shades	??	HSL-49	TX 102	
SH-60B	Dick Tracy character	Det. 3 Dons	HSL-49	TX 106	162990
SH-60B	Large scorpion on tail	None	HSL-49	TX 100	
SH-60B	A skull and rotor	Trans World Rotors / Warheads on Foreheads	HSL-49 CTF-58	TX	
SH-60B	A winged skull	The Warriors	HSL-49, USS Thach	TX 100	
SH-60B	A bull with horns	None	HSL-51	TA 712	164815
SH-60B	A large number Four and Fork	Det. 4	HSL-51	TA 714	164817
SH-60B	A red skull inside a cog	HSL-51 Det. 1	HSL-51	TA 705	162120

Type	Artwork	Name	Squadron	Modex	BuNo.
SH-60B	A Samurai warrior and Mt. Fuji on tail	Warlord 700	HSL-51	TA 700	161564
SH-60B	A Spade on a blue field	None	HSL-51	TA 704	162341
SH-60B	A three headed dragoon on a Japanese rising sun flag	Names of Members on Det.1	HSL-51	TA 707	162338?
SH-60B	A yellow cartoon cat w/ a Australian flag	Lucky Son Warlords	HSL-51	TA 706	
SH-60B	Characters of unit Maintainers dancing around the H-60	Maintainers ??	HSL-51	TA 711	164814
SH-60B	Demon dragon	Det. 5, HSL-51, DDG-85	HSL-51	TA 714	164817
SH-60B	Japanese Warlord, Musashi	Warlord 02	HSL-51	TA 02	161564
SH-60B	Japanese Warlord, Musashi		HSL-51	TA 02	162112
SH-60B	Mt. Fuji and Rising Sun banner and samurai on tail	None	HSL-51	TA 700	161564
SH-60B	Samurai eyes on red sono door	Det. 3 #%#!	HSL-51	TA 710	163240
SH-60B	Smiley face on bottom radome	Always There, Always	HSL-51	TA 716	164857
SH-60B	Transformer logo on sono panel	2008 Det. Six	HSL-51	TA 703	161555
SH-60B	Transformer logo on sono panel	2008 Det. Six	HSL-51	TA 707	162985
SH-60B	US, Australian and Japanese flags w/ green lion	None	HSL-51	TA 703	161555
SH-60B	US, Australian and Japanese flags w/ green lion	None	HSL-51	TA 711	164814
SH-60B	An Hindu deity sitting on a lily pad	International Fleet Review 2001-USS Cowpens	HSL-51 Det. 2	No. 04	
SH-60B	Large tiger paw w/ claws tearing through fuselage	None	HSL-60, CHWR	NW 600	161556
SH-60B	A winged skull	?		No. 106	
SH-60F	CONA markings MOH Lt Clyde Lassen VN War		HS-10	RA 17	164073
SH-60F	Anime Dragoon	None	HS-11	AB 10	
SH-60F	Medieval armor and dragon anniversary marks.	Dragonslaters-50 Years of Excellence	HS-11	AB 611	
SH-60F	A cat clawing his way out of the drop tank	None	HS-15	AE 610	
SH-60F	A knight w/ 9/11 breast plate and sword	None	HS-4	NK 610	164098
SH-60F	Teenage Mutant Turtle	None	HS-4	NK 610	164098
SH-60F	An eagle and Indian on tail and an Indian Chief on the fwd J-box cover	Crazy Horse	HS-6	NH 610	
SH-60F	Large Indian head	None	HS-6	NH 610	163287
SH-60F	OIF door art	None	HS-7	AC 610	164610
SH-60F	A map of Iraq, a helo, and a bulldog	Dusty Dogs 7-Operations Iraqi Freedom	HS-7, CVN-75		
SH-60F	Giant mace w/ eight ball on tail	World Famous Eightballers	HS-8	NG 610	164077
SH-60F	A black Samaria w/ sword on nose	Shogun	HS-8, CVN-70, CAG-9	NG 610	
SH-60F	Neptune character and palm tree on tail	None	HSC-25	No. 00	
SP-2E	Caricatures of the crew and Alfred E. Newman/ a whale on the nose gear door	2 %	VP-8	LC 11	128345
SP-2H	Comic caricature	Jolly Green Giants	VP-18	LG 3 or13	145907?
SP-2H	A pin-up on the glass of the bow observer's nose turret	None	VP-2	YC 12	
SP-2H	A scenic view and a dog	Thanks Fido?	VP-2	YC 11	135606
SP-2H	Playboy bunny	None	VP-2	YC-12	147953
SP-2H	Polar bear	Polar Bear Express	VP-24	LR 5	135588
SP-2H	A coyote	Coyote Patrol	VP-56	LQ 7	148344
SP-2H	Cartoon Viking	None	VP-56	LQ 5	148344
SP-2H	Snoopy	None	VP-56	LQ 7	147950
SP-2H	Gator	Phillips 69'ers	VP-7	LB 11	147962
SP-2H	NAVAIR 50th Anniversary	None			148350
SP-5A	Pin-up and mission marks	1,000th P2v Neptune	VP-48	SF 9	
SP-5A	Vulture	Valliant Vultures	VP-48	SF 2	126499
SP-5A	Daisy Mae	None	VP-49	LP 5	127713
SP-5B	Big red razorback hog and nine little hogs	Crew names under each hog	VP-40	QE 8	140142
SP-5B	Ace of spades on tail gun	None	VP-45		

Type	Artwork	Name	Squadron	Modex	BuNo.
SP-5B	Road Runner & mission marks	*The Road Runner*	VP-48	SF 2	147926
T-1A	Two buzzards	*Patience-My Foot I'm Going to Kill Something*	NAS WASHINGTON DC	6A 4214	144214
T-28B	An Old Crow cartoon	None	VT-2	2G 777	137707
T-2C	75th Anniversary Scheme	*City of Kingsville*	VT-23		158602
T-2C	cartoon of T-2C Buckeye in a spin on the nose	None			159713?
T-34C	Blue Angel markings	*Lil' Cyndi*	SFWSL	AD 1	160640
T-45C	A hound dog on the tail	*Salty Dog*	VT-7, TW-1	A 182	165624
T-45C	A hound dog on the tail	*Salty Dog*	VT-9	A 182	165624
TA-4J	75th Anniversary	*Golden Eagles*	VT-22	No.__ 275	158085
TA-4J	Tasmanian devil	*Taz*	VT-7	A 701	
TBF-1C	Betty Boop cartoon	*Blopsy*	VC-76	No. 83	73495
TBM-1C	Five pin-ups	None	VC-10	B 1	
TBM-3	A Confederate soldier	*Rebel*	VMTB-143, USS *Gilbert Islands*	P 83	
TBM-3	A goose	*The Loose Goose*	VMTB-143, USS *Gilbert Islands*	P 81	
TBM-3	A praying dog	*Amen*	VMTB-143, USS *Gilbert Islands*	P 78	68952
TBM-3	A praying dog	*Amen*	VMTB-143, USS *Gilbert Islands*	P 78	23316
TBM-3	Alligator drawing	*Florida Gator*	VMTB-143, USS *Gilbert Islands*	P 85	
TBM-3	Oily mess	*Turmoil*	VMTB-143, USS *Gilbert Islands*	P 86	
TBM-3	Pin-up	*Doris Mae*	VMTB-143, USS *Gilbert Islands*	P 77 or 87?	
TBM-3	Pin-up	None	VMTB-143, USS *Gilbert Islands*	P 79	
TBM-3	Turkey on bomb	*Fertile Myrtle*	VMTB-143, USS *Gilbert Islands*	P 84	69058
TBM-3	Stork carrying baby	*Expectant*	VMTB-232		
TBM-3	Portrait of a lady	None	VMTB-233, USS *Kitkun Bay*	No. 60	
TBM-3	Hobo cartoon	None	VT-17 Lt Cdr Frank Whitaker		
TBM-3	A pair of dice	None	VT-6, CV-19 USS *Hancock*	U 4	
TBM-3	A ticket	*Round Trip*	VT-80	No. 107	
TBM-3	Belly dancer	*Bayou Belle*	VT-83	F 407	23549
TBM-3	Girl' n glass	*Satan's Helper*	VT-83	F 417	23470
TBM-3	Vulture in tux	*Cultured Vulture II*	VT-83	F 413	
TBM-3	Wolf cartoon	None	VT-83	F 413	
TBM-3E	Pin-up and mission marks	None	VT-34	C 27	
TS-2F	A ruptured duck on No. 2 engine	None	CVA-/	752	136752
UC-45J	A green dragon	None	NARTU, NAS Jax, FL	6F 9230	39230
UH-1B	Snoopy and Pattie cartoon on gun mount	*Peppermint Pattie*	HAL-3		
UH-1B	Yellow Smiley Face on gun mount	None	HAL-3	No. 314	65-09476
UH-1E	Two vultures sitting on a branch	*Patience Hell*	HML-167 or HML-367	No. 16	
UH-1E	Cobra snake	None	HMLA-367	VT 21	
UH-1N	A Huey, a Transformer, and a pin-up	*Under Estimated*	HMLA-167, 22nd MEU (SOC) LHA-3 *Kearsarge*	EM 40	160438
UH-1N	Red demons, fire, and pin-up	None	HMLA-167, 22nd MEU (SOC) LHA-3 *Kearsarge*		
UH-1N	Twin towers flag and girl silhouette	None	HMLA-267		
UH-1N	Anime girl	*Chicks Dig Hueys*	HMLA-269	HF 37	160444
UH-1N	Fat female in bra	*Real #1 Virgin*	HMLA-269	HF 39	159189
UH-1N	Miss Liberty and dogs	*Cry Havoc and let slip the Dogs of War*	HMLA-269	HF 39	
UH-1N	Pin-up in a bikini top and flight suit	*The Real H-1 Upgrade*	HMLA-269	HF 39	159189
UH-1N	Twin pin-ups standing back to back	None	HMLA-269	HF 41	
UH-1N	Pin-up in Stars and Stripes bikinis w/ M-16	*Bad Religion*	HMLA-269, USS *Saipan* LPA-2		
UH-1N	Pin-up in Stars and Stripes bikinis w/GAU-16	*The New Huey Upgrade*	HMLA-269, USS *Saipan* LPA-2		
UH-1N	Four gunfighters fr. The old west w/ rattle snakes and a skull	None	HMLA-369		

Type	Artwork	Name	Squadron	Modex	BuNo.
UH-1N	Red background w/ skull and cross bones	Edge's Revenge	HMLA-775	WR 07	158270
UH-1N	Snoopy sitting on his dog house	CONA Markings Vietnam USMC Major Pless MoH Aircraft	HMLAT-303	WB 15	160454
UH-1N	Artwork on hood	None	HMM-162	YS 40	149876
UH-1N	Pin-up and dragon	None	HMM-162		
UH-1N	A large green dragon on the a/c nose	None	HMM-162?		
UH-1N	Betty Boop cartoon	Always Ready-Always Willing	HMM-162?		
UH-1N	Leather and Lace pin-up w/ a stack of skulls	None	HMM-162?		
UH-1N	Pin-up on nose	None	HMM-261	EM 40	160438
UH-1N	A Storm Trooper	?	HMM-261, 22th MEU, Al Asad	EM 40	
UH-1N	Skull and crossed bones	None	HMM-261, 22th MEU, Al Asad	EM 41	
UH-1N	Horse on motorcycle	None	HMM-263	EG?	158266
UH-1N	A pin-up w/ 50 Cal MG	?	HMM-263, 22nd MEU	EG 40	159685
UH-1N	Harley Quinn character	Lady Luck	HMM-263, 22nd MEU	EG 41	158263
UH-1N	Angel w/ 50 Cal. MG	None	HMM-263, 24th MEU	EG 21	160459
UH-1N	Artwork on hood w/ white ball	None	HMM-264	EH 41	
UH-1N	Pin-up	UH-1N Escort Service	HMM-264	EH 12	159192
UH-1N	A flaming winged helo w/ POW and MIA flags	POW MIA Freedom Ghost Ship	USMC	No. 6167	
UH-1N	Flaming skull	Soul Chaser	USMC		
UH-1N	Pin-up w/ halo	None	USMC		158230
UH-1N	A pin-up warrior on hood	None	USMC OIF, Iraq		
UH-1N	A pin-up in combat boots and a big bottom	Big Buns	HU-2	No. 09?	
UH-25B	Penguin	None	HU-2	UR 56	128519
UH-25C	Roadrunner	None	HU-2	HU 43	149088
UH-2A	Little Annie Fannie jumping rope?	None	HC-5	TD 2	149021
UH-2A	Vargas Girl on forward engine pod	None	HC-7, Det. 104		
UH-2A	Witch on broomstick	Capt'n Hardy's Broomstick-Trick or Treat	HU-1, Det. N, USS Hornet	UP 7	149782
UH-2A	Bull on nose	??			
UH-2C	Mission marks (six plane guard res)	None	HC-1	UH 105	149758
UH-2C	Critter in top hat on door	Shaka	HSL-31	TD 14	149031
UH-34	Snoopy flying a commode w/ rotor on top and prop on the back	Hell Beats Walking	H&MS-36	No. 3	
UH-34D	Andy Capp comic character	None	HC-7		
UH-34D	A tiger	Tiger in the Tank	HMM-361		
UH-34D	? character	?	HMM-362	YL 41	147150
UH-34D	A crow and a flying coffin	Crowin' Coffin	HMM-362	YL 22	
UH-34D	A white rabbit	HMM-363-IWO Easter Rabbit	HMM-363		
UH-34D	Red apple w/ worm	None	HMM-363		
UH-34D	Alfred E. Newman and Penguin	What 'me Winter Over?	VX-6	JD 4	148122
UH-34E	A Viking with sword	War Lord	HMM-362	YL 5	
UH-34E	Blue eyed angel	My Innocent Angel	HMM-362	YL 14	
UH-34E	Santa	None	HMM-362	YL 1	
UH-34E	Buzzard	Trans-Paddie Airways	HMM-362, MAG-16, 1969	YL 18	
UH-34E	Snuffy Smith	Snuffy	MAG-16, 1969		
UH-34E	Penguin emblem	None	VXE-6	JD 26	144655
UH-34E	Penguin	King Pin II	VXE-6	XD 25	144657
UH-46A	Art work on forward dog house	None	HC-3	SA 05	151956
UP-3A	Shoe' character	Loon	VXN-8		150528
UP-3A	Skating fox	The Arctic Fox	VXN-8		151384
UP-3A	Snoopy	World Traveler	VXN-8	JB	150528

Type	Artwork	Name	Squadron	Modex	BuNo.
UP-3A	Tasmanian devil	Tasmanian Devil	VXN-8		150527
US-2B	Snoopy	Fightertown USA	NAS Miramar		136546
US-3A	Cat on COD pod	You Pod It- We Cod It	VS-24		157998
US-3A	Miss Piggy	Miss Piggy II	VS-37/28/VRC-50	RG 712	157998
US-3A	Miss Piggy	Miss Piggy	VS-37/28/VRC-50	No. 712	157998
VP-3A	Valkyrja and stars	Valkyrja	NAS Keflavik		150495
VP-3A	Disney cat w/wings	Catbird	VR-Det Sigonella		150496
VP-3A	Disney cat w/wings	Catbird	VR-Det Sigonella		150515
WC-121N	Dragon	Draggin' Lady	VW-1	TE 2	145934
WC-121N	Flo cartoon on nose by door	None	VW-1	TE 5	145931
WC-121N	Outhouse and 'Flo'	City of Cavite	VW-1	TE 5	145931
WC-121N	Skunk	We're So Sweet Nobody Loves Us	VW-1	TE 8	145938
WC-121N	Snoopy	WWI Ace	VW-1	TE 1	145935
WC-121N	Roadrunner	Beep! Beep! Road Runner	VW-1	TE 7	145928
WC-121N	Hurricane symbol	Blanche	VW-4	MH 6	137896
WC-121N	Hurricane symbol	Camille	VW-4	MH 3	141323
WC-121N	Hurricane symbol	Camille	VW-4	MH 4	137894
WC-121N	Hurricane symbol	Dora	VW-4	MH 1	143198
WC-121N	Hurricane symbol	Faith	VW-4	MH 8	145929
WC-121N	Hurricane symbol	Ivea	VW-4	MH 1	143198
WP-3A	Hurricane symbol	Agnes	VW-4	MH 2	149675
WP-3A	Hurricane symbol	Brenda	VW-4	MH 3	149676
WP-3A	Hurricane symbol	Edith	VW-4	MH 1	149674
ZPN-1IO	Pin-up on a mine	Minnie the Miner	ZP-14	K 110	

APPENDIX B

NOSE ART LISTED ALPHABETICALLY BY NAME

Name	Type	Squadron	Modex	BuNo.
1 o'clock Jump	F6F-5N	VMF(N)-542	F(N) 78	
1,000th P2V Neptune	SP-2H			148350
1000th Are We Proud	PV-1			
114 Years of CPO Leadership	F-18E	VFA-143, CVW-7, USS Eisenhower	AG 114	166599
114 Years of CPO Leadership	F-18F	VFA-211	AB 114	165807
18th NOLO	F6F-5K	VU-3K		
1945-2005 Torpedo Bomber Squadron Two One	S-3B	VS-21	NF 710	160604
2 %	SP-2E	VP-8	LC 11	128345
2008 Det. Six	SH-60B	HSL-51	TA 703	161555
2008 Det. Six	SH-60B	HSL-51	TA 707	162985
265 Prepare for Glory	CH-46E	HMM-265	EP 00	
265 Prepare for Glory	CH-46E	HMM-265, LHD-2, USS Essex	EP 10	
4 Sale ---- Cheap	EC-130Q	VQ-3		156173
400th Orion	P-3C	VP-5	LA	158926
463rd BOMBERS	CH-53D	HMH-463	YH 12	
500th P-3 Orion	P-3C	VP-26	LK 1	161011
65 Years of Grey Knight Excellence	P-3C	VP-46	No. 315	
9-11, NYPD, FDNY, FLIGHT 93	EA-6B	VAQ-209	AF 500	158029
Abroad for Action	PB4Y-2	VPB-121	Y 450	59450
Absolute Justice	F-18E	VFA-115, CVW-14, USS Lincoln	NK 203	165784
Accentuate the Positive	PB4Y-2	VPB-108	No. 441	59441
ACM Det. Key West	F-4S	VMFA-321	MG 04	157261
ACM Det. Key West	F-4S	VMFA-321	MG 06	156980
ACM Det. Key West	F-4S	VMFA-321	MG 06	155580
Affirmed 1978	F-18A	VFA-97	NH 210	163106
After Your Ass	F4U-4	VF-871	B 305	
Aged to Perfection	CH-46E	HMM-162	YS 05	
Agnes	WP-3A	VW-4	MH 2	149675
Air Mail	A-1H	VA-152	NL 208	137502
Air Savannah	CH-46D	HC-6		153699
Aircraft 10	CH-46E	HMM-165	YW 10	
Aladdin	S-3B	VS-32	AB 700	159419
All In	MH-60S	HSC-23	WC 40	166298
Aluminum Falcon	PBY-5A	VP-61	No. 59	48426
Always Ready–Always Willing	UH-1N	HMM-162?		
Always There, Always	SH-60B	HSL-51	TA 716	164857
Amber MXMXMXM	EP-3E	VQ-1	RP 33	
Amber	CH-53E	HMH-361	YN 21	
Amen	P2V-2N	VXE-6	XD 4	122466
Amen	TBM-3	VMTB-143, USS Gilbert Islands	P 78	68952
Amen	TBM-3	VMTB-143, USS Gilbert Islands	P 78	23316
American Dream	CH-46E	HMM-263	EG?	
Amoozin' but Confoozin'	PBY-5A	NAS JAX	No. 43	34043?
Anchors Away	PB4Y-1	VPB-116		90483
Anchors Away	PB4Y-2	VPB-108		59483
Angel in Di-Skies	PB4Y-2	NAS Kaneohe Bay		
Angel	AV-8B	VMA-331	VL	162722
Angel	HO3S-1	HU-1	UP 25	
Annie-Mo	F4U-5NL	VC-3	NP 21	124453
Annie-Mo	F4U-5NL	VC-3	NP 21	124???
AO-TE'A-ROA	LC-130R	VXE-6	JD 17	155917
Arab Airlines-See Japan	A-1D	VA-115, CVA-33 Kearsarge	A 502	
Arctic Basin II	P-2H	Weapons Test, NAS Pax. River		
Available Jones	PB4Y-1	VB-109/VD-1/VD-4	No. 49	32149
Avery's Aviator	F-18C	VFA-83	AA 302	165215

Name	Type	Squadron	Modex	BuNo.
Awk	F9F-2P	VC-61	PP 12	
B_____ Clover	EC-54U	USCG	9147	9147
Babe	F4U-4	VF-74, USS *Bon Homme Richard* CVA-31	L 408	
Baby Bing	PV-1	VPB-136		
Baby III	SB2C	VMB-? Banshees	No. 702	
Baby Leonora	F4U-4	VF-783	D 201	81849
Baby Shirley	PB4Y-1	VPB-115	No. 50	32150
Baby	A-1J	VA-145	AK 501	142033
Bachelor's Delight	PB4Y-2	VPB-109	V 521	59521
Bad Iron	CH-46D	HC-11 Det. 7	VR 74	152553
Bad Karma	CH-53E	SFOR-Opertn. Phoenix Gauntlet, Congo	No. 41	
Bad Kitty	CH-46E	HMM-268		
Bad Religion	UH-1N	HMLA-269, USS *Saipan* LPA-2		
Bad to the Bone	CH-46E	HMM-268	YQ	
Bad to the Boneyard	SH-2F	HSL-32 Det. 3		
Bakersfield Sheriff	F4U-4	VF-871	B 303	
Baldy	F4F/FM-2	VC-7		
Baldy	FM-2	VC-27		
Baldy and Tortilla Flat	PB4Y-2	VPB-106 and VPB-197	X 398	59398
Baldy, Tortilla Flat	PB4Y-2	VPB-106 and VPB-197	X 398	59398
Baldy's Baby	F4U-4	VF-871	B 301	97230
Bales' Babe	PB4Y-1	VPB-106 and VPB-115	No. 243	32243
Baltops 96	SH-2G	HSL-94		
Bamboo Clipper	EC-121K	VW-11	MJ 293	141293
Barbara Ann II	OY-1	USMC *Saipan*		60507
Bare Riders	SH-2G	HSL-37 Det. 6	TH?55?	
Bart of Arabia	RA-3B	VQ-2	JQ 00G	
Bartman- 'Eat my shorts Saddam'	RQ-2B	2nd RPV Platoon,		
Battle Hog	CH-46E	HMM-265	EP 03	154020
Bayou Belle	TBM-3	VT-83	F 407	23549
Beachcomber (The Lone Wolf) Murray	PB4Y-1	VPB-102	No. ___3	38943
Beep! Beep! Road Runner	WC-121N	VW-1	TE 7	145928
Belle Bottom	PBM-5	VP-731	SF 2	85146
Belle of the Pacific	PBM-5		E 8	
Berlin Express	PB4Y-1	VPB-103	B-13 N	32014
Betty / Pride of McMurdo	LC-130R	VXE-6	XD 07	148319
Beware Det. 7	SH-2D	HSL-33		
Big Buns	UH-1N		No. 09?	
Big Dick too hot to Handle	PB4Y-1	VPB-111	No. 747	38747
Big Dick	F9F-5	VF-72	L 211	
Big Dolly Hauler	CH-46E	HMM-365	YM 15	
Big Easy	CH-46E	HMM-163, 13th MEU	YP 15	157702
Big Hog MK. II CAG	F4U-4	CAG-74	CAG	
Big Hog	F4U-1A	VF-17	No. 1	17649
Big Johnson 50. Cal.-Might Short E...T...	CH-53D	HMH-363	YZ	
Big Snow Propaganda	PB4Y-2	VPB-116		
Big Willy Airlines	CH-46E	HMM-365, 26th MEU (SO) Afghanistan	YM 15	
Bingo King	A-4F	VA-164	NP 402	155022
Black Cats	CH-53E	HC-1	No. 743	
Black Death / Millie Lou	F6F-5N	VMF(N)-542	F(N) 76	78669
Black Eagle	PBY-5A	VPB-71	E 68	46517
Black Jack You Lose	CH-53	USMC		
Black Mac	A-4E	VMA-331	VL 6	150016
Blackjack	F-8H	VFP-63	PP 101	147049
Blanche	WC-121N	VW-4	MH 6	137896
Blind Bomber	PB4Y-2	VPB-109	No. 514	59514
Blithe Spirit	R5C-1			
Blonde Blitz	PV-1		No. 5	
Blondie	F-4B	VMF-542		
Blopsy	TBF-1C	VC-76	No. 83	73495
BLPFSTK	F9F-5	VF-71	L 106	127180
Blue Belle	PB4Y-1P	VD-5		
Blue Deuce	MH-60S	HSC-2	HU 02	166294
Blue Diamond	PB4Y-2	VPB-106	X 396	59396
Blue Ghost	C-1A	CVT-16 USS *Lexington*	No. 754	136754
Blue Nose 88	F-14A	VF-11	AE 110	161869
Blue Racer	OS2U-3			
Blues in the Night	F6F-5N	VF-83	No. 502	
Bobbie D	F4U-4	VF-713	H 211	

Name	Type	Squadron	Modex	BuNo.
Bob's Job	F4U-4	VF-871	B 308	
Boeing Racing	CH-46E	HMM-162	YS 00	157713
Bogey Baiters	AD-5W		No. 783	
Boggs Bandits Beatin' The Odds	SH-2F	HSL-34 Det. 7		
Bombcat No Escort Required	F-14A	VF-41	AJ 101	162689
Bombs Away	CH-46E	HMM-163	YP 07	153377
Bon Lee	F4U-4	VF-884	A 414	81530
Bond Girl	AH-1W	HMLA-269, USS *Saipan* LPA-2	HF 07	
Bonesaw	S-3B	VS-30	AA 700	159390
Boo??	CH-46E	HMM-163	YP 01	157655
Boomerang	PBM-3D	VPB-16		48198
Bosom Buddy	PB4Y-1P	VD-1	No. 28	
Boss Burton's Nitemare	PB4Y-1	VPB-102	No. 843	38843
Bouncin' Betty	PB4Y-2	NARU New York	R	66311
Bouncing Bertha	C-117D	NAVSP Danang,		
Bounty Hunter	CH-46E	HMM-165	YW 12	
Brenda	WP-3A	VW-4	MH 3	149676
Brock Landers	CH-53E	HMM-263 24th MEU	No. 40	161989
Brooklyn Bombshell	PB4Y-1	FAW-7	B-8	
Brooklyn Butcher	FG-1D	VMF-512, USS *Gilbert Islands*	No. 21	
Brown Bagger's Retreat	PB4Y-1	VPB-107	No. 7	65385
Buccaneer Bunny	PB4Y-2	VPB-121	Y 478	59478
Bud Man	F-4J	VF-31	AC 103	155513
Bull of the Woods (Bulldog)	PB4Y-1		No. 9?	31987
Bulldog?	F-8J	VF-24	NP 201	150311
Bulldogs Det. IV	SH-2F	HSL-32		
Bullet Hero / The Bullet	CH-46E	HMM-264		157656
Bush Shaker	PB4Y-1	VPB-116		38844
Busted Stuff	F-18C	VFA-83, CVW-7, USS *Eisenhower*	AG 303	164244
Caser Augustus	F-18C	VFA-15	AJ 305	164661
Calamity Jane	PB4Y-1	VD-3	No. 96	
Call House Madam	PB4Y-1	VPB-116	No. __2	90482
Camel Smoker	F-14A	VF-24	No. 210	163409
Camille	WC-121N	VW-4	MH 3	141323
Camille	WC-121N	VW-4	MH 4	137894
Capt. Elrod Hammering Hank	AV-8B	VMA-211, USS *Tarawa*	CF 50	
Capt'n Hardy's Broomstick-Trick or Treat	UH-2A	HU-1, Det. N, USS *Hornet*	UP 7	149782
Carol Ann 3	PBM-5		J 12 Y	
Caroline	CH-46E	HMM-263	EG 04	
Cat-Al's Destruction	CH-46E	HMM-265	EP 06	
Cat Snatch Fever	F-14A	VF-84	AJ 201	162692
Catbird	VP-3A	VR-Det Sigonella		150496
Catbird	VP-3A	VR-Det Sigonella		150515
Coyote Patrol	SP-2H	VP-56	LQ 7	148344
Cecil Doyle	F-18D	VMFA(AW)-121	VK 04	165867
Charles the 1st?	C-1A	CVA-43 USS *Midway*	No. 039	146039
Charlie's Block Heads	CH-53D	HMH-462		
Cheers	A-6A	VA-175	NE 503	156997
Chicken Hawk	CH-46E	HMM-262	ET 12	156437
Chicken Man	A-4E	VMA-211	CF 3	149983
Chick's Chick	PB4Y-1	VPB-106 and VPB-115		32238
Chick's Dig Hueys	UH-1N	HMLA-269	HF 37	160444
Chief Wahoo	F6F-5N	VMF(N)-542	F(N) 84	
Chief	F-18C	VFA-83	AA 301	165212
Chill Out	CH-46E	HMM-268	YQ 12	156446
Chilly Willy 24	MV-22	HX-21, NAS Pax River, MD		165383
Chilly / Spirit of Willy Field	LC-130R	VXE-6	XD 04	159130
Chippy Ho! II	F-18C	VFA-195	NF 400	163703
Chippy Ho!	F-18C	VFA-195	NF 400	163758
Chippy Ho	F-18C	VFA-195	NF 400	164905
Chloe	PV-1	VMF(N)-531	No. 53	33253
Choppers Inc.	CH-53E	HMH-361	YN 69	
Chow Hound	FG-1D	VFB-83		
Christine	AH-1W	HMLA-269, 24th MEU, LHA 4 *Nassau*	EG 34	
Chunky Chelsea	CH-46E	HMM-261	EM 07	154037
City of Auckland	LP-2H	VXE-6	JD 1	140437
City of Cambridge	T-2C	VT-23	3H 340	158882
City of Cavite	WC-121N	VW-1	TE 5	145931
City of Kingsville	T-2C	VT-23		158602
City of Oneida	T-2C	VT-23	B 319	158606

Name	Type	Squadron	Modex	BuNo.
Classic	E-2C	VAW-124	AJ 601	161552
Climb Aboard _____	CH-46E	HMM-261, 22nd MEU (SOC)	EM 11	
Climaboard	PB4Y-1	VB-109/122/123	No. 40	32140
Club Bohica	HH-46A	HC-5	RB 10	150962
Comair Wolfpac II	PB4Y-1	VPB-101/FAW-1O loan VPB-104	No. 276	32276
Come and Get It	CH-46E	HMM-365		
Come Get It	PB4Y-1	VB-109	No. 68	32068
Come 'n' Get It	PB4Y-2	VPB-121		59409
CONA markings Vietnam USMC Major Pless MoH aircraft	UH-1N	HMLAT-303	WB 15	158270
Coors	EP-3A	VQ-2	No. 25	
Coral Princess / Target for Tonight	PV-1	VMF(N)-531	No. 51	33251?
Cornfed	CH-53D	USMC		
Cover Girl	PB4Y-1	VB-105	B-14	38948
Cover Girl	PB4Y-1	VB-105	B-14	38948
Cover Girl	PB4Y-1P	VD-4	No. ?	321xx
Cover Girl	PB4Y-2	VPB-116	No. 760	59760
Crazy Horse	SH-60F	HS-6	NH 610	
Crew names under each hog	SP-5B	VP-40	QE 8	
Crickets	A-1H	VA-115 USS *Hancock*	NF 504	137612
Crosby Can Wait, I Was Drafted	PV-1			
Crowin' Coffin	UH-34D	HMM-362	YL 22	
Cry Havoc and let slip the Dogs of War	UH-1N	HMLA-269	HF 39	
Cry Havoc and let slip the Phrogs of War	CH-46E	HMM-261	EM 01	153368
C-------The------?	CH-46E	HMM-162?	YS 00?	153402
Cujo	A-6E	VA-155	NE 400	152916
Cultured Vulture II	TBM-3	VT-83	F 413	
Cutty Sark	EC-121K	VW-11 1963	MJ 939	145939
Cutty Sark	EC-121P	VW-11 1965	MJ 937	145937
Daisy June	F4U-1D	VMF-511	I m 82	
Daisy Mae	BD-2	VJ-2 NAS Pax. River	2-X-14	7039
Damn you Jim J	CH-46A	HMM-262		
Dangerous Dan / Eight Ball	F4U-1	VMF-213	No. 8	
Dangerous Lady	PB4Y-1	VD-5 OR VPB-111?	No. 58?	
Daphne C.	F4U-1	VMF-213	No. 13	
Daphne C.	F4U-1	VMF-213	No. 15	No. 03829
Daphne C.	F4U-1	VMF-213	No. 7	No. 02350
Daredevils	SH-2G	HSL-35 Det. 7		162576
Daring Dame	PB4Y-1	VPB-117	No. 740	38740
Dawdling Dromedary	SH-3H	NAS Pax River		152104
Dazy May?	PB4Y-1	VPB-116	No. 734	38734
Dead Bone	CH-46D	HMM-165		
Dealer	F-18D	VMFA(AW)-332	EA 00	164967
Death Angell II	CH-46E	HMM-261	EM 05	155307
Death Dealer	F-18D	VMFA(AW)-225	CE 01	
Death 'n' Destruction	F6F-5	VF-83	No. 115	72534
Deep Throat II	KA-3B	VAQ-130	TR 70	138953
Defabe	F4U-1	VMF-213	No. 11	
Defending Freedom to the very Last Day	S-3B	VS-30	AA 700	
Demon Child	CH-46E	USMC		
Demon Dilbert	PB4Y-1	VPB-102	No. 64	
Desert Duck	SH-3H	HC-2, USS *Nimitz*	AJ	
Desert Fox	F-14B	VF-32	AC 100	162916
Desert Rats	SH-2F	HSL-34 Det. 5		
Desperado	A-6E	VA-155	NE 410	152916
Det. ???	SH-2F	HSL-37 USS *Rathburne*	TH 57	149780
Det. 3 #%#!	SH-60B	HSL-51	TA 710	163240
Det. 3'S MIA Tai Express–Aloha	SH-2G	HSL-84 Det. 3		
Det. 4	SH-60B	HSL-51	TA 714	164817
Det. 5 Wolfpack	SH-2F	HSL-34	HS	149024
Det. 5, USA	HH-46A	HC-11 Det 5	VR 73	150954
Det. One	SH-60B	HSL-48	HR 510	163905
Det. Seven	SH-2F	HSL-32, Det. 7	HV 135	151321
Der. 3 DONS	SH-60B	HSL-49	TX 106	162990
Der. One	SH-2F	HSL-74 Det. 1	NW 44	149__72
Det. 5, HSL-51, DDG-85	SH-60B	HSL-51	TA 714	164817
Detroit Flying Tigers	CH-46D	HC-6 Det. 3	HW 17	154824
Deuce Deuce	CH-53E	HMM-264	EH 22	
Deuce's Wild!	MH-60S	HC-11 Det. 2	VR 66	166307
Deuce's Wild!	MH-60S	HC-11 Det. 2	VR 62	
Deuce's Wild	AP-2H	VAH-21	SL 2	148353

Name	Type	Squadron	Modex	BuNo.
Devil Dog	PB4Y-1P	VD-3	No. 5	
Dick's Dixie	PB4Y-1P	VD-5 or VPB-115/117	No. 298	65298
Did Someone Say Djibootie & Wish You Were Here 100 Proof	CH-53E	HMM-365, MCAS Jacksonville, NC	YM 22	
Dinah Might	PBM-5	VPB-27	E 2/ E 019	59019
Dinosaur the Last of a Dying Breed	SH-2F	HSL-32 DET. 2		
Dirty Birds	MH-60S	HSC-26	HW 65	165748
Dirty Dawgs	MH-60S	HC-6	HW 63	165772
Dirty Dozen	CH-46E	HMM-265	EP 01?	
Dirty Gerty	PB4Y-1	VPB-117	No. 757	38757
Disaster/Dirty Sanchez	AV-8B	VMA-223	WP 09	165385
Doc's Delight	PB4Y-1	VPB-111 and VPB-117/106	No. 746	38746
Doing it Phroggy Style	CH-46E	HMM-266	ES 15	154009
Doing What we do Best-Carry the Gas	CH-53E	HHM-461	CJ 09	
Donald Yost??	F-18D	VMFA(AW)-121	VK 10	
Donald's Ducks	PB4Y-1	VPB-104	No. 74	32074
Donnie Girl	PBY-5	VP-91		
Don's Hopped Up Model A	F4U-4	VF-871	B 310	
Dons Jail	PB4Y-2	VPB-123		
Don't Mess With Jasmine	CH-53E	HMH-464	EN 11	162001
Dora	WC-121N	VW-4	MH 1	143198
Doris Mae	TBM-3	VMTB-143, USS *Gilbert Islands*	P 77 or 87?	
Dot	F4U-4	VF-791	A 211	81712
Dottie	CH-46E	HMM-263	EG 5	157651
Double Nuts	CH-46A	HMM-265		
Draggin' Lady	WC-121N	VW-1	TE 2	145934
Dragonslaters- 50 Years of Excellence	SH-60F	HS-11	AB 611	
Dusty Dogs 7–Operation Iraqi Freedom	SH-60F	HS-7, CVN-75		
Easy Come Easy Go	CH-46E	HMM-266	ES 07	154020
Easy Day Jeff	F-18F	VFA-103	AG 200	166620
Easy Maid	PB4Y-1	VPB-116	R 923	38923
Easy on the Eyes- Hard on the Soul	AH-1W	HMLA-269, USS *Saipan* LPA-2	HF 06	160815
Easy Way Airlines	C-1A	CVA-43 USS *Midway*	No. 000	146035
Eat My Shorts Al Qaeda	CH-46E	HMM-266	ES 00	153318
Eazy Wind	CH-46E	HMM-263	EG 02	153872
Eazy Wind	CH-46E	HMM-263	EG 12	157667
Eazy Wind	CH-46E	HMM-263	EG 02	153872
EDF Markings	E-2C	VAW-123	AB 601	165293
Edge's Revenge	UH-1N	HMLA-775	WR 07	
Edith	WP-3A	VW-4	MH 1	149674
Eight Ball	PV-1	VMF(N)-531		
Eightballers	CH-60S	HSC-8	NG 0	165765
Eightballers	CH-60S	HSC-8	NG 8	
El Coyote	NC-121K	VXN-8	JB 924	145924
El Coyote	RP-3A	VXN-8		149667
El Coyote	RP-3C	VXN-8	No. 01	153443
El Paisano	EC-121K	FASRON 102/VXN-8		126513
El Paisano	NC-121K	VXN-8		131659
Eloise	C-54D	NAS Argentia	No. 489	56489
Els Notcho	PB4Y-2	VPB-108	Z 460	59460
Endless Summer Tour	MH-60S	HSC-21	VR 74	166319
Eve of Destruction / Deception Lass	EA-6B	VAQ-141	AJ 621	163527
Eevelyn	EP-3E	VQ-2	JQ 26	157320
Expectant	TBM-3	VMTB-232		
Eye's of the Storm	S-3B	VS-24	AJ 701	159743
Faith	WC-121N	VW-4	MH 8	145929
Fanny Hill	A-4C	H&MS-15	YV 81	147681
Fanny Hill	A-4C	VA-22	YV 81	147681
Fanny Hill	A-4C	VA-94	NF 401	147681
Fats	PB4Y-1P	VD-1	No. 07?	
Fear the Reaper	AH-1W			
Fearless Fosdick	PB4Y-1	FAW-7 VB-110	B 5	32233
Feeling Lucky	CH-46E	HMM-264 398th AEG, Liberia USMC	EH 05	157656
Feeling Lucky	CH-53E	HMH-464	EN 05	
Fertile Myrtle	TBM-3	VMTB-143, USS *Gilbert Islands*	P 84	69058
FFG-8 USS McInerney?	SH-60B	HSL-44	No. 36	
Fifi	SH-2F	HSL-32	HV 133	161642
Fightertown USA	US-2B	NAS Miramar		136546
Fighting Crew 10	PBM-5S2	VP-731	SF 3	84713
First in Phantoms	F-4J	VF-74	AA 201	153777
Flak Bait	F4U-1D	VMF-? Ie Shima		

Name	Type	Squadron	Modex	BuNo.
Fleet D-Fender	F-18A+	VFA-87	AJ 400	162886
FLIR Cat	F-14A	VF-103	AA 213	161608
Florida Gator	TBM-3	VMTB-143, USS *Gilbert Islands*	P 85	
Fly 3 Big Bob	F-18F	VFA-103	AG 201	166621
Flying Carpet	PB4Y-1P	VD-4	No. ?	321xx
Flying Circus II	PB4Y-1	VPB-109		32148
Flying Circus	PB4Y-1	VB-109	No. 48	32148
Flying Cloud	EC-121K	VW-11	MJ 292?	141292?
Flying Dragon	HH-2D	NAF Bloomfield, CT	No. 9033	149033
Flying Scud	EC-121K	VW-11	No. 299	141299
Flying Submarine	AQM-3Q			Q15
Flying Tail?	PB4Y-2	VPB-118/106	No. 379	59379
Forsaken	CH-46E	HMM-365	YM ?	
Four 0 Seven	A-7B	VA-72	AB 407	154375
Franken-Prowler	EA-6B	VAQ-141	AJ 500	158542
Franken-Prowler	EA-6B	VAQ-141	AJ 502	158542
Franken-Prowler	EA-6B	VAQ-141, CVN-71 *Roosevelt* 2008	AJ 503	158542
Franken-Tiger	F-5B	VFC-111	AF 117	810834
Freedom	CH-46E	HMM-263	EG 12	157667
Frisco Kid	F4U	VFB-10	No. 29	92132
Frito Bandido 2	AH-1J	HML-367	VT 47?	
Froggingroovin'	CH-46E	HMM-774	MQ 408	158462
From USS JFK to Smithsonian Inst.	EA-1F	VAQ-33	AB 752	132506
Frumious Bandersnatch	F6F-3	VF-15		
Frumious Bandersnatch	PB4Y-1	VPB-104		38774
Gadget	F6F-3	VF-6	No. 19	40467
Gal Friday??	CH 46E	HMM 162, 26th MEU	YS 14	153983
Galant Fox 1930	F-18A	VFA-97	NH 201	163143
Gallopin' Ghost of the Braz. Coast	PB4Y-1	VPB-107	No. 11	32052
Gassman	S-3B	VS-24	AJ 706	160602
Gator	F-8J	VF-24	NP 213	
Gaye	F4U-4	VF-713	H 210	
Gear Down And Locked	PB4Y-2	VPB-124		59519
Get Some	CH-46E	HMM-365, Kandahar, Afg.		
Gewp Gewp	QF-4N	NWST Mugu	No. 143	152970
Gewp Gewp	QF-4N	NWST Mugu	NWAC 40	150465
Gewp Gewp	QF-4N	NWST Mugu	EWAT 140	150465
Ghostriders Det. 7	MH-60S	HSC-28	No. 41	166322
Ginger II	F4U-4	VF-783	D 206	81956
Ginger	SH-2F	HSL-35	TG 41	
Go Get 'em Pal	PV-1	FAW-4 HEDRON, NAS Attu, AK	No. 19	
Going My Way	PV-1	VPB-133		49599
Golden Eagles	TA-4J	VT-22	No. __ 275	158085
Golden Falcons	MH-60S	HSC-12	NE 0	167832
Golden Light	EC-121P	VW-11	MJ 320	141320
Gone Fishin' in the Gulf	CH-46E	HMM-166	YX 09	152574
Gone with the Wind	EC-130Q	VQ-3		156173
Gooney Bird	C-117	NAV Arctic ResLab	N722NR	17156
Gotcha Rattled	PV-1	VPB-128		
Grammaw	EA-6B	VAQ-139, USS *Reagan*	NK 6??	
Grand Slam	F4U-1D	VMF-512, USS *Gilbert Islands*	No. 22	82732
Green Cherries	PB4Y-2	VPB-109	V 502	59502
GT 66, Cap. Martini-'We Will Never Forget'	AH-1Z	HMLA-369		
Gumby	EA-6B		AC 500	
Gus's Gopher	F4U-1	VMF-213	No. 10	
H&MS-17 Non Lifers	CH-34C	H&MS-17		
Hang I Can Beat a Routen Japs MYS	PV-1	VPB-136	X 12	
Hangar Lily	F6F-5	CAG-19	No. 99	
Hard Hearted Hanna	F4U/FG-1D	VMF-512, USS *Gilbert Islands*	FE 62	82842
Harley Quinn	CH-46E	HMM-268	YQ 12	154805
Haulin' ass	CH-53E	HMM-264 398th AEG, Liberia USMC		
Hawk	F6F-3		No. 17	41476
Hawk	F6F-3		No. 17	66237
HC-11 Air Hog Det. 1	CH-46E	HC-11 Det. 5/ USS *Rainer*	VR-65	153319
Head Savage	RA-5C	RVAH-5	No. __ 601	156632
Heart Less	A-6E	VA-36	AJ 536	155600
Heather Jean	CH-46E	HMM-261	EM 03	157660
Heavenly Body	F4U-1A	VMF-321	No. 842	
Heavenly Body	PB4Y-1	VPB-107	No. 1	
Heavy Lifters	CH-53D	HMH-463	YH 12	157168

Name	Type	Squadron	Modex	BuNo.
Heavy Metal Mistress	CH-46	USMC LHA-2 *Saipan*		
Hefty Betty	A-1D	VA-923	D 504	122737
Hell Beats Walking	UH-34	H&MS-36	No. 3	
Hell Raisers CG-61	SH-60B	HSL-44 Det. 4	HP 4__	
Helldorado	PB4Y-1	VB-109	No. 37	32137
Hell's Angel	PB4Y-1	VD-1 and VPB-102	No. 95	31995
Hell's Belle	PB4Y-1	VPB-115	No. 25	32225
Here Comes the Pain	CH-46E	HMM-262	ET 00	153365
Here it comes Charlie	OV-10	VAL-4		
Heroes on a Clamshell	HH-46A	HC-5	RB 06	
Hewego	PV-1	VPB-133 or maybe VPB-150	No. 1	
High Maintenance	CH-53E	HMH-461	CJ 20	163062
High Maintenance	CH-53E	HMH-461	CJ 13	162518
High Noon	F-14A	VF-213	NH 206	
High Rollers	MH-60S	HSC-85	No. 07	165743
Hijack This!!!	F-18E	VFA-115, CVW-14, USS *Lincoln*	NK 212	165791
Hillbilly	CH-46E	HMM-261	EM 06	153402
Hippin Kitten II	PB4Y-2	VPB-108	Z 480	59480
HMM-161 The First- 55Years of Winning the Nations Battles	CH-46E	HMM-161	YR 55	
HMM-363-IWO Easter Rabbit	UH-34D	HMM-363		
Hogan's Goat	PB4Y-2	VPB-109	V 515	59515
Holt's 'Patches'	PB4Y-2	VPB-119	W 413	59413
Homesick Angel	PBY-6A	NAS Kaneohe Bay		46680
Honey Bunny	F9F-2P	VC-61 Det. E	PP 40	
Hoorayy	CH-46E	HMM-162		
Hooters–Melbourne FLA.–More Than a Mouthful!	CH-46E	HMM-774	MQ 407	154000
Hose Monster	KC-130F	VR-22		148895
Hostile Intent	CH-46E	HMM-263, USS *Wasp*	EG 15	156476
Hot Body	PB2Y-3	VP-13	13-27	7127
Hot to Go	F4U-4	VF-871	B 313	
Hotel California & Golden Arches Airlines	CH-46E	HC-3 Det-106	SA 12	154832
HSL-32 Gopfers Det. 1	SH-2G	HSL-32		
HSL-33 1973-1994	SH-2F	HSL-33		
HSL-33 Det. 9	SH-2F	HSL-33		
HSL-34 Det. 8 The Labrats!	SH-2F	HSL-34 Det. 8 USS *Iwo Jima*		
HSL-46 Det. 8 Bulldogs USS Winston S. Churchill DDG-81	SH-60B	HSL-46, Det. 8		
HSL-47 Det. 6 Do It The _____	SH-60B	HSL-47	TY 71	
HSL-51 Det. 1	SH-60B	HSL-51	TA 705	162120
I am Jack's Battlephrog	CH-46E	HMM-163	YP 12	156429
I Gave so Others Could Fly	F-14D	VF-31	NK 105	159610
Ichy??	F4U-1D	VMF-351	FF 61	
I'll Get By	PB4Y-2	VPB-106		
I'll Get By	PV-1	VPB-133		
Impatient Lady	PB4Y-2	Tinian	No. 480	
Impatient Virgin	F4F-4	VMF-112	No. 29	
Impatient Virgin	PB4Y-1	VPB-102	No. 920	38920
Imperial Battle Force	CH-46E	HMM-163	YP 03	153956
In Memory of Flight 11 American Airlines	F-18C	VFA-151	NE 312	164740
In the Mood	CH-53E	HMH-461		
Indian Made	PB4Y-2	VPB-106		59586
International Fleey Review 2001–USS Cowpens	SH-60B	HSL-51 Det. 2	No. 04	
Iraqi Widow Maker	A-6E	VA-155	NE 407	149946
Iron Butterfly	AP-2H	VAH-21	SL 4	145902
Iron Butterfly	CH-53E	HMM-263 24th MEU	No. 43	163060
Island Knights	MH-60S	HSC-25	RB 00	166356
It's from that Sailor I Knitter a Sweater for Last Spring	PV-1	VPB-135		48891
It's My O'Keary_____	CH-53E	HMH-466		
It's Time for you Punishment	AH-1W	HMLA-269	HF 19	152823
Ivea	WC-121N	VW-4	MH 1	143198
Jack's Rabbits	P-2E	VP-661	LV 2	128371
Jackson's Jail	PB4Y-2	VPB-123 and VP(HL) ATU-12	X 510	59510
Jake	SH-60B	HSL-49	No. 101	
Jaws 90	HH-65A	USCG Cutter Boutwell	No. 90	6590
Jeff	Mchi. M-5	263rd Squadriglia NAF Porto Corsini	No. 32	M13021
Jerry Gue	PBY-5A	VP-81		
Jester??	CH-46E	HMM-263	EG 12	157667
Jet Cats	F9F-2B	VMF-311	WL 2	123451
Jimmy Junior	PV-1	VPB-144		34877
Jinny	F4U-1	VMF-215	No. 34	
Jody??	F4U-5N	VC-3	NP 4	

Name	Type	Squadron	Modex	BuNo.
Joe _____	CH-46E	HMM-265	EP 07	
Joe Foss	F-18D	VMFA(AW)-121	VK 01	165413
Joe's Jokers	F-18A	VMFA-115	VE 200	162904?
Jolly Green Giants	SP-2H	VP-18	LG 3 or13	145907?
Joy Rider	PB4Y-2	VPB-106	X 370	59370
Jr	F9F-5	VF-153	H 307	
Jr	F9F-5	VF-153	H 308	125437
Jr	F9F-5	VF-153	H 313	126230
Judy IV?	F4U-4	VF-884	A 406	
June	F4U-4	VF-874	D 401	
Jungle Bunny?	CH-46D	HMM-364	YK 21	
Junya	CH-53D	HMH-363	YZ 15	
Just call me Fifi!	SH-2F	DET-1		
Justice 4 All	F-18E	VFA-115, CVW-14, USS *Lincoln*	NK 214	165792
K? Shitters??	CH-53D	HMH-463	YH	
Kartell Khurshers-Det. III- FLG-41	SH-60B	HSL-45	TZ 57	164178
Kate's Nickel	F-14B	VF-103	AA 103	161435
Kathusaletm	F9F-2	VF-781	D 119	123669
Katy Did	F4U-1A	VMF-422		
Keepin' 'em Sharp	CH-46E	HMM-365	YM 02	
Kenneth Ford	F-18D	VMFA(AW)-121	VK 05	165411
Kentucky Gal	AH-1J	HMA-773	No. 410	157801
Kentucky Wildcat	CH-46E	HMM-265		
Kid Vega	PV-1	Burbank factory		
Killer Whale	KA-3B	VAH-13	NF 031	142659
Killer Whale	EA-3B	VQ-2	No. 004	146454
Killer Whales	EA-3B	VQ-2	JQ 010	144852
Killer Whales	EA-3B	VQ-2	No. 004	146454
King Bee	A-4E	VMA-331	VL 1	151177
King Cobra	P-3C	VP-60	LS 1	
King Pin II	UH-34E	VXE-6	XD 25	144657
King Sol's Royal Jesters	PB4Y-1	HEDRON 2, FAW-5 or VPB-113	No. 4	
Kiwi Special	NC-54R	VXN-8 Project Magnet	JB 396	90396
Kool Kiwi	LC-47H	VXE-6	JD 14	17221
Korea	F4U-4	VF-192	B 208	
L.A. City Limits	F4U-1A	VF-17	No. 7 and No. 34	17932
La Cherrie	PB4Y-2	VPB-108 and VPB-121	No. 489	59489
La Cherrie	PB4Y-2	VPB-123	No. 382	59382
La Navaja	F-18C	VFA-15	AJ 314	164657
Labella	F-4J	VF-31		
Labrador Special	HNS-1	USCG		39045
Lady Ace 01	CH-46E	HMM-165, Al Asad	YW 01	155309
Lady Ace 03	CH-46E	HMM-165	YW 03	154027
Lady Ace 04	CH-46E	HMM-165	YW 04	153346
Lady Ace 07	CH-46E	HMM-165	YW 07	153969
Lady Ace 12	CH-46E	HMM-165, Al Asad	YW 12	156457
Lady Ace 14	CH-46E	HMM-165, Al Asad	YW 14	
Lady Ace Double Buts	CH-46E	HMM-165	YW 00	154023
Lady Ann	PBY-5A	HEDRON FAW-3		
Lady B' Good	OV-10A	VMO-2	UU 01	155409
Lady Carol W.	F4U/FG-1	VMF-214	No. 883	??883
Lady Jessie	A-4E	VA-164	AH 406	152048
Lady Jessie	A-4E	VA-164	AH 407	151180
Lady Jessie	A-4F	VA-164	NP 401	155018
Lady Jessie	A-4F	VA-164	NP 401	155022
Lady Jessie	A-4F	VA-164	NP 401	155029
Lady Luck II	PB4Y-2	VPB-108	No. 446	59446
Lady Luck III	PB4Y-2	VPB-108	Z 459	59459
Lady Luck Old No.7	CH-46E	HMM-264 398th AEG, Liberia USMC	EH 07	
Lady Luck	CH-46E	HMM-165, Al Asad		
Lady Luck	PB4Y-1	VPB-111	No. 892	38892
Lady Luck	UH-1N	HMM-263, 22nd MEU	EG 41	158263
Lady Luck	CH-53E	HMM-264	EH 20	
Lady of Leisure	PB4Y-2	VPB-123		59438
Lady Satan	OY-1	VMO-4, *Iwo Jima*		No. 02766
Lambaster	PB4Y-2	VPB-109	No. 528	59528
Larry's Legion	RF-8G	VFP-62	AJ 913	145645
Lassie	PBJ-1J	VMB-433		35144?
Last Ride 1975-2005	F-14B	VF-143	AG 101	

Name	Type	Squadron	Modex	BuNo.
Last Ride 1975-2005	F-14B	VF-143	AG 102	162921
Last Ride EAD	CH-46E	HMM-264, 26th MEU, USS *Iwo Jima* LHD-7	EH 10	
Lazy May-Z	PB4Y-1	FAW-7	No. 10	
Leann Lena	PBY	VP-53 Green Island		
Lester	F-18C	VFA-15	AJ 306	164258
Let's Roll	CH-53E	HMH-464	EN 21	163063
Life	F9F-2P	VC-61	PP 155	123595
Lil' Abner	BD-2	VMJ- Paris Island		7040
Lil' Cyndi	T-34C	SFWSL	AD 1	160640
Lil' Effie	PB4Y-1	VPB-102?	No. 843	38843
Linda	F7F-3N	VMF(N)-513	WF 24	
Little Bill's Lucky Lady	PB4Y-1	VPB-115	No. 215	32215
Little Butch	JM-1		No. 2	
Little Green Apples	PB4Y-1P	VD-1	No. 67	32067
Little Joe	F6F-3	VF-51	X 3	
Little Joe	PB4Y-1	VPB-107	No. 4	
Little Lady	F4U-4	VF-113	V 301	
Little Miss Rita	A-1D	VF-194	B 417	126921
Little Snatch	PB4Y-1	VPB-111	No. 386	38836
Live to Fly the Chopper	CH-46E	HMM-263	EG 14	153999
Lizard's Last Romp	A-6E	VA-95	NH 501	164383
Logistics Excellents Since 1960	C-2A	VRC-40	JK 50	162144
Lonesome Polecat	F4U-1	VF-17	No. 9 & No. 33	48772?
Look	F9F-2P	VC-61	PP 154	123510
Look	F9F-2P	VC-61	PP 54	123536
Lookin' for some Action!	AH-1W	HMLA-269		
Looks like we hit the Jap-Pot	PV-1	VPB-135	No. 2	48909
Loon	UP-3A	VXN-8		150528
Loose Livin'	PB4Y-1	VPB-115	No. 304	32304
Lorie	F4U-4	VF-871	B 310?	
Lot of Jean?	CH-46E	HMM-163		
Lotta Tayle	PB4Y-2	VPB-121	Y 484	59484
Lou Byrd II	LC-117D	VXE-6	JD 7	17188
Louie's Love Nest	F4U-4	VF-871	B 302	
Louisiana Lil'	PB4Y-2	VPB-121	Y 475	59475
Low Blow	PB4Y-1	VPB-111	No. 853	38853
Lt Stillmans' Fightin' Lady	PB4Y-1	VPB-102	965	38965
Lucifer	F4U-1	VMF-213	No. 38	
Luck of the Irish	KA-3B	VAH-10	AP 613	138974
Lucky Lady	HO3S-1			
Lucky Son Warlords	SH-60B	HSL-51	TA 706	
Lucky-Leven	PB4Y-2	VPB-106/ HEDRON 14-2	X 3	59397
Lucy Quipment	CH-53E	HMH-464	EN 01	
Lucybelle	F4U-1D	VMF-214	No. 86	
L-UK-TUR?	Curtiss H-12	Pensacola Squadron IV	No. 67	A-767
Luscious Lil'-Nan	F4U-1D	VMF-321	No. 831	
Macahyba Maiden / Madam	PB4Y-1	VPB-107	No. 4	32055
Mac's Hack	F4U-4	VF-871	B 304	
Mad Dog	F-4B	VF-51	NL 113	149457
Madeline	EA-6B	VAQ-135	NH 500	158544
Maggie's Drawers	FG-1D	CV-9 *Essex* CAG-83: VBF-83?	No. 191	
Magic Lantern Kama Panama City	SH-2F	HSL-94		
Mah Baby	F4F/FM-2	VC-10	B 6	
Mail-　?	LC-47H	Operation High Jump		17197
Mail Bag	CH-53E			
Maintainers_____??	SH-60B	HSL-51	TA 711	164814
Mamie Stover	A-4C	H&MS-15	YV 83	147829
Man-Child	CH-53E			
Marine's Dream	F4U-1	VMF-214	No. 576	No. 02576
Mark's Farts II	PB4Y-2	VPB-118	No. 405	59405
Mark's Farts	PB4Y-1	VB-104		38761
Mars Star	CH-46E	HC-3 Det. 104	SA 40	154000
Martha	F4U-1	VMF-214	No. 883	??883
McKees Insane Assiam	PBY-5A	VP-81	No. 07	
Me Retire Never	C-54P	NARTU, NAF Washington, DC	6A 865	50865
Me Retire Never	C-54Q	NARTU, NAF Washington, DC	6A 490	56490
Mean Jeanne	F-18C	VFA-83, CVW-7, USS *Eisenhower*	AG 311	164240
Melvin's Massacre	F4F-4	VMF-221/121	No. 77	12094
Memories	F4U-4	VF-871	B 311	

Name	Type	Squadron	Modex	BuNo.
Micky Krause Club	F-4J	VF-101	AJ 101	153900
Micky Krause Club	F-4J	VF-101	AJ 110	153808
Midnight Cocktails	F4U-2	VMF(N)-532	No. 212	
Midway Magic	C-1A	CVA-41 *Midway*	600	146038
Mig Eater	F-4J	VF-11	AA 100	157308
Miller's High Life	PB4Y-1	VPB-101	No. 280	32280
Milwaukee City Limits	F4U-1D	VMF-322		
Minnie the Miner	ZPN-110	ZP-14	K 110	
Minsi II	F6F-5	VF-15		
Minsi III	F6F-5	VF-15		70143
Minsi III	F6F-5	VF-15	CAG	94203
Mischief Maker III	PB4Y-1	VPB-115	No. 74	32274
Miss Hayward	A-1A	VA-923	D 5__	
Miss 28th Seabee	JM-1	US NAVY		
Miss B. Havin	E-2C	VAW-124	AJ 601	161552
Miss Behavin'	PB4Y-2	VPB-118	No. 392	59392
Miss Behavin' II	PB4Y-2	VPB-118		59470
Miss Behavin'	CH-46E	HMM-165, USS *Boxer*	YW 05	157661
Miss Belle	C-1A	CVA-62 USS *Independence*, VRC-40	No. 62	146044
Miss Camille	F-18C	VFA-83, CVW-7, USS *Eisenhower*	AG 301	164214
Miss Happybottom	PBM	VPB-32	V2	
Miss Lotta Tail / Handy Andy & Poisin Ivy gun turr.	PB4Y-2	VPB-109	V 522	59522
Miss Lottatail	PB4Y-2	VPB-118	No. 410	59410
Miss Mary Jane	A-1D	VF-194	B 401	126905
Miss Milovin	PB4Y-2	VPB-121 /VPB-116/ VP(HL)-12	R 617	59617
Miss Molly	F-14A	VF-111	NL 200	161621
Miss Molly	F-14A	VF-111	NL 200	161621
Miss Natch	PB4Y-2	VPB-118	No. 405	59405
Miss Pandemonium	PB4Y-2	VPB-124		59____
Miss Piggy II	US-3A	VS-37/28/VRC-50	RG 712	157998
Miss Piggy	US-3A	VS-37/28/VRC-50	No. 712	157998
Miss Pussy Galore	A-1H	VA-165	AK 209	134577
Miss Sea-Ducer	PB4Y-2	VPB-116	R 582	59582
Miss US Flak	PV-1	VPB-142	No. 436	?33436
Miss Vay	F-18C	VFA-83, CVW-7, USS *Eisenhower*	AG 302	164210
Miss You (Dee) (2)	PB4Y-2	VPB-118 and VPB-197?	No. 432	59432
Miss You (1)	PB4Y-2	VPB-118		59381
Miss-Able	PBY-5A	NAS Kaneohe Bay		___??4
Miss-Conduct	FG-1D	VMF-422	No. 28	76481
Mission Belle	PB4Y-1	VB-109	No. 112	32112
Miss-Take	PBY-5A	NAS Kaneohe Bay		
Mitzi-Bishi	PB4Y-1	VPB-106	No. 091	___091
Mixed Emotions	A-6A	VMA(AW)-224	NL	155655
Modest Maiden	F-18C	VFA-83, CVW-7, USS *Eisenhower*	AG 306	164225
Modest Miss	PB4Y-1	VPB-111	No. 733	38733
Modest O' Miss II	PB4Y-2	VPB-118	No. 448	59448
Modest O' Miss	PB4Y-2	VPB-118	No. 402	59402
Molon Lade	EA-6B	VAQ-131	NE 500	163525
Mon Cheri	PB4Y-2	NARU Niagara	H 207	59631
Moon Equipped	F-14A	VF-101	AD 101	161134
Mr. Ed	AV-8B	HMM-264 (Reinforced)	EH 04	
Ms. Heidi	F-14D	VF-31	NK 106	164343
Mutha Goose	LC-47H	VXE-6	JD 4/14	17221
Mutt 2ⁿᵈ	Mchi. M-5	263rd Squadriglia NAF Porto Corsini	No. 36?	
My Innocent Angel	UH-34E	HMM-362	YL 14	
My Lil' Sixshooter	F-14D	VF-31	AJ 107	163902
My Lovia??	F4F-4		No. 17	
My Own Joan II	F6F-3	VF-33	No. 13	25813
Nadine	E-2C	USCG CGAW		159112
Names of members on Det. 1	SH-60B	HSL-51	TA 707	162338?
Napalm Nellie	AP-2H	VAH-21	SL 3	148337
Natural Born Killers	CH-53E	HMH-464	EN 16	
Naval Body	PB4Y-2	VPB-121	Y 406	59406
Navy 1	S-3B	VS-35	NK 700	159387
Navy's Gravy	PB4Y-1	Tinian	No. 292	65292
Navy's Torchy Tess	PB4Y-2	VPB-118	No. 383	59383
Neptune's Virgin	PB4Y-1	VPB-117/104	No. ___1	38761
Never Forget	F-18E	VFA-115, CVW-14, USS *Lincoln*	NK 210	165789
Never Hoppen Twice	PBM-5	VP-731	SF 8	85148?
Never Hoppen	PBM-5	VP-731	SF 8	84748

Name	Type	Squadron	Modex	BuNo.
Nickle Boat	PBM-3C	VP-74	74-P-5	48144
Night Flyers- Lost Boys	SH-2F	HSL-35 Det. 5	TG 43	150140
Nite Hop	PB4Y-1	FAW-7	No. 2	
Nite Life	PBY-5A	VP-81	No. 45	
No Brew	CH-53E	USMC	No. 04	
No Foolin'	PB4Y-1	VB-109	No. 18	32118
No Strain II	PB4Y-1	VPB-102	No. __93	38783
No Strain III	PB4Y-2	VPB-124/ NAS Kaneohe Bay		59540
Nobody Else's Butt	PB4Y-2	VPB-123	X 520	59520
Not Just Mid-way! It'll be All-The-Way	PV-1	Burbank factory		
Northern Lights	SH-2F	HSL-94	NW 22	161644
Now Touring Uh, Hu, Gh, Cool	CH-46E	HMM-163		
Nuclear Task Force One	C-1A	CVN-65 USS *Enterprise*		146021
NY Yankees	CH-46D	HMM-261	EM 07	
Ocean Scanners	SH-2F	HSL-32	HV 134	150163
Octane Sniffer	F9F-2B	VF-191	B 104	123633
Off With Their Heads	AH-1W	HMLA-269	SN 21	
Ol' Blunderbuss	PB4Y-2	VPB-121	Y 564	59564
Ol' Shep	SH-3H	HS-7, *Saratoga*, Aug 1980	No. 730	148045
Ol' Slippery	QF-86H	NMC Point Mugu, CA	No. 31	53-1381
Old Blue from Point Mugu	C-121J	PMTC		131643
Old Milwaukee	CH-46D	HC-6	HW 04	152555
On Call 24/7	AH-1Z	HMLA-167, 22nd MEU (SOC)?		
Oop, Ack, Baby!	F-14A	VF-154	NK 104	161618
Oop, Ack, Baby!	F-14A	VF-21	NK 205	161601
Orient Express 40/ Westpac 92	SH-2F	HSL-35/ USS *John A. Moore*	TG 40	161904
Orion Update	P-3C	NADC PAX		158928
Our Baby	PB4Y-2	VPB-106	X 525	59525
Out of Bounds	PB4Y-2			
Outlaws	SH-2F	HSL-32 DET. 2, USS *Capodann*		
Over Exposed	PB4Y-1P	VD-4	No. 19	32119
Overlord CG-60 Normandy	SH-60B	HSL-42	HN 434	162132
Pacemakers	F6F-5	VF-781	L 69	
Pagong	CH-46E	HMM-265		
Paisano Dos	NC-121K	VXN-8		145925
Paisano Tres	RP-3D	VXN-8	No. 02	158227
Palpitatin' Paulie	F4U-1D	VMF-441	No. 422	
Panama Hattie	PBM-5E	VP-74		
Paoli Local	F6F-5	VF-27	No. 10	
Paper Doll	F9F-2	VF-781	D 121	123702
Paper Doll	F6F-5	VF-27	No. 7	
Paper Tiger II	A-1H	VA-25	NE 572	135297
Party Babe	A-4C	VA-34	AA 300	148483
Party One	F-18E	VFA-87	AJ 400	
Pasquotank Roadrunners	EC-130E	USCG		1414
Passarola	PB4Y-1	VPB-107	No. 3	32056
Passionate Shirley	F4U-4	VF-871	B 306	
Pastime	PB4Y-2	VPB-124 and VPB-121	X 504	59504
Patches	PV-1	VPB-148	No. 727	
Patience Hell	UH-1E	HML-167 or HML-367	No. 16	
Patience-My Foot I'm going to Kill Something	T-1A	NAS Washington D.C.	6A 4214	144214
Patrick & Murry	CH-46D	HMM-161		
Payback can be a Real Pain in the...	CH-53E	HMH-461, 22nd MEU, HMM-261 (REIN)	EM 21	162521
Peace _____?	CH-46E	HMM-162	YS 04	
Peace Feeler	PB4Y-2	VPB-116	R 755	59755
Peanut Airlines	C-117D	Cam Rhan Bay	No. 087	39087?
Peepin' Tom	F9F-2P	VC-61	PP 70	
Peg O' My Heart	F4U-4	VF-871	B 309	
Pegasus 7	C-121J	VXE-6	JD 7	131644
Peggy	F4U-4	VF-783	D 202	81991
Penguin Express	LC-130F	VXE-6	JD 19	148319
Penetration Guaranteed	SH-2G	HSL-36	HY 343	161913
Penny	F4U-1D	VBF-83	No. 205	
Peppermint Pattie	UH-1B	HAL-3		
Persuader	PB4Y-1			
Pete	LC-130F	VXE-6	XD 06	148320
Petulant Porpoise	J4F-2	EDO	E 175	32976
Phabulous Phantoms 1973-1991	F-4S	VMFA-321	MG 000	153904
Phillip's 69'ers	SP-2H	VP-7	LB 11	147962
Phoenix 6	C-121J	VXE-6	JD 6	131624

Name	Type	Squadron	Modex	BuNo.
Phoenix	LC-130F	VXE-6	XD 03	148321
Pic II	F9F-2P	VC-61 Det. N *Bon Homme Richard* CVA-31	PP 46	
Pic	F9F-2P	VC-61	PP 153	123708
Piccadilly Pam	PB4Y-1	FAW-7 UK	B 12	
Piccadilly Pam	PB4Y-1	VPB-103/114	B-12 M	90474
Pirate Princess	PB4Y-2	VPB-121	Y 492	59492
Pirate Princess	PB4Y-2	VPB-123	X 476	59476
Pirate Queen	PB4Y-2	VPB-118	No. 404	59404
Pirate	F-8J	VF-24	NP 207	150670
Pistol Packin' Mama III	PB4Y-2	VPB-121?	Z 56	5956_
Pistol Packin' Mama	PBY-5	VP-11		
Pistol Packin' Mama	PV-1	VPB-144		34805
Plane Ramrod- Cherry Carry	CH-46E	HMM-261	EM 05	157665
Polar Bear Express	SP-2H	VP-24	LR 5	135588
Polar Star	HH-52A	USCG		1383
Polly Adler	A-4C	H&MS-15	YV 82	147809
Pop's Cannon Ball	PB4Y-1	VPB-117	No. 735	38735
POW MIA Freedom Ghost Ship	UH-1N	USMC	No. 6167	
POW/MIA	CH-46E	HMM-261?		
Princess	CH-46A	HMM-262		
Project Highjump	C-47	Operation High Jump		
Puddle Jumper	PBM-5	VP-731	SF 6	
Puff the Magic Dragon	A-1J	VA-165	AK 204	142059
Puff the Magic Dragon	A-6E	VA-165	NG 501	159314
Pukin' Tr___-All In	CH-46E	HMM-163	YP 00	156434
Punch and Judy	PV-1	VPB-131		
Punkie	PB4Y-2	VPB-109	No. 501	59501
Queen of Spades	F-14A	VF-41	AJ 101	162689
Queenie	SBD-5	USMC	No. 713	
Quick Step	EC-121K	VW-11	MJ 309	141309
R_____ C_____	CH-46D	HC-3 Det. 103	SA 31	154826
Radar Love	EA-6B	VAQ-137	AB 502	163522
Ragin' Bulls	SH-2F	HSL-32	HV 136	149030
Ram On	F-18C	VFA-83	AG 307	
Ram Rod	F-18C	VFA-83, CVW-7, USS *Eisenhower*	AG 300	164201
Ramblin' Rebel	F9F-2	VF-72, USS *Bon Homme Richard* CVA-31	L 209	
Ramp Tramp	PBM-5	VP-731	SF 3	84675
Raptor	F-18C	VFA-15	AJ 300	164627
Raptor	MH-60R	HSM-71	No. 710	166520
Rattler	F-8J	VF-211	NP 110	150347
Rattler	F-8K	VF-111	AK 10?	146951
Ray's Roost	F4U-4	VF-871	B 307	
Ready on Arrival	EA-6B	VAQ-137	AB 501	163047
Ready Willing and Able	PB4Y-1	VPB-117	No. __9	38759
Reaking Destruction Since 1964	CH-46E	HMM-261	EM 02	156469
Real #1 Virgin	UH-1N	HMLA-269		159189
Rebel	TBM-3	VMTB-143, USS *Gilbert Islands*	P 83	
Rebel's Delight	F4U-4	VF-871	B 312	97053
Red Baron	CH-46E	HMM-268	YQ 02	153350
Red-Hot Riden-Hood III	PB4Y-2	VPB-119		
Red's Playmate	PB4Y-1	VPB-116		38777
Redwing	PB4Y-2	VPB-106	X 505	59505
Reluctant	F4U-1D	VMF-213		
Reputstion Cloudy	PB4Y-1	VPB-111	No. 906	38906
Retir'n @ 30	S-3B	VS-24	AJ 704	159732
Rhinos Revenge??	AH-1W		No. 27	
Rhumb Runner you Buy we Fly	SH-2F	HSL-36 Det. 2		
Ridin High	PB4Y-1	VPB-116		38779
Riding Dirty	CH-46E	HMM-268	YQ 01?	
Right in Tojo's Face	PV-1	VPB-136	X 4	
Ring Dang Doo	F4U-1A	VMF-217	No. 033	50033?
Ring Dang Doo	F4U-1A	VMF-217	No. 185	50033?
Ringer	F4F-4	VMF-221		
Rittmeister Arnold York von Richt	F4B-3	VF-1, CV-3 *Saratoga*	1-F-2	
Robbie's Rowdies	P-2E	VP-661	LV 3	128345
Rookie	EA-6B	VAQ-137	AB 500	163527
Rookie	EA-6B	VAQ-137	AB 500	162936
Rosa	F-18C	VFA-146	NG 300	163777
Round Trip	TBM-3	VT-80	No. 107	
Rovin' Redhead	PB4Y-1P	VD-1 and VD-5 1946	No. 22	65299

Name	Type	Squadron	Modex	BuNo.
Rowdy Rouges	SH-60B	HSL-46, Det 3	TT 461	
Rugged Beloved	PB4Y-1	VPB-111	No. ___3	38913
Rugged	SB2C-3	VB-80, CV-19 USS *Hancock*	No. 1	
Ruthie	PBY-5	VP-91		
Ruth-Less	F6F-3	VF-38		
S_____ Dragon	CH-53E	HMH-361		
Saber Hawks	SH-60B	HSL-47	TY 65	
Saddams Nightmare	CH-46E	HMM-264	EH 07	156477
Saguaro Sweet Heart	CH-46E	HMM-265		
Salty Dog	T-45C	VT-7, TW-1	A 182	165624
Salty Dog	T-45C	VT-9	A 182	165624
Salty	CH-46D	HC-8, USS *Kearsarge*	BR 16	151950
San Antonio Rose	F-14B	VF-103, CAG-17	AA 100	162918
Santa Clause Special	PM-2	Coco Solo, Panama CZ, 1937		
Satan's Helper	TBM-3	VT-83	F 417	23470
Satan's Wagon	PB4Y-1	VD-1	No. 82	
Save	EKA-3B	VAQ-130	AH 616	147648
Sayonara Kitty Hawk	A-1H	VA-115	NH 501	137552
Scarface	AH-1J	HMA-773	No. 407	157785
Scooter	A-4A	VA-36	AC 400	142227
Sea Beasts/Torrid Toots	PB4Y-1	VPB-107	No. 6	
Sea Deuce	PV-1	VPB-133	No. 2	
Sea Hag	PB4Y-1	FAW-7	B-8 H	
Secretariat 1973	F-18A	VFA-97	NH 200	163098
Semper Fi	FG-1D	VMF-512, USS *Gilbert Islands*	No. 25	
Senorita Ventura	PV-1	VPB-144	No. 730	34730
Sex Machine	F4U-4	VF-713	H 202	
Sexy Six	F4D-1	VF-74	AF 106	139113
Sha-BOOM	F6F-3	USS *Essex*	No. 24	
Shady Lady	PB4Y-1	VPB-111	No. 745	38745
Shady Lady	PBY-5A	HEDRON FAW-3		
Shaka	UH-2C	HSL-31	TD 14	149031
Shanghai Lil'	PB4Y-2	VPB-109		
Shin Pai Nai	PBM-5S2	VP-731	SF 9?	84735
Shogun	SH-60F	HS-8, CVN-70, CAG-9	NG 610	
Shootin' Blanks	CH-46E	HMM-365	YM 04	
Shoot-you'er Faded	PV-1	VPB-144	No. 741	34741
Shore Leave	AS332 Puma	NAVSEALIFT COMM, USS *Richard E. Byrd*	P-4	N330KW
Short Bus	CH-46E	HMM-163	YP 04	
Show Bird	F-18C	VFA-82	AB 300	165200
Shush Boomer	A-1J	VA-165	AK 210	135272
Sicilian Citrus Express	EC-121K	AEWBARRONPAC	No. 313	141313
Sick Eagle	C-1A	CVA-34 USS *Oriskany*		136760
Silver	Q-2A			
Sister	SBD-4	VMSB-233	No. 16	6783
Sitka	OL-8	Alaskan Survey		A-8076
Six's Avenger	PB4Y-1	VPB-105	B-4 R	38751
Skid Kidz Rule	AH-1W	HMLA-269, 24th MEU, LHA 4 *Nassau*		
Skipper's Orchid	FG-1D	HQSS-22	No. 99	
Sky Cow	PB4Y-1	VB-109	No. 21	32121
Sky Pig	CH-53E	HMH-772	EG 24	
Slayer	CH-46E	HMM-263	EG?	
Sleepless Knight	F4U-5N	VC-3	NP 6	122186
Sleepy Time Gal!	PBY-5A	VP-91 Kaneohe Bay		___34
Sleepy Time Gal	PB4Y-1	VD-4	No. 22	32122
Sleepy Time Gal	PB4Y-2	VPB-118	R 470	59470
Sleepytime Gal	PB4Y-1	VPB-116/VD-5	No. 977	38977
Sleezy Beast	PB4Y-1			
Slick Chick	PB4Y-1	VD-5		
Slidin' Home	PB4Y-1	VPB-117	No. 901	38901
Slippery Sally II–HMM-261 Returns to Iraq	CH-46E	HMM-261	EM 14	156470
Smilin Through II	CH-46E	HMM-263, 24th MEU	EG?	
Smokey's Lucky Witch	FM-2	VC-10	B 27	
Smooth Character	CH-46E	HMM-365		
Snafu I	QF-9H	NWST China Lake		130886
Snapper Control	E-2C	VAW-115	NF 600	165301
Snoopy	SH-3H	HS-7, *Saratoga*, Aug 1980	No. 733	148052
Snoot and Hollywoods Little Deuce Coupe	CH-46E	HMM-261		
Snuffy	UH-34E	MAG-16, 1969		
Snuffy's Mischief Maker	PB4Y-1	VPB-115	No. 82	32182

Name	Type	Squadron	Modex	BuNo.
So Solly	PB4Y-1	VPB-117	No. __36	38736
So Sorry	PB4Y-1	VPB-115	No. 69	32169
Soda H2O	SC-1	NAF Mustin Fld, Philadelphia	No. 2	
Somewhere Between Haven and Hell	CH-53E	HMM-165, 31st MEU	YW 63	
Sonic Youth Goo	CH-53E	HMH-461		
Soul Chaser	UH-1N	USMC		
Sound oh Philly BRO DB	F-4J	VF-74	AJ 211	153784
South Paw Connection	CH-46E	HMM-265		
Southern Cross	PB4Y-1	VPB-107		
Southwest Tour '90	EC-130Q	VQ-4		156172
Sovereign of the Seas	EC-121K	VW-11	MJ 330	141330
Spark Plug	Curtiss R-type	First Yale Unit?, Huntington Beach, L.I., NY		
Speedy Gomez	F4U-4	VF-871	D 3XX	
Spirit of '76	PB4Y-1	VD-1/VPB-102	No. 76	31976
Spirit of America	RF-4B	VMFP-3	EF 10	153101
Spot Baby	CH-53E	HMH-461	CJ 01	
Spring Break 2003	AH-1W	HMLA-269		
Spuds	QF-4N	VX-30	No. 122	148360
St. Pauli Girl	F-18C	VFA-83, CVW-7, USS *Eisenhower*	AG 307	
St_____	CH-46E	HC-8 Team 6	BR 56	153339
Staghound	EC-121K	VW-11	MJ 332?	141332?
Stanley?	PB4Y-2	VPB-111	R 786	59786
Stapps Snappers	RF-8G	VFP-	No. 911	
Stateside Structure	PB4Y-1	VPB-116		38755
Sting Ray	F-8K	VF-111	AH 115	146931
Stinky	F4U	VMF-122		
Stoop an' Drop It	PB4Y-1	VPB-106	No. 075	32075
Storm	EP-3E	VQ-2	No. 26	157320
Strikecat	F-14A	VF-41	AJ 101	160394
STS107/ Deus Et Patria	F-14B	VF-32	AC 107	163224
Sub Stompers	SH-2F	HSL-34	HS 234	
Subduer	PB4Y-1	VPB-107	No. 5 & 10	32057
Subhunter Det. Three	SH-2F	HSL-34	HS 230	149748
Sugar Queen	PB4Y-1	VB-109	No. 41	32241
Sugar	PB4Y-1	VPB-108/VD-3/VPB-122/123	No. 98	32098
Sultans of Swing	CH-46D	HC-6		154028
Summer Storm	PB4Y-2	VPB-118	No. 380	59380
Sundowner	F-8E	VF-111	AH 105	150916
Super Phrog Airlift??	CH-46E	HMM-163		
Super Race Huh! Look at the Score Tojo: Navy-97 – Japs-0	PV-1	Burbank factory		
Super Snooper	PB4Y-2	VPB-108	No. 498	59498
Superior/Surprise (3/60)	EC-121K	VW-11	MJ 305	141305
Supreme Zu Zu	PB4Y-2	VPB-124		59___
Surprise _____ Tojo	PV-1		No. 20	
Surprise	EC-121P	VW-11	MJ 312	141312
Survey	F6F-5P	VMF-512, USS *Gilbert Islands*	No. 29	77690
Swan Song	CH-46E	HMM-263	EG 2	153372
Sweet Cheeks	AH-1W	HMLA-269, 24th MEU, LHA 4 *Nassau*	EG ?	
Sweet Little Miss	F-14D	VF-31	AJ 110	164346
Sweet Sixteen Untouched and ready for Action	CH-46E	HMM-266		
Sweet Sue	F4U-4	VF-884	A 413	80788
Sweet Sue	F4U-4	VF-884	A 403	82027
Sweetiepie	OS2U-1	VS-1D13, Adak, Alaska		
Tag	R5C-1	TAG, NAS Honolulu	No. 51	
Tail Chaser	PB4Y-2	VPB-121	Y 491	59491
Takahe	LC-47H	VXE-6	XD 7	17163
Taming the Beast in the Middle East	SH-2G	HSL-32 Det. Five, USS *Valdez*	HV 145	162583
Tarfu	PB4Y-2	VPB-106	X 433	59433
Tasmanian Devil	UP-3A	VXN-8		150527
Taz	TA-4J	VT-7	A 701	
Terrorist	CH-46E	HMM-163	YP 13	
Texas Touch	CH-46E	HMM-265		
Thanks Fido?	SP-2H	VP-2	YC 11	135606
Thanks for the Ride 1980-2005	F-14D	VF-11	AG 200	163227
That's the Finish for that Sub Pilo	PV-1			
That's All Folks-The War Pig	CH-46E	HMM-165, USS *Boxer*	YW ?	
The Arctic Fox	NC-121K	VXN-8	JB 325	141325
The Arctic Fox	NP-3D	VXN-8	No. 03	154587
The Arctic Fox	RP-3A	VXN-8		150500
The Arctic Fox	UP-3A	VXN-8		151384

Name	Type	Squadron	Modex	BuNo.
The Beast	A-6E	VA-155	NE 412	161107
The Beast	PB4Y-1	VPB-106	No. 085	32085
The Big Stick	A-6E	VA-65	AJ 500	161675
The Blow Must Go	SH-60B	HS-8	No. 455	
The Cat is Back	F-14A	VF-2	NE 101	159630
The Champagne Flight-Potts a Puck	CH-37C	HMH-461	CJ 10?	
The Citadel	CH-53E	HMH-464	EN 00	161180
The Crown	LC-130F	VXE-6	JD 21	148321
The Deuce-Because Two are better than One	CH-46E	HMM-165, Al Asad	YW 02	157703
The Dude Chuck Norris	F-18C	VFA-15	AJ 310	164673
The Emperor	LC-130F	VXE-6	JD 20	148320
The Flying Pig II	CH-37C	HMH-461	CJ 10?	
The Furtrappers	SH-2F	HSL-35 Det. 5		
The Great American Bulldogs	AV-8B	VMA-223	WP 01	165354
The Greatful Dead	CH-46A	HMM-362	YK 21	
The Green Banana	PB4Y-1	VPB-105	B-1 'O'	63944
The Green Dragon	OP-2E	VO-67		
The Green Garuda	OP-2E	VO-67	MR 9	131525
The Green Slime	CH-53D	HMH-463		
The Guardian	CH-46E	HMM-265		
The Hanio Hawkeye	RF-8A	VFP-63 Det. 43	PP 989	
The Hannah Special	SB2C-4E	VB-6, CV-19 USS *Hancock*	U 14	
The Happy Hooker	C-1A	CVA-59 USS *Forrestal*	No. 59	136761
The Incredible Hulk	CH-53D	NAS Pax River		
The Kamikaze Miss	PB4Y-1P	VD-1	No. 24	
The Kee Bird	PB4Y-1	VPB-103	B-15	32028
The Kickin' Chicken	CH-53E	HMH-466	YK 70	
The King	LC-130F	VXE-6	JD 19	148319
The Knight??	F9F-2	VF-151	H 314	
The Ko Sisters	A-4C	H&MS-15	YV 84	148464
The Lady	PB4Y-1	VPB-102	P 483	90483
The Last Great Act	SH-2G	HSL-?	No. 20	
The Last Intruder	A-6E	VA-75	AA 501	162179
The Lemon	PB4Y-1P	VD-1		38764
The Leper Colony	EC-130Q	VXE-6	No. 00	159348
The Lewd Nude	PB4Y-1	VPB-117	No. 741	38741
The Loose Goose	TBM-3	VMTB-143, USS *Gilbert Islands*	P 81	
The Mad Cossack	FG-1D	VMF-512, USS *Gilbert Islands*	No. 26	
The Mad Cossack	FG-1D	VMF-512, USS *Gilbert Islands*	No. 11	
The Mad Frenchman	PB4Y-2	VPB-121	R 566	59566
The Malta Dog & Brunheild	EC-121K	VW-2	XD 9	131389
The Marines #53 Proof	CH-53E	HMM-162 (REIN) LHA-4 USS *Nassau*	YS 26	
The Mig Killer	F-4B	VF-161	NF 105	153915
The Mirage of Willcox Dry Lake	PBM-5	VPB-22?	5 22B	
The Mongoose/Gale	CH-46F	HMM-263	EG 2	156472
The Muckalone	PB4Y-1	VPB-111	No. 895	38895
The New Huey Upgrade	UH-1N	HMLA-269, USS *Saipan* LPA-2		
The Nomads	SH-60B	HSL-45	TZ 47	165707
The Outlaw	PB4Y-2		No. __40	
The Peace Maker	CH-46E	HMM-162	YS 07	153395
The Phoenix	CH-46H	HMM-261	EM 05	153369
The Princess	F4U-4	VF-871	B 316	81057
The Putney Swamp	CH-46A	HMM-362	YK 21	
The Ram	A-4C	VA-66	AK 301	145122
The Rape'n Rabbit	CH-46A	HMM-265	EP 12	
The Rat	F-4J	VF-142	NK 212	?155875
The Real H-1 Upgrade	UH-1N	HMLA-269	HF 39	159189
The Reckoning	CH-46E	HMM-162	YS 01	
The Red Ass	JM-1	VMJ-3	No. 3	90507
The Reluctant Maiden	FM-2	VC-14	D 9	
The Road Runner	SP-5B	VP-48	SF 2	147926
The Shark	RP-3D	VXN-8		152738
The Sioux Chief	F4U-1	VMF-115		
The Snooper	PB4Y-1	VPB-116		__50
The Soaring Fin	PB4Y-2	VPB-118	No. 388	59388
The Solid Character	PB4Y-1	VPB-105	B-2 P	
The Sorrow & The Rage 9-11-2001	CH-46D	HC-6	HW 62	
The States or Bust	PBJ-3	VMB-433		64949
The Stinger	PB4Y-1	VPB-117	No. __42	38742
The Superchief	PB4Y-2	VPB-106	X 563	59563

Name	Type	Squadron	Modex	BuNo.
The Suzy Parmer	A-4E	VA-23	No. 335	
The Thing	P2V-2	FASRON 112		
The Turtle	P2V-1	Flight Test	No. 082	89082
The Victory Line	R5C-1	TAG, NAS Honolulu	No. 66	
The Warriors	SH-60B	HSL-49, USS *Thach*	TX 100	
The Weak shall inherit... Nothing	CH-46E	HMM-774	MQ 435	154801
Their Horses are Swifter... to Devour	CH-46E	HMM-774	MQ 435	154801
There can be only One	SH-60B	HSL-48, Det. 1	HR ?	
They don't make them any Tougher than Us	PV-1	VPB-139	No. 32	34640
Thief of Baghdad	F14A+	VF-24	No. 212	163411
Thor	EC-121K	VW-2	No. 8	135761
Thumper	PV-1	VPB-132	132-B-1	
Thunder Mug / 'Olde 8 Ball'	PB4Y-1	VB-109	No. 08	32108
Thunder Pig	CH-53E	HMH-462		
Thunder-Rockin' Out	SH-60B	HSL-43 Det.7		
Thunder	F-8H	VFP-63		147916
Thunder	F-8J	VF-24	NP 203	149145
Thunderclap	CH-46E	HMM-165, USS *Boxer*	YW 11	
Thundercloud	PB4Y-1	FAW-7 UK	B-3 Q	63916
Thundering Hog II	F4U-1D	VMF-422	No. 20	
Thundering Hog	F4U-1D	VMF-422		
Tiger 7	A-1A	VA-702	A 507	
Tiger in the Tank	UH-34D	HMM-361		
Tiger Lady	PB4Y-2	VPB-106	X 384	59384
Tiger	F-8K	VF-111	AK 103	146961
Tin Yan Ty Foon	PB4Y-1	VPB-116		38800
Tina Rose	F-14A	VF-154	NF 102	
To the 21st Century and Beyond-HC-130J Project	HC-130J	USCG Elizabeth City	USCG 2004	
To the 21st Century and Beyond-HC-130J Project	HC-130J	USCG Elizabeth City	USCG 2005	
Tokyo–USA	PB4Y-1	VPB-115		
Tomcat Fast FAC	F-14A	VF-41	AJ 101	162608
Tomcats and Targets	F-14D	VF-31	AJ 106	164343
Tonight... We Ride	F-18C	VFA-105	AC 400	164246
Tonkin Gulf Yacht Club	A-4B	VA-95	AK 03	142783
Too Cool	CH-46E	HMM-261	EM 11	154851
Top Hook	EA-6B	VAQ-139	NK 620	
Topcats we'er No. 1	S-3A	VS-30	AG 700	
Topgun	F-4N	VMFAT-101	SH 36	152230
Torchy Lena	PB4Y-2	VP-109 post war	X	59397
Tornado from Hell	JM-1	VJ-15 NAF Bermuda	15-B-8	41-35586
Touché!	F4U-1D	VMF-422		
Touché!	PB4Y-1P	VD-1	No. 25	
Tour Farewell Sold Out	SH-2F	HSL-33/ USS *G. Philip*		150179
Tourist	PB4Y-1P	VD-1	No. 23	
Trackers FFG-46 Rentz HSL-43 Det. 6 Fear the Monkey	SH-60B	HSL-43 Det.6	TT 26	
Trade Wind	EC-121K	VW-11	MJ 308	141308
Trade Wind	EC-121P	VW-11	MJ 936	145936
Trans World Rotors/ Warheads on Foreheads	SH-60B	HSL-49 CTF-58	TX	
Trans-Paddie Airways	UH-34E	HMM-362, MAG-16, 1969	YL 18	
Traveller 1856	F-18A	VFA-97	NH 206	162860
Triple Nickels	A-6E	VA-42	AD 555	162202
Triple Nuts	C-1A	CVA-64 USS *Constellation*		146053
True Tacamo Warriors	EC-130Q	VQ-4		156172
Turmoil	TBM-3	VMTB-143, USS *Gilbert Islands*	P 86	
Twin Acres	FG-1D	VMF-422	No. 22	
Twitchy Bitch	PB4Y-2	VPB-118	No. 430	59430
Two Can Do It	MH-60S	HSC-26	HW 72	165778
Typhoon	PB4Y-2	VPB-123	No. _48	59548
Tyr	EC-121K	VW-2	XD 7	135746
US Mule	A-1D	VC-33	SS 803	126985
Ug__ _____	CH-53E	USMC	No. 20	
UH-IN Escort Service	UH-1N	HMM-264	EH 12	159192
Ultimate Warrior	F-18A+	VFA-87	AJ 410	
Ultimate Warrior	F-18A+	VFA-87	AJ 410	163105
Ultimate Warrior	F-18C	VFA-87	AJ 411	164669
Umbriago II	PB4Y-1	VPB-105	B-13	
Umbriago	PB4Y-2	VPB-106	X 390	59390
Unapproachable	PB4Y-1	VPB-104/115/120	No. 8__	32080
Uncle Tom's Cabin	PB4Y-1	VPB-117 @ Tacloban, P.I.	No. 737	38737

Name	Type	Squadron	Modex	BuNo.
Under Estimated	UH-1N	HMLA-167, 22nd MEU (SOC) LHA-3 *Kearsarge*	EM 40	160438
Unitas XXXVI Titians	SH-2F	HSL-94		
Urabu	PB4Y-1	VPB-107	No. 12	32065
Urge Me	PB4Y-1	VB-109		32145
Use our Gas or go to Shell	AJ-2	VC-6	NF 13	134069
USS Antietam Donkey Rollers	SH-60B	HSL-43 Det.5		
USS Fife DD-991 Successum Merere Conemur	SH-60B	DD-991, USS *Fife*		
V??	CH-53E	HMH-461	CJ 13	
Vagrant Virago	PB4Y-2	VPB-123	X 487	59487
Valery	SH-2F	HSL-32 Det. Five, USS *Valdez*	HV 137	152203
Valiant Vultures	SP-5A	VP-48	SF 2	126499
Valkyrja	VP-3A	NAS Keflavik		150495
Vark of Arabia	F-14A	VF-114	NH 100	
Velox	EC-121P	VW-11	MJ 326	141326
Venom	AV-8B	VMA-231	CG 01	163662
Venom	AV-8B	VMA-231	CG 01	163662
Vicious Virgin	PBM-5	VH-6		
Village of Wickford	DB-26J	VU-2	JE 3	77165
Vinceve Ast Mort	CH-46E	HMM-265	EP 10	
Vinceve Ast Mort	CH-46E	HMM-265, LHD-2, USS *Essex*	EP 00	156442
Viper Maintenance	SH-60B	HSL-48	HR 500	
Viper	A-4M	VMA-131	QG 00	160024
Virgin Jackie	FG-1A	VMF-222	No. 993	13993
Viva's Valentine	CH-46E	USMC Iraq, 2007		
Vortex	F4U-5N	VC-3	NP 1	
Vulgar Display of Power	CH-53E	HMH-363	YZ 12	
Vulgar Display of Power	CH-53E	HMH-464	EN 06	
Vulgar Display of Power	CH-53E	HMM-261	EM 22	162491
Vulnerable Virgin	PB4Y-1	VB-104	No. 77	32077
Vulnerable Virgin	PB4Y-2	VPB-118	No. 449	59449
W.W. I Ace	WC-121N	VW-1	TE 1	145935
Wanted Outlaws	SH-60B	HSL-42		
War Eagle	A-6E	VA-155	NE 403	155595
War Eagles	CH-46E	HMM-774	MQ 407	155310
War Is Hell	CH-46E	HMM-265		
War Lord	UH-34E	HMM-362	YL 5	
War Pig 00	EA-6B	VAQ-142	NL 520	160437
Warlord 02	SH-60B	HSL-51	TA 02	161564
Warlord 700	SH-60B	HSL-51	TA 700	161564
Water Rats	HH-46A	NAS Pax River		150947
Water Spy	PB4Y-2	VPB-116		59682
Way to go_____Joe	PV-1	Burbank factory		
We Can Take Care of 'em Up Here	PV-1	Burbank factory		
We Give Green Stamps	AJ-2	VC-6	NF 3	
We got your Back	CH-46E	HMM-262	ET 16	
We Never Forget	CH-53E	HMM-461, 22nd MEU, HMM-261 (REIN)	EM 22	161995
We're So Sweet Nobody Loves Us	WC-121N	VW-1	TE 8	145938
We Weill Never Forget	F-18E	VFA-115, CVW-14, USS *Lincoln*	NK 204	165785
Weapons Free	CH-53E			
We'er Det. 8____ Our Mission_____	SH-2G	HSL-33	TF 10	
We'll Soon do the Laughing	PV-1			
We're All Behind You Sailor	PV-1			
We're Coming for You	F-18E	VFA-115, CVW-14, USS *Lincoln*	NK 211	165790
We're Tokyo Bound Doc	PV-1			
West Coast Choppers	CH-53E	HMH-465	YJ 67	
West Win	EC-121K	VW-11	MJ	
We've got their Number but We Can	PV-1			
What 'me Winter Over?	UH-34D	VX-6	JD 4	148122
What Me Worry	F4D-1	VMF(AW)-114	AB 208	134964
What the Deuce	CH-53E			
Where are you at?	PB4Y-2	VPB-123	No. ?35 or ?85	
Whirlybird Cowboy	HH-52A	USCG		
Whiskers	A-4C	VA-34		145141
Whit's Shits	PB4Y-1	VB-104		32081
Who You Gonna Call Mine Busters	RH-53D	HM-14		
Why, Where, When	PB4Y-1P	VD-1	No. 29	
Wicked Wanda Med-Red HSL-32 Det. 8	SH-2F	HSL-32, USS *Truett*		162577
Wide Open?	CH-53E	HMM-264, 26th MEU(SOC)	EH 23	

Name	Type	Squadron	Modex	BuNo.
Wild Cherry II	PB4Y-1P	VD-1	No. 27	
Wild Deuce	PB4Y-2	VP-28	CF 2	
Wild Her	PB4Y-1	FAW-7	No. 8	
Wild?	CH-46E	HMM-165		
Will Not Be Forgotten	F-18E	VFA-115, CVW-14, USS *Lincoln*	NK 200	165781
William Freeman	F-18D	VMFA(AW)-121	VK 06	
William Marontate	F-18D	VMFA(AW)-121	VK 11	164652
Willie Jump Jump	P2V-2N	Operation Skijump II	TT 16	
Willie's Wildcat II	PB4Y-1	VPB-116		38845
Willie's Wildcat	PB4Y-1	VPB-116		32310
Wilshie Duit	LC-117D	VXE-6	JD 10/7	99853
Wisconsin	CH-46E	HMM-163		
Witch Craft	PB4Y-1P	VD-4	No. 43	32143
Witch of the Wave	EC-121K	VW-11	MJ 327	141327
Wolf Pack One	SH-60B	HSL-45	TZ 45	161554
Wolf's Witch	F4U-4	VF-871	B 315	
Wolof	NOP-2E	NADC		128397
World Famous Eightballers	SH-60F	HS-8	NG 610	164077
World Famous Maulers	S-3B	VS-32	AB 701	159751
World Tour	SH-60B	HSL-44	HP 453	162347
World Traveler	UP-3A	VXN-8	JB	150528
Worrybird	PB4Y-1	VPB-116	R 960	38960
Yankee Tiki Au Te Hau	LC-47H	VXE-6	JD 14	17221
Yokosuka Queen	F4U-5N	VC-3	NP 24	124442
You Pod it- We Cod it	US-3A	VS-24		157998
Your Ace in the Hole	SH-2F	HSL-34 FF-1085 DET. 4	HX 230	161656
Your Pad or Mine	HH-46D	HC-5 Det.1	RB 03	
Yvonne III	F4U-4	VF-791	A 207	82084
Zowie	PBM-5	VP-731	SF 7	
Zulu Invader	SH-2F	HSL-32	HV 135	151321

APPENDIX C

LOCATION OF ARTWORK ON AIRCRAFT

The circled numbers on the aircraft profiles represent the approximate location for the artwork referred to in the appropriate text. The penguin nose art of VX-6 (VXE-6), as shown on this page, represent the changes in style of penguin artwork over a span of thirty-five years.

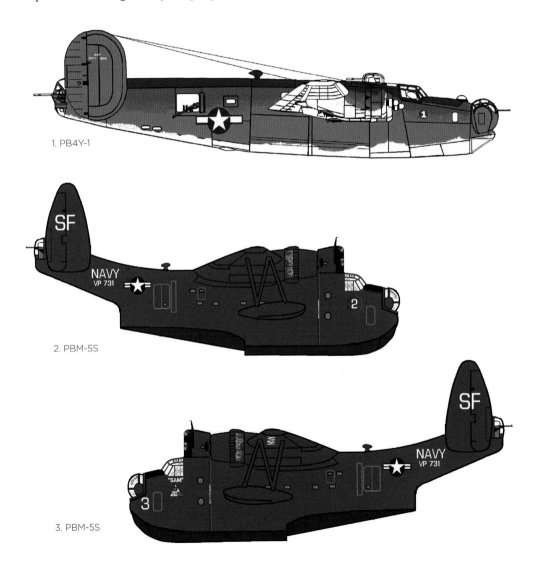

1. PB4Y-1

2. PBM-5S

3. PBM-5S

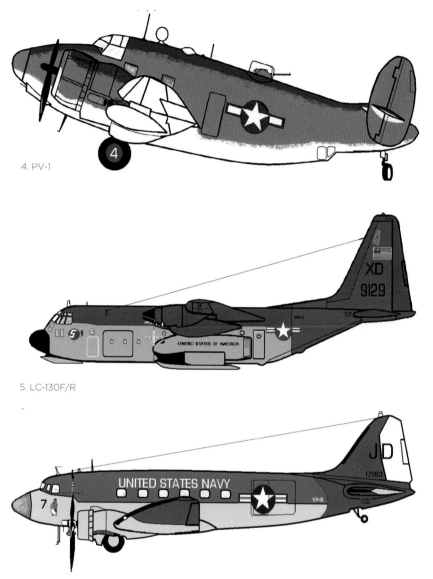

4. PV-1

5. LC-130F/R

6. LC-47H

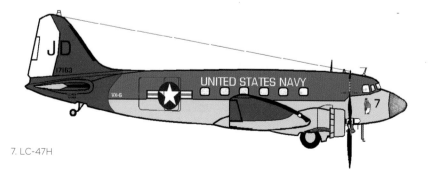

7. LC-47H

8. P2V-2N

9. N9H

P2V-2N No. 8, 1955

LC-47H No. 6 & 7, 1962

LC-130 No. 5, 1983

THE MARK OF THE BEAST

Naval Aviation nose art is an ongoing evolution. One way to trace the evolution of nose art is by looking at the shark, tiger, cat, and other beast markings found on naval aircraft. Many are familiar with the legend of Col. Claire Chennault's *Flying Tigers*, and how their planes with the snarling tiger mouths were so well-received by the Chinese people and the media during the Second World War. In fact, some of the volunteers that served with Chennault's 1st American Volunteer Group (AVG) earlier in the war were US Navy pilots. Therefore, it stood to reason that it would not

be long before the US Navy would adopt its own related aircraft markings. The first unit to adopt this style of art was VF-27 on board the *Princeton* (CVL-23). However, their effort was cut short by the sinking of that ship during the Battle of Leyte Gulf. There were also numerous other examples of tiger or shark mouths painted on individual naval aircraft during the Second World War. But VF-27 remains the sole exception, where a unit painted the enter squadron inventory of aircraft. In VF-27s case all the unit's aircraft were adorned with a snarling cat's mouth. After the 1945 nose art in the Navy was not used or encouraged.

Even during the Korean police action this type of art was not found on many airplanes. The exception was VF-871, a reserve unit activated for the conflict. Supposedly at least two of this unit's F4U-4s had huge red lips and green eyes painted on their cowlings. However, this has not been substantiated by photographic evidence. This type of artwork was not used again until the post-Korean War era. The F-11A Tiger squadron, VF-21, reinstated the use of this type of nose art first used by VF-27. FITRON 21 introduced the Tiger into service on the East Coast and painted the tiger teeth and eyes on the nose of all their aircraft. However, this effort was again short-lived when the squadron transitioned to a new platform (A4D-1 Skyhawks) and discontinued the practice of painting tiger nose art. The next attempt to paint tiger or shark teeth on naval airplanes was to become a long-term and successful affair. The West Coast squadron VF-111 took up the tradition by painting their F-8 Crusaders with shark's mouths and eyes. They started this in the early 1960s and the tradition continued through until 31 March 1995, when the unit was decommissioned. Over the years VF-111's Crusaders, then their F-4 Phantom IIs, and finally their F-14 Tomcats have all been decorated with this scheme.

There was a small-scale resurgence during the Vietnam Conflict of this type of nose art. VA-93, an A-7 Corsair II unit, which operated off the CVA-61 Ranger, is one example. Also, the US Marine Corps fast FAC squadron, H&MS-13, carried the tiger-shark mouths on their TF-9J Cougars while operating out of Chu Lai in 1967–68. Some of these aircraft were replaced with TA-4F and as the

VAQ-33's EA-3B displays the shark-mouth artwork. Not all of the squadron's aircraft were painted with the shark mouth. (*Don Spering A.I.R.*)

The *City of Cambridge* of VT-23 with the shark-mouth motif. VT-23 first adopted this form of art when it took custody of Marine TF-9 Cougars from Vietnam with this style of artwork. (*Don Spering A.I.R.*)

Cougars returned to the states they were turned over to training squadrons, like VT-23. For a while, VT-23's Commanding Officer retained these aircraft in their Vietnam markings. There have been other examples of this art style on naval aircraft. Certain squadrons would have either one or more of their planes painted, but never the whole unit's inventory. The two training squadrons, VT-5 and the aforementioned VT-23, are notable examples. In fact, in the mid-1970s VT-23 went one step further by christening their aircraft, T-2C Buckeyes, with names. Some of the Buckeyes were named after cities or towns from which their instructor pilots haled.

Looking through this appendix it will be noted that fighter-type aircraft with this style of nose art are most prevalent. Very few patrol or scout aircraft can be found with this style of art. By far the F-14's of VF-111 are the most numerous examples, with sixteen airplanes listed. This also gives testament to the durability and longevity of the Grumman design, which has been in service for over thirty years.

During the War on Terror's Operation Enduring Freedom and the Second Gulf War, this style of art reappeared for a short time. VAW-123's (Screwtops) E-2C Hawkeyes of CVW-1 onboard the CVN-71 *Theodore Roosevelt* had at least three of their five aircraft painted with shark mouths on both of the engine cowlings. Also, the AV-8B Harriers of VMA-311 onboard the USS *Tarawa* LPA-1 in the Persian Gulf had a least three of their jump jets decorated with snarling 'tomcat' nose art.

During PhanCon 99 another QF-4N *Bloodhound 45* carries on the tradition at Point Mugu with a particularly ugly, snarling shark mouth. This nose cone with a shark mouth is cannibalized from one Phantom to another as the situation dictates. (*Frank Hamby*)

This TA-4F, BuNo. 153674, carries a fierce-looking shark mouth when photographed in July 1979. The aircraft flew with VX-4 as XF 22. (*Don Spering A.I.R.*)

Above and *Below*; Two aircraft belonging to the USS *Kitty Hawk* Air Wing during their September 1999 deployment to Japan. The dragon on the CAG FA-18 Hornet, above, and the sea hawk on the tail of the HS-14 SH-60B, below, certainly reflect an Oriental flavor. (*Dr Stephen Wolf*)

One of two HH-2D Seasprites modified for Anti-Ship Missile Defense (ASMD) role. The bulbous APS-115 radar in the nose has what appears to be a hideous dragoon face on it. This aircraft was based at Bloomfield, CT as a Kaman test and development airframe during November 1971. This Seasprite was again modified in March 1972 as an YSH-2E test vehicle, and was flown extensively at NADC Warminster, PA. However, the face art was not retained on the modified airframe. (*Don Spering A.I.R.*)

One of the most spectacular paint schemes on a Navy aircraft appeared on *Chippy Ho!*, an F-18C of VFA-195, in 1995. This CAG bird's nose was decorated with a large hawk's head and talons appeared on the under-wing fuel tanks. Capt. Dana Potts took these magnificent air-to-air photos of *Chippie Ho II* over Japan. The aircraft is an F/A-18C, BuNo. 163703, and carries some of the most flamboyant artwork ever displayed on a Navy aircraft—even for a CAG Bird. Both *Chippie Ho!* Hornets wore modex NF 400 from Air Wing Five off the USS *Independence* (CV-62). (*Dana Potts*)

Above: F-14A, BuNo. 161859 appears to be wearing some type of shark mouth in April 1990 at NAS Oceana. Noting that this aircraft belongs to VF-11's Commanding Officer, it was logical that this artwork is a hog's mouth based on the wild boar insignia of the *Red Rippers*. (*Lionel Paul*)

Below: This AV-8B Harrier performs a vertical take-off onboard the USS *Tarawa* in March 2003. These Harriers will participate in both Operation Enduring Freedom and Operation Iraqi Freedom. At least three of the ships aircraft would carry the low-vis tomcat's snarling mouth. (*US Navy photo by SNJO David Senn*)

VAW-121's E-2C Hawkeye prepares to launch from CVN 73 USS *George Washington*, 12 February 2004. Note the colorful shark mouth decorating the number one engine's intake. (*US Navy photo by PHAN Joan Kretschmer*)

This RF-8G operated from the USS *Roosevelt* during the Vietnam War. Not all this unit's aircraft carried the shark-mouth artwork. Note the logo 'Eyes of the Fleet' and cartoon eyes on the forward raised portion of the wing. (*Nick Williams via Jim Meehan*)

A T-34C belonging to VF-101 is decorated with a shark mouth at NAS Oceana during September 1998. (*Author's Collection*)

An F-14 belonging to VF-101 was photographed at the last Azalea Festival airshow in April 2002, at NAS Norfolk, VA. The *Grim Reapers* were the Fleet Aircrew Replacement squadron for the F-14 Tomcat. As the regular Tomcat squadrons decommission, this unit has begun the practice of remembering their sister squadrons by marking their own aircraft with the decommissioned unit's markings. In this case, BuNo. 161287 is carrying the shark-mouth nose markings of the former VF-111, which was decommissioned in 1995. (*Author's Collection*)

Type	Artwork	Name	Squadron	Modex	BuNo.
A-3B	Shark's mouth	None		# 902	138902
A-4A	Shark's mouth	None	TEST		137816
A-4C	Shark's mouth	None	VA-43	AD 302	142150
A-7A	Shark's mouth	None	VA-93	NF 310	152667
A-7A	Shark's mouth	*Bicentennial markings*	VA-93	NF 300	152673
A-7A	Shark's mouth	None	VA-93	NF 307	152678
A-7A	Shark's mouth	None	VA-93	NF 301	153152
A-7A	Shark's mouth	None	VA-93	NF 302	153208
A-7A	Shark's mouth	None	VA-93	NF 305	153215
A-7A	Shark's mouth	None	VA-93	NF 313	153228
A-7A	Shark's mouth	None	VA-93	NF 316	153244
A-7A	Shark's mouth	None	VA-93	NF 305	154485
A-7A	Shark's mouth	None	VA-93	NF 314	154506
A-7B	Shark's mouth	None	CVA-61 *Ranger*	NE 321	
A-7B	Shark's mouth	None	VA-203		154371
A-7B	Shark's mouth	None	VA-93	NF 311	153191
A-7B	Shark's mouth	None	VA-93	NF 312	153226
A-7B	Shark's mouth	None	VA-93	NF 306	154545
A-7B	Shark's mouth	None	VA-93	NE 315	
A-7E	Shark's mouth	None	VA-66	AG 301	157488
A-7E	Shark's mouth	None	VA-93	NF 315	159639
A-7E	Shark's mouth	None	VA-93	NF 312	159656
A-7E	Shark's mouth	None	VA-93	NF 310	159985
A-7E	Shark's mouth	None	VA-93	NF 305	160001
A-7E	Shark's mouth	None	VA-93	NF 304	160537
A-7E	Shark's mouth	None	VA-93	NF 303	160538
A-7E	Shark's mouth	None	VA-93	NF 302	160541
A-7E	Shark's mouth	None	VA-93	NF 301	160544
A-7E	Shark's mouth	None	VA-93	NF 300	160545
A-7E	Shark's mouth	None	VA-93	NF 301	160554
A-7E	Shark's mouth	None	VA-93	NF 300	160730
A-7E	Shark's mouth	None	VA-93	NF 315	160880
A-7E	Shark's mouth	None	VA-93	NF 314	160874
AH-1J	Shark's mouth	None		HF 6	157769
AH-1W	Shark's mouth	None	HMLA-167	TV 39	162545
AH-1W	Shark's mouth	None	HMM-264	EH 40	160804
AH-1W	Shark's mouth	None	HMM-264	EH 42	
AV-8B	Shark's mouth	None	HMM-163/VMA-311	? 55	
AV-8B	Shark's mouth	None	HMM-163/ VMA-311	? 51	
AV-8B	Shark's mouth	*Venom*	VMA-231	CG 01	163662
AV-8B	Shark's mouth/ Camel mission marks	None	VMA-513	YP 56	164145
AV-8B	Shark's mouth	None		? 15	
C-2A	Shark's mouth	None	VRC-50	? 21	162162
CH-53E	Shark's mouth	_____?	USMC	# 22	
E-2C	Shark's mouth on two engines	None	VAW-121	AA 600	
E-2C	Shark's mouth on two engines	None	VAW-123	AB 600	163693
E-2C	Shark's mouth on two engines	None	VAW-123	AB 603	165298
EA-3B	Shark's mouth	None	VQ-2	# 003	146453
EA-3B	Shark's mouth	*Killer Whale*	VQ-2	__ 004	146454
F-11A	Shark's mouth	None	VF-21	AM	138633
F-11A	Shark's mouth	None	VF-21	AM 201	141732
F-11A	Shark's mouth	None	VF-21	AD 205	141740
F-11A	Shark's mouth	None	VF-21	AM 207	141742
F-11A	Shark's mouth	None	VF-21	AM 208	141744
F-11A	Shark's mouth	None	VF-21	AD 204 AM 204	141745
F-11A	Shark's mouth	None	VF-21	AM 210	141757
F-11A	Shark's mouth	None	VF-21	AD 212	141765
F-11A	Shark's mouth	None	VF-21	AD 203	141765
F-11A	Shark's mouth	None	VF-21	AM 204	141803
F-11A	Shark's mouth	None	VF-21	AD 204	141807
F-11A	Shark's mouth	None	VF-21	AD 219	141808
F-11A	Shark's mouth	None	VF-21	AD 201	141812
F-14A	Boar's teeth	None	VF-11	AM 201 AE 101	161859
F-14A	Shark's mouth and Superman motif	None	VF-111	NL 201	160660

Type	Artwork	Name	Squadron	Modex	BuNo.
F-14A	Shark's mouth	None	VF-111	NL 213	160664
F-14A	Shark's mouth	None	VF-111	NL 200	160666
F-14A	Shark's mouth	None	VF-111	NL 210	160669
F-14A	Shark's mouth	None	VF-111	NL 202	160670
F-14A	Shark's mouth	None	VF-111	NL 203	160672
F-14A	Shark's mouth	None	VF-111	NL 203	160674
F-14A	Shark's mouth	None	VF-111	NL 205	160676
F-14A	Shark's mouth	None	VF-111	NL 207	160680
F-14A	Shark's mouth	None	VF-111	NL 211	160684
F-14A	Shark's mouth	None	VF-111	NL 212	160686
F-14A	Shark's mouth	None	VF-111	NL 213	160688
F-14A	Shark's mouth	None	VF-111	NL 202	160690
F-14A	Shark's mouth and pin-up	*Miss Molly*	VF-111	NL 200	161621
F-14A	Shark's mouth	None	VF-111	NL 200	162594
F-14B	Shark's mouth	None	VF-101	AD 101	161287
F-14B	Shark's mouth	None	VF-101	AD 101	163222
F-14B	Shark's mouth	None	VF-101	AD 133	
F-14B	Shark's mouth	None	VF-101	AD 164	
F-14D	Lion's face	None	VF-213	NH 101	164603
F-18A	Shark's mouth	*Traveller 1856*	VFA-97	NH 206	162860
F-18C	Golden dragon wrapped around tails	None	VFA-192	NF 300	163417
F-18C	Golden dragon wrapped around tails	None	VFA-192	NF 300	163777
F-18C	Golden dragon wrapped around tails	None	VFA-192	NF 300	164909
Type	Artwork	Name	Squadron	Modex	BuNo.
F-18C	Eagles head on nose	*Chippy Ho! II*	VFA-195	NF 400	163703
F-18C	Eagles head on nose	*Chippy Ho!*	VFA-195	NF 400	163758
F-18C	Eagle body on fuselage and tail	*Show Bird*	VFA-82	AB 300	165200
F-4B	Shark's mouth	None	VF-111		150632
F-4B	Shark's mouth	None	VF-111	NL 200	151000
F-4B	Shark's mouth	None	VF-111	NL 203	151489
F-4B	Shark's mouth	None	VF-111	NL 200	152986
F-4B	Shark's mouth and MIG kill	None	VF-111	NL 201	153019
F-4B	Shark's mouth	None	VF-152	NF 200	153059
F-4J	Eagle/Bicentennial marks	None	VX-4	XF 76	153088
F-4N	Shark's mouth	None	VF-111	NL 204	150466
F-4N	Shark's mouth	None	VF-111	NL 201	152278
F-4N	Shark's mouth	None	VF-111		153012
F4U-4	Green eyes and lips (two a/c)	None	VF-871		
F6F-3	Shark's mouth	None	VF-21	# 29	
F6F-3	Cat's mouth/scores	None	VF-27	# 17	
F6F-3	Cat's mouth/scores	None	VF-27	# 13	
F6F-3	Cat's mouth/scores	None	VF-27	# 23	
F6F-3	Cat's mouth/scores	None	VF-27	# 9	
F6F-5	Cat's mouth/scores (two)	None	VF-27	# 2	40832
F6F-5	Cat's mouth	*Paoli Local*	VF-27	# 10	
F6F-5	Cat's mouth	*Paper Doll*	VF-27	# 7	
F6F-5	Cat's mouth	None	VF-27	# 1	
F6F-5	Cat's mouth/scores	None	VF-27	# 3	
F7F-3N	Cat's face	None			
F-8A	Shark's mouth	None	VF-32	AC 201	143747
F-8B	Shark's mouth	None	NADC Johnsville		145443
F-8D	Shark's mouth	None	VF-111	AJ	147055
F-8D	Shark's mouth	None	VF-111	NE 452 AJ 110	147056
F-8E	Shark's mouth	*Sundowner*	VF-111	AH 105	150916
F-8E	Shark's mouth	None	VF-111	AH 124	
F-8H	Shark's mouth and double nuts	None	VF-111	AJ 100	147048
F-8H	Shark's mouth	None	VF-111	AJ 106	148677
F-8H	Shark's mouth	None	VF-111	AH 101	148703
F-8H	Shark's mouth	None	VF-111	AJ 105	148684
F-8H	Shark's mouth	*Blackjack*	VFP-63	PP 101	147049
F-8K	Shark's mouth	*Sting Ray*	VF-111	AH 115	146931
F-8K	Shark's mouth	*Tiger*	VF-111	AK 103	146961
F-8K	Shark's mouth	?	VF-111	AH 20	147022
F-8K	Shark's mouth	None	VF-111	AJ 107	147051

Type	Artwork	Name	Squadron	Modex	BuNo.
F-8K	Shark's mouth	None	VF-111	AJ	147925
F-8K	Shark's mouth	None	VF-111	AJ 101	147909
F9F-2B	Panther's head	None	VMF-311	WL	127207
F9F-5	Shark's mouth	None	VMA-232	WP 1	126013
HE-1	Shark's mouth	None	Henderson Field		30228
HH-2D	Dragon's mouth	*Flying Dragon*	NAF Bloomfld. CT	# 9033	149033
Type	Artwork	Name	Squadron	Modex	BuNo.
HS-2L	Flying fish w/teeth and gills	None	NAS Miami, FL		5566
OY-1	Shark's mouth	None	USMC		75172
P-2E	Shark's mouth on jet pods	None	VP-6	PC 7	128356
P-3C	Dragon's mouth	None	VP-56	LQ 76	156527
P-5A	Shark's mouth and eyes	None	VP-46	RC 6	135473
P5M-1	Shark's mouth and eyes	None	VP-45	LN 7	135471
PB4Y-2	Shark's mouth and hill billy	*Baldy and Tortilla Flat*	VPB-106 and VPB-197	X 398	59398
PBM-3	Shark's mouth	None	VPB-216	# 5	45255
Q-2A	Shark's mouth	*Silver*			
QF-4N	Shark's mouth	None	NAWC China Lake	#45	152269
QF-4N	Shark's mouth	None	NWST Mugu	NWAC 45	151461
QF-4N	Shark's mouth (large)	None	NWST Mugu	145	153030
QF-9H	Shark's mouth and mission marks	*Snafu I*	NWST China Lake		130886
QF-9J	Shark's mouth and biplane	None	NAF Redwing		144272
RF-8G	Shark's mouth and dragon/hound	None	VFP-62	AE 908	146889
RF-8G	Shark's mouth	None	VFP-62	AE 910	
RF-8G	Shark's mouth	None	VFP-63	AE 602	146892
RQ-2B	Shark's mouth	None	VMU-1	D2	
S-2E	Shark's mouth	None	VS-24	AU 117	153572
S-2E	Shark's mouth	None	VS-24	AU 114	153571
S-2G	Shark's mouth	None	NAS Quonset	# 10	152333
S-2G	Shark's mouth	None	VS-30	AR 103	152842
SH-60B	Screaming eagle	None	HS-14	NF 610	164617
SH-60B	A running wolf	None	HSL-45	TZ 45	161554
SP-5B	Shark's mouth	None	VP-48	SF 3	135482
T-28C	Shark's mouth	None	VT-5	2S 519	140068
T-28C	Shark's mouth	None	VT-5	2S 706	140520
T-28C	Shark's mouth	None	VT-5	2S 509	140526
T-28C	Shark's mouth	None	VT-5	2S 714	140631
T-2C	Shark's mouth	None	VT-23	3H 341	158604
T-2C	Shark's mouth	*City of Oneida*	VT-23	B 319	158606
T-2C	Shark's mouth	*City of Cambridge*	VT-23	3H 340	158882
T-2C	Shark's mouth	None	VT-23		158894
T-34C	Shark's mouth	None	NAS Oceana	# 903	160501
T-34C	Shark's mouth	None	VF-101	AD 001	160273
T-34C	Shark's mouth (all black)	None	VF-101	AD 01	160509
T-34C	Shark's mouth	None	VF-101	AD 03	160646
T-34C	Shark's mouth	None	VT-3	E 0473	160473
TA-3B	Shark's mouth	None	VAQ-33	GD 121	144856
TA-4J	Snoopy and Shark's mouth	None	VF-101	AD 137	154301
TA-4J	Shark's mouth	None	VX-4	XF 22	153674
TF-9J	Shark's mouth	None	H&MS-13	YU 1	
TF-9J	Shark's mouth	None	H&MS-13	YU 4	147377
TF-9J	Shark's mouth	None	H&MS-13	YU 2	147384
TF-9J	Shark's mouth	None	H&MS-13	YU 3	147386

This QF-9J Cougar, BuNo. 144272, has a bright-red scheme which is enhanced by a shark mouth and small biplane emblem on the nose of the aircraft. Also, an emblem on the tail depicts a red phoenix in a gun sight and the legend 'NAF Redwings'. (*Bergagnini*)

VF-111's F-14A Tomcat, BuNo. 160666, attached to the USS *Kitty Hawk* during January 1982. (*Meehan*)

VFA-82's Big Bird was another example where an animal is incorporated into the paint scheme. This unit is part of CVW-1, and as of 22 January 2004 they were supporting Operation Iraqi Freedom and the War on Terrorism. (*US Navy photo by Lt Cdr P. R. Catalano*)

APPENDIX E

US COAST GUARD

The US Coast Guard is only transferred to the Navy when needed, especially during times of a national emergency; however, since the 'Coasties' cooperate so closely with the Navy during SAR and drug interdiction missions, we include a partial list of their nose art.

Type	Artwork	Name	Squadron	Modex	Serial
E-2C	Drug bust score board	*Nadine*	USCG CGAW		159112
EC-130E	Roadrunner	*Pasquotank Roadrunners*	USCG		1414
EC-54U	Three leaf clover	*B_____ Clover*	USCG	9147	9147
HC-130J	Lil' Martian and cartoon C-130	*To The 21st Century And Beyond*	Elizabeth City	USCG 2004	2004
HC-130J	Lil' Martian and cartoon C-130	*To The 21st Century And Beyond*	Elizabeth City	USCG 2005	2005
HH-52A	Cartoons and map	*Polar Star*	USCG		1383
HH-52A	Yosemite Sam	*Whirlybird Cowboy*	USCG		
HH-52A	None	*Chicago*	USCG Chicago		1394
HH-60	Shark's mouth	None	USCG Cape Cod	# 6025	6025
HH-65A	A shark on the side	*Jaws 90*	Cutter Boutwell	# 90	6590
HNS-1	Eskimo and penguin	*Labrador Special*	USCG		39045
HO3S-1	None	*Gander Express*	USCG		75610
PBM-3C	Cartoon animal under cloud	None	USCG	S 6582	6582
PBY-5	None	*Aleutian Belle*	USCG	V-189	2990
PBY-5	None	*Forever Amber*	USCG post-war		4831?
RD-1	None	*Mizar*	USCG 1920'S		
RD-2	None	*Adhara*	USCG	#129	
RD-4	None	*Cappella*	USCG	#137	

1 August 2009: a HH-60 helicopter from the Coast Guard Air Station Cape Cod bows to the crowd after performing a water rescue in New York harbor. Peter Benchley's novel, *Jaws,* which took place off the Massachusetts coast, Cape Cod, is probably the reason this Jayhawk carries a shark mouth for its nose art. (*USCG photo/Chief Petty Officer Bob Laura*)

Above: *Jaws 90* was onboard the USCG Cutter Boutwell (WHEC 719) in the North Arabian Gulf during Operation Iraqi Freedom. While in the Gulf, the HH-65A and the Boutwell's missions were surveillance, SAR, and transporting cargo and personnel. (*USCG photo by PA2 David Mosley*) Below: *Jaws 90* back at NAS Barber's Point, HI, after returning from Iraqi Freedom on 25 June 2003. This HH-65A Dolphin had a great white shark painted on the starboard cowling during the aircraft's deployment to Operation Iraqi Freedom. (*USCG photo by PA2 David Mosley*)

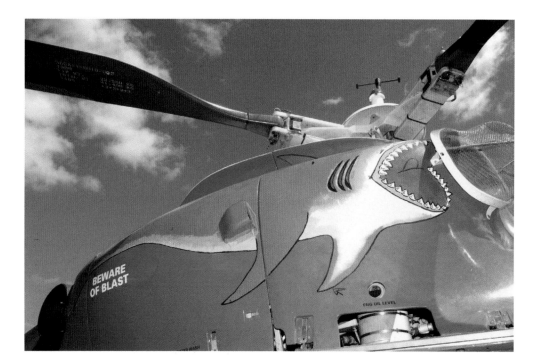

This aircraft, a USCG HH-52A, serial number 1383, with *Polar Star* artwork on the starboard aft fuselage was assigned to the Aviation Training Center in Mobile, AL. This unit supplied Seaguard aircraft detachments to Coast Guard cutters and icebreakers going north to Alaska. They provide air-sea rescue and airborne ice-flow observation to assist the Coast Guard in performing its mission in Polar Regions. The aircraft has been everywhere between Mobile and Alaska if the map is to be believed. (*William Tate*)

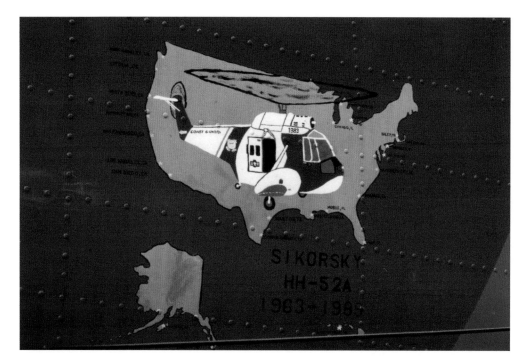

Nadine, an E-2C Hawkeye assigned to the Coast Guard Airborne Warning Squadron 1 (CGAW-1), provides support for the law-enforcement community in stopping the flow of illegal drugs into the United States. This plane displays the squadron's contribution to this effort: 4.3 tons of snow (cocaine) seized, 5.2 tons of Marijuana seized, nineteen aircraft intercepted, nine boats intercepted, and fifty-two convictions. (*William Tate*)

Below: By March 1988, all CGAW-1 Hawkeyes also carried the 'Just Say No' motto on both sides of the fuselage.

EMERGENCY RESCUE SQUADRONS

The US Army Air Force in the Second World War formed Emergency Rescue Squadrons to assist the US Navy in the rescuing of downed aircrew over the water. The 1st ERS operated in the Mediterranean Theater from February 1944. The squadron was equipped with nine OA-10As, two L-5s and three B-25s. This unit had detachments at Casablanca, on the island of Corsica, and at Foggia, Italy. For the squadron's outstanding contribution during the invasion of Southern France they were awarded the Presidential Unit Citation. In January 1945, the 1st ERS sent a detachment to India which later became the 7th ERS and operated in the China-Burma-India Theater. The OA-10As used on these 'Dumbo' flights were almost identical to the Navy's PBY-5A. Although these are technically not US Navy aircraft, there was such a great deal of response from the USAAF members of the PBY Catalina International Association that we decided to add an appendix which included their OA-10 nose art information.

Type	Artwork	Name	Squadron	Serial
OA-10	Pin-up in bikini	Gypsy	7th ERS	
OA-10	?	Web Foot Maggie	7th ERS	
OA-10	Pin-up?	Pickup Girl	7th ERS	
OA-10	Pin-up?	The Snatch	7th ERS	
OA-10	None	Fearless Fosdick	1st/7th ERS	41-18772
OA-10	A question mark	Who Cares	1st ERS	43-47959
OA-10	None	The Sea Hag	1st ERS	
OA-10	Cartoon Snafu	Snafu Snatchers	2nd ERS	44-33879
OA-10 Mission marks ?	I'll Be Seein' You	6th ERS	44-34056	
OA-10 Miss Lace pin-up	Miss Pick Up	5th ERS	44-33915	
OA-10	Nurse with life preserver	Nurse-Maid	2nd ERS	44-33928
OA-10	Pin-up	I'll Be Seeing You	2nd ERS	44-34056
OA-10	A cripple duck	The Lame Duck	2nd ERS	
OA-10	None	Junie	2nd ERS	44-33929
OA-10	None	The White Pussy	2nd ERS	
OA-10	Pin-up	Rosie	2nd ERS	
OA-10	Pin-up	Bouncing Bette	2nd ERS	44-33990
OA-10	None	Miss Mary Ann	2nd ERS	
OA-10	None	Roamin' Roma II	2nd ERS	
OA-10	Pin-up	S_____	2nd ERS	
OA-10	None	Lazy Daisy	1st ERS	43-43856
OA-10	The ark	Mizpah		44-34070
OA-10	Name on tail	Old Ironsides	7th ERS	44-33976
OA-10	Cartoon duck	Lame Duck	7th ERS	44-34000
OA-10 ?	Sophisticat	5th ERS	44-39923	

OA-10A *Snafu Snatcher*, of the 2nd Emergency Rescue Squadron, is now at the USAF Museum. The 2nd ERS was tasked with Dumbo operation in the South and Central Pacific during the Second World War. Below the raft are symbols denoting thirty-five air-sea search-and-rescue missions. (*John Schneider*)

Below left: OA-10A, the *Coconut Queen*, on Tinian in 1945; there is no other information on this artwork other than the picture, taken by Lt Joe H. Jobe of VPB-109's Crew Sixteen.

Above right: This OA-10, *Who Cares*, in Foggia, Italy, during 1944. It was attached to 'B' Flight of the 1st ERS. The plane's name was the suggestion of her flight engineer, John Schneider, who is standing in front of the aircraft. This design had yellow letters with black outline. This PBY was shot down by enemy AAA on 16 November 1944. (*John Schneider*)

FLY GIRL: TAIL ART

Shayne Meder has been painting art work on Navy H-60 Seahawks for the last ten years or more. She likes to refer to it as tail art. Shayne has always loved art, and when it came back in vogue, she painted nose art on B-52s in the 1980s. Her first Seahawk was done for HSL-47 in 1999. The flag and hawk motif was done on the SH-60Bs' in metallic blue tail. The sea hawk was taken from the unit's logo, which depicts a hawk and crossed sabers. Most of the time, the squadrons do not place a lot of restrictions on Shayne and her team as far as the artwork is concerned.

In HSL-45's case the artists were asked to include the unit's colors, which were blue and yellow. The squadron's wolf mascot and lightning bolts from the squadron insignia were also incorporated. The Wolf Pack was very pleased with Shayne and her team's effort—so pleased that they were asked back three more times to paint the Skipper's new aircraft.

Shayne and her crew usually clean and remove the salt, oil-hydraulic fluid, and exhaust stains from the airframe as the first step in the process of applying the tail art. Next they mask off the area to be painted. The main base colors are repainted before the details are added. Shayne then airbrushes the more intricate artwork, such as the HSL-45's wolf's head and torso. Team member and husband Scott Donnell always tackles the stenciling and perfecting the 'shadow' technique in the appropriate colors. He also is the best at prepping the tail rotor assembly and scouring over oily rivets.

Scott has helped on every Seahawk except the one in Guam. Roxane Bond, who has assisted on at least six of the H-60s, is also an artist, and she helps with some of the airbrushing or when more detail is needed. Shayne and her group have painted at least three SH-60Bs for HSL-45. They sometimes return to re-touch the artwork, or, if the aircraft is transferred out of the unit, they will come back and paint a different aircraft.

Shayne has been asked many times how she and her associates are paid for painting the aircraft. She says that she receives 'absolutely zero' in monetary gain:

> The Navy usually helps with expenses and some supplies, but we are mostly paid with the smiles and gratitude we receive from the sailors and crewmen of the units we serve and a thanks for a job well done. The sailor's appreciation is heartwarming and no amount of money can replace that.

They volunteer their time to do the work, and this is the way they show their support for the military. As seen during the Second World War, this style of aircraft artwork is a great morale builder and a unifying element for a command.

Above: This is a rear view of Wolfpack One while returning from a cross-country flight from Sedona, AZ. The wolf's-head artwork has not been painted yet on the forward right-hand J-box cover. (*US Navy photo by Photographer's Mate Rebecca Moat*)

Left: Shayne was called on to improve the original unit design, which appeared somewhat less than a predator. (*Doug Allen*)

Here, Shayne is at work on the SH-60B of the HSM-77 Saberhawks. (*Shayne Meder*)

Above: Wolfpack No. 2 was a repaint of HSL-45's SH-60B (BuNo. 161554) with the new wolf-flag motif on the forward right hand J-box cover. (Shayne Meder) Below: (*US Navy photo by Mass Communication Specialist SN Shannon Cassidy*)

Below: Shayne and her husband, Scott Donnell, stand with the finished product.

Left: Fellow artist Roxane Bond, together with Shayne and Scott, make up the FlyGirl painting team, which has painted the tail art or artwork on at least seventeen Navy Seahawks, a CH-46E Sea Knight, and one EA-6B. (*Doug Allen*)

Below is a close up of the Fly-Girl team's scorpion on Seahawk BuNo. 163546. (*Shayne Meder*)

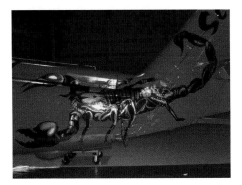

An SH-60B from the *Scorpions* of HSL-49 hovers alongside the destroyer DDG-83 USS *Howard* during a family day cruise on 2 August 2006. (*US Navy photo*)

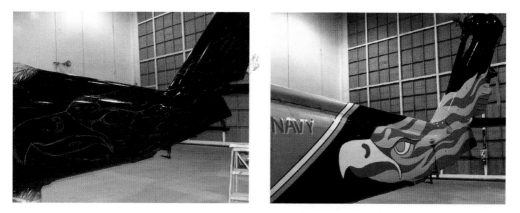

This is a MH-60R from HSM-41, BuNo. 166402, and Shayne's husband would have already prepared the aircraft surfaces for painting. Shayne then sketches out the blue sea hawk. (*Shayne Meder*)

This is the CAG bird from the Sea Hawks of HSM-41, flying along the rocky coast of California after its new paint job. (*Romeo-Shayne*)

This is a detail shot of the artwork of a raptor skeleton on the Commanding Officer's Seahawk of HSM-71. Shayne's attention to detail is one reason why her team is so much in demand with US Navy H-60 squadrons. (*Shayne Meder*)

Roxane Bond and Shayne Meder hand-painting the feathers on *Crazy Horse*, a MH-60S attached to HSC-6 *Screamin' Indians*. Many of HSC-6 Seahawks are christened with the names of a famous American Indian Chiefs. (*Shayne Meder*)

Here, Shayne paints some pin-up art for HMMT-164 on a Kevlar armor plate from a Marine CH-46E Sea Knight. (*Shayne Meder*)

This MH-60S Seahawk of the Island Knights (HSC-25) is performing a vertical underway replenishment for the USS *George Washington*. The carrier is involved in stability and security operations in the Western Pacific. (*US Navy, MCSSM Michael Mulcare*)